HC
151
.H65
1986

Hope, Kempe R.

Economic development
in the Caribbean

ECONOMIC DEVELOPMENT IN THE CARIBBEAN

ECONOMIC DEVELOPMENT IN THE CARIBBEAN

Kempe Ronald Hope

PRAEGER

New York
Westport, Connecticut
London

Library of Congress Cataloging-in-Publication Data

Hope, Kempe R.
  Economic development in the Caribbean.

  Includes index.
  1. Barbados—Economic conditions. 2. Guyana—
Economic conditions—1966–   . 3. Jamaica—Economic
conditions. 4 Trinidad and Tobago—Economic conditions.
I. Title.
HC151.H65   1986   330.9729′052   86-9290
ISBN 0-275-92181-6 (alk. paper)

Library of Congress Catalog Card Number 86-9290
ISBN: 0-275-92181-6

First published in 1986

Praeger Publishers, 521 Fifth Avenue, New York, NY 10175
A division of Greenwood Press, Inc.

Printed in the United States of America

∞

The paper used in this book complies with the Permanent Paper Standard issued by the National Information Standards Organization (Z39.48-1984).

10 9 8 7 6 5 4 3 2 1

To
DAWN, EUCLYN, AND KEMPE, Jr.

PREFACE

The chapters in this volume cover the primary and significant aspects of development problems and policies in the Caribbean. Some of them were originally prepared for publication in journals or other volumes, and they have now been rewritten, updated, and revised, where appropriate, to reflect current trends and policies. They present comparative analyses of economic growth and change with particular reference to the Commonwealth Caribbean nations of Barbados, Guyana, Jamaica, and Trinidad and Tobago — the so-called more-developed Caribbean countries, whose socioeconomic structure tends to mirror, though on a somewhat larger scale, that of the smaller developing countries in the region.

The economies of the Caribbean Basin have, in the past, been more or less neglected in the international literature. Some attempts were made by a few Caribbeanists and research institutes to rectify the situation, but output has always been, and continues to be, hampered by the lack of financial support for such research, even from the Caribbean governments and agencies that have a vested interest in such research.

The idea for this book emerged, therefore, from a recognition of the paucity of book-length studies on Caribbean economic development as well as the current international interest in the Caribbean countries. Both of those reasons prompted my colleagues to encourage me to revise and compile some of my papers into a comprehensive book on the Caribbean economy. I accepted the challenge and worked intermittently on the project from 1983 to 1985.

The approach taken in this book follows from my experience with, and comparative study of, development policy in the Caribbean. My experience has convinced me that one of the most serious problems in the formulation of sound economic policy is the extent to which Caribbean politicians and their advisers understate or ignore the real costs of using a purely ideological framework to achieve developmental goals. The majority of Caribbean leaders placed inordinate faith in the power of ideology to provide them with the key to development. But development has been elusive, to say the least, and some Caribbean countries have succumbed to economic crisis and are now chained to dismal prospects, making survival a matter of priority and a stark reality. Those Caribbean nations that have managed to escape have done so by virtue of their effective management and/or by de-emphasizing ideology in their economic policy. Consequently, I have come to the conclusion that had policy-makers been aware of some of the consequences of their decisions, the policy choices would have been different and the decisions would have been better ones for broader based long-term development, rather than short-term personal political gratification.

My debts in the preparation of this book are too many to list. However, I must make particular mention of the graduate students in my public sector economics course at the University of the West Indies from 1983 to 1985. They listened politely to my lectures that drew heavily on the preliminary drafts of this work, and they all provided penetrating criticism as well as encouragement to continue and complete the project.

Several of my colleagues offered comments and were most helpful in improving the presentation of the issues. I would especially like to thank Professors Jesse Burkhead, Wilfred David, Rawle Farley, and Ivor Mitchell. Any omissions or errors remain my sole responsibility, however.

Finally, I would like to thank Mrs. Sue Cleary and Evadnie for their tireless efforts in typing the manuscript through its several drafts and for putting up with my sometimes unconscionable demands upon their time to meet my deadlines.

ACKNOWLEDGMENTS

I am grateful for permission to include some of my previous work, versions of which were published in other places. The following are the relevant acknowledgments:

Chapter 1 originally appeared in *Man and Development*, Vol. 3 (June 1981); Chapter 2, in *World Futures*, Vol. 18, nos. 3–4 (1982); Chapter 3, in the *Scandinavian Journal of Development Alternatives*, Vol. 3 (December 1984); Chapter 6, in the *International Journal of Tourism Management*, Vol. 1 (September 1980); Chapter 7, in *Food Policy*, Vol. 6 (November 1981); Chapter 8, in *Cities*, Vol. 1, no. 2, pp. 167–74 (November 1983), published by Butterworth Scientific Ltd., P.O. Box 63, Westbury House, Bury Street, Guildford, Surrey GU2 5BH, UK; Chapter 9, in *Labour and Society*, Vol. 8 (July–September 1983); Chapter 11, in *Economia Internazionale*, Vol. 32 (November 1979); Chapter 12, in *Third World Planning Review*, Vol. 4 (February 1982); Chapter 14, in the *Bulletin for International Fiscal Documentation*, Vol. 34 (July 1980); Chapter 15, in *Savings and Development*, Vol. 6, no. 4 (1982); Chapter 16, in the *New West Indian Guide*, Vol. 59, nos. 3–4 (1985); Chapter 18, in *Public Administration and Development*, Vol. 3 (January 1983).

CONTENTS

TABLES

PART I

CONCEPTUAL ASPECTS OF DEVELOPMENT AND ECONOMIC CHANGE

1

The Concept of Economic Development: Toward a New Interpretation

For more than a decade now, growing worldwide attention has been focused on the development of poor nations. The United Nations has sponsored development decades. Rich countries pay lip service to development, if not much largesse; and millions of poor people in several countries have set development as their most sought-after goal.[1] Indeed, this is the first time in history that it has been possible to conceive of development for some countries in the world economy.[2]

But what is development? And how do we recognize it when it occurs? These questions do not have easy answers. There is much disagreement over what development is all about and how it should be measured and accomplished. In this chapter, an attempt is made to provide some of the answers.

WHAT IS DEVELOPMENT

For many years, almost everyone looked at the development of poor countries solely in terms of economic goals. Development meant a rising Gross National Product (GNP), increasing investment and consumption (the twin pillars of traditional economics), and a rising standard of living. A theory was elaborated on the basis of Western experience during the nineteenth century. According to that theory, at some point a developing economy would become strong enough and complex enough to take off toward the industrial heights scaled by so many countries in the Northern Hemisphere.[3]

The tools of this type of development also were, quite clearly, anything that could help get the engines of investment, production, and consumption moving in the individual poor country. This meant an inflow of capital goods from rich countries. It also meant technical advice, borne either by experts from abroad or by students returning home with degrees in economics from North American and European universities, and the creation of economic institutions that would provide people in the developing countries with the ability to read and write and then to produce more economic and technical know-how.

Round and round the system would go, getting steadily richer, until the poor country could truly be said to be developing. This theory of economic development worked remarkably well in some countries. In South Korea and Taiwan, for example, production of goods and services leaped upwards—helped, of course, by U.S. aid and defense outlays—until these countries began to leave poverty behind.[4]

However, elsewhere, some flaws appeared in the theory. For one thing, the poor countries challenged the notion that development could be measured purely in terms of growth in Gross National Product. In country after country, it became obvious that there were serious questions to be asked about economic justice, social equality and political development, the nature and rate of change, the internal consistency of the development process, and income distribution.[5]

Hence, the challenge resulted in a search for a new meaning and approach to development—a relative meaning and approach to development. "The task was therefore one of finding a new measure of development to replace the growth or national income measure, or, more precisely, to enable the national income to be given its true, somewhat limited, significance as a measure of development potential."[6]

Many theorists and the leaders of the developing Third World countries, therefore, agreed on the principle that underdevelopment is not just the lack of development. They argued, instead, that before there was development there was no underdevelopment and that the relation between development and underdevelopment is not just a comparative one, in the sense that some places are more developed or underdeveloped than others. Rather, they argued that development and underdevelopment are related both through the common historical process that they have shared during the past several centuries and through the mutual, that is, reciprocal, influence that they have had, still have, and will continue to have on each other throughout history.[7]

The emphasis therefore shifted and development began to be regarded as a total process involving economic, social, political, and cultural elements, its principal aim to improve not only the economic, but also the social, cultural, and environmental welfare of a nation. This was to be brought about not through reliance on external assistance but through national effort embodied in local community participation and targeted at removing all signs of external economic dependence.

This new definition of development stresses the importance of local considerations in the formulation of development policies and programs.

Local needs and values would determine the direction development takes in a particular country, and local institutions would be responsible for carrying it out.[8]

Some evaluations of development activities have both exemplified and influenced this emerging new approach to development.[9] Their similar diagnoses of the ills of the development system represent a much deeper understanding than did the one-sided explanations frequently offered in the postwar period for the failure of policies and programs, for example, lack of infrastructure, industrialization, education, and modern agricultural policies. Furthermore, there has been a rapidly growing awareness on the part of developing countries generally of the need for joint action to improve their bargaining position and to protect their economic interests.[10] This apparently resulted in a United Nations resolution, on May 1, 1974, for a "Declaration and Program of Action on the Establishment of a New International Economic Order."

Essentially, the current thrust toward development can be viewed as a process in eradicating the state of economic dependence that was brought about when some nations became rich at the expense of others. Hence, what is now required is an elaboration by the developing countries of this comprehensive strategy for strengthening their mutual cooperation in all aspects of their economic relations. Such an elaboration of the strategy should include, *inter alia*, measures designed specifically to promote the flows of trade and finance among the developing countries; to encourage joint ventures involving the technology and know-how of developed nations, both market economy and socialist; to build up an independent and viable scientific and technological base; and to take the first step toward harmonizing their respective economic development programs.[11]

Development in this context is seen as development of every man and woman—of the whole man and woman—not just the growth of things, which are merely means. Development is geared to the satisfaction of needs, beginning with the needs of the poor who constitute the world's majority, and at the same time, is designed to satisfy peoples' needs for expression, creativity, conviviality, and self-determination.

Development, therefore, is a whole; it is an integral, value-loaded, cultural process. It encompasses the environmental, social relations, education, production, consumption, and well-being. It is endogenous and springs from the heart of each society, which relies first on its own strength and resources and defines in sovereignty the vision of its future, cooperating with societies sharing its problems and aspirations. In general, development should aim at achieving a more equitable distribution of the benefits of growth in the whole economy,[12] and as such it must be thought of in terms of evolution, rather than in terms of creation.

Development does not start with goods; it starts with people and their education, organization, and discipline.[13] Without these three, all resources remain latent, untapped potential. Here, then, lies the central problem of development and the reason why development cannot be an act of creation, why it cannot be bought or accelerated through aid. It requires a process of evolution.

If aid is given to introduce certain new economic activities, these will be beneficial and viable only if they can be sustained by the already existing educational level of fairly broad groups of people. They will be truly valuable only if they promote and spread advances in education, organization, and discipline.[14]

It follows from this that development entails a direct internal attack which takes poverty seriously. Development will not go on mechanically. It must concern itself with people because people represent the primary source and the ultimate beneficiaries of the development process.

CONCLUSIONS

It is never simple during the course of an ongoing historical movement to realize that a particular problem is going to be approached in a different way. However, there can be little doubt that a thorough survey of opinion on the problem of development policy would show that at the end of the 1960s and the beginning of the 1970s a new consensus had begun to emerge, and like most new approaches, it arose not in a vacuum but in response to the demonstrable failure of past beliefs and practices.[15] These outdated beliefs and practices were deemed, at the time, necessary for the continuation of the evolution into the realm of sustained economic growth and industrialization.

However, anyone who is concerned with the welfare of the world's developing countries must recognize that business cannot continue as usual in the process toward development. Development policies that in principle ought to have made for a more equitable distribution of income have served merely as additional instruments for increasing the wealth and power of existing elites. Even more serious, new elites, many of whom owe their power to development programs, have become adept at manipulating economic and political institutions to serve their private ends.

It has been found that increases in political participation do not lead predictably to a more equitable distribution of income, probably because only a major redistribution of political power is likely to affect income distribution significantly.[16] The only hope for significant improvements in the standard of living of the inhabitants of the developing countries is reform of the policies of development.

NOTES

1. Robert Hunter, *What is Development* (Washington, D.C.: Overseas Development Council, 1971), p. 1.

2. Ibid.

3. Among many expositions of this doctrine see, for example, W.W. Rostow, *Stages of Economic Growth* (London: Cambridge University Press, 1959); P.N. Rosenstein-Rodan, "Notes on the Theory of the 'Big Push,'" in *Economic Development for Latin America*, edited by H.S. Ellis (London: Macmillan, 1961), pp. 57–81; and Harvey Leibenstein, *Economic Backwardness and Economic Growth* (New York: Wiley, 1957).

4. Robert Hunter, *What is Development*, p. 2.

5. Ibid.

6. Dudley Seers, "The New Meaning of Development," *International Development Review* 11 (December 1969), p. 3.

7. See, for example, André Gunder Frank, *On Capitalist Underdevelopment* (Bombay: Oxford University Press, 1975), p. 1; and Dudley Seers, "The New Meaning of Development," *International Development Review* 19, no. 3 (1977), pp. 2–7.

8. Alan R. Kasdan, *The Third World: A New Focus for Development* (Cambridge, Mass.: Schenkman, 1973), p. 10.

9. See Franklin Lisk, "Conventional Development Strategies and Basic-Needs Fulfillment," *International Labour Review* 115 (March–April 1977), pp. 175–91.

10. UNCTAD, *Trade and Development Issues in the Context of a New International Economic Order* (Geneva: UNCTAD IV Seminar Program Discussion Paper, February 1976), p. 1.

11. For more on this issue of cooperation see Samuel L. Parmar, "Self-Reliant Development in an 'Interdependent' World," in *Beyond Dependency: The Developing World Speaks Out*, edited by Guy F. Erb and Valeriana Kallab (Washington, D.C.: Overseas Development Council, 1975), pp. 3–27; and Paul Streeten, "The Distinctive Features of a Basic Needs Approach to Development," *International Development Review* 19, no. 3 (1977), pp. 8–16.

12. Dudley Seers, "The New Meaning of Development," pp. 5–6.

13. E.F. Schumacher, *Small is Beautiful: A Study of Economics as if People Mattered* (London: Abacus-Sphere Books, 1974), pp. 140–41.

14. Ibid.

15. Derek T. Healey, "Development Policy: New Thinking About an Interpretation," *Journal of Economic Literature* 10 (September 1972), p. 792.

16. Irma Adelman and Cynthia Taft Morris, *Economic Growth and Social Equity in Developing Countries* (Stanford: Stanford University Press, 1973), pp. 107–40.

2

The New International Economic Order, Basic Needs, and Technology Transfer: Toward an Integrated Strategy for Development in the Future

Current approaches to development emphasize such concepts as self-reliance, rural development, local values and community participation, economic independence, basic needs, technology transfer, and the need for a New International Economic Order (NIEO). Without a doubt, the new concepts of development, particularly the emphasis on economic independence, have, for the first time, resulted in some shift in the balance of economic power in favor of a few developing countries. This shift in the balance of economic power was initiated by the embargo of the oil-exporting countries in late 1973. This was followed by a rapidly growing awareness on the part of developing countries of the need for joint action to improve their bargaining position and to protect their economic interests.[1] However, the result was a call for the NIEO.

This chapter analyzes and continues to assess underlying new perceptions of development, with emphasis on basic needs and the transfer of technology, within the framework of the perceived NIEO. The essential thrust herein is to highlight the current emphasis on the NIEO and analyze the necessity for an integrated strategy for development in the future, embodying basic needs and technology transfer to achieve the objectives of the proposed NIEO. Before that is done, however, it may be worthwhile to first discuss the conceptual premise of the NIEO.

THE NEW INTERNATIONAL ECONOMIC ORDER: ELEMENTS AND OBJECTIVES

The concept of a NIEO embodies institutional arrangements that promote the economic and social progress of the developing countries in the context of an expanding world economy. It is a framework of rules and institutions, regulating the relations among sovereign nations.

The primary elements of the approach toward a NIEO are threefold.[2] First, and most importantly, measures are being sought to reduce, and eventually eliminate, the economic dependence of developing countries on developed-country enterprises in the production and trade of developing countries, thus allowing those countries to exercise full control over their natural resources. A second element is that of promoting the accelerated development of the economies of developing countries on the basis of dependence on their own internal efforts. Thirdly, appropriate institutional changes are being sought to introduce some measure of global management of resources in the long-term interests of humanity.

The NIEO therefore is intended to stand for a new way of ordering the international economic system so as to bring about, first, improved terms of trade between the present-day center and periphery countries (in other words, the First World and the Third World countries); secondly, more control by the periphery over the world economic cycles that pass through them; and, thirdly, increased and improved trade among the periphery countries themselves.[3]

The NIEO concept has emerged primarily because of the perceived defects of the existing international economic order which, it is argued, has resulted in an economic crisis perpetuating poverty and inequality, both between countries and within each country.[4] The economic crisis, which is centered in the major developed market economy countries, has adversely affected the economies of both developed and developing countries. Indeed, many of the poorer developing countries are facing a drastic deterioration in their economic positions. The economic crisis has therefore made even more urgent the implementation of effective international policies for development. At the same time, it was felt that the concern of many of the developed countries for assured supplies of essential raw materials would make them more responsive than hitherto to the negotiation of new development policies.

The results of these concerns in the world at large have resulted in the need for some changes in the framework of international economic relations becoming more widely recognized and, hence, more likely to be effectuated than was the case heretofore.[5]

The NIEO which the developing countries seek is intended to facilitate a direct attack on the central issue of widespread poverty. But it is generally felt that such an order could be without any impact at all on the majority of people in many developing countries unless those countries themselves installed national arrangements both to optimize their gains from an improved external regime and also to bring about an equitable internal distribution of an increasing national product. However, it is recognized that many of the measures which are required to improve the internal economic order depend upon improved international arrangements in trade and finance.[6]

Without these improved internal arrangements, in addition to required cooperation between the developed and developing countries, then, there would be no complementarity with respect to meeting the objectives of the NIEO. As applied to the NIEO, this principle of complementarity means that something other than a mere redistribution of resources among nations is required. It means that all of the elements of the NIEO, internal and external, must be achieved by close cooperation among the developed and developing countries with as much emphasis as possible on self-reliance.

The NIEO is intended to replace the current economic order. It is not a static concept but a dynamic and evolving process. Its defining characteristic is the attempt to eliminate economic injustice by equalizing economic opportunity, conducive to unfolding productive capacities capable of responding to basic needs in all parts of the world.

The notions of beyond dependence and toward self-reliance define the striving toward the NIEO, more than any specific international demand or resolution. But, though the formulation of NIEO objectives are subject to change and evolution, the NIEO framework itself is expected to stay. A future without a NIEO is considered inconceivable.[7]

BASIC NEEDS AND TECHNOLOGY TRANSFER POLICY ISSUES RELATED TO THE NIEO

The primary objectives of a basic needs approach to development is to provide oportunities for the full physical, mental, and social development of the individual.[8] This approach focuses on mobilizing particular resources for particular groups, identified as deficient in these resources, and concentrates on the nature of what is provided rather than on income.[9] The basic needs approach does not rely solely on income generation or transfers; it places primary emphasis on the production and delivery to the intended groups of the basic needs basket through supply management and a delivery system.[10]

The basic needs approach differs conceptually from other poverty-oriented development strategies.[11] First, whereas conventional antipoverty programs are directed at target poverty groups within an economy, the basic needs approach is founded on the premise that poverty in most developing countries is widespread and that action should therefore be directed at the population as a whole. Secondly, this approach is concerned both with significantly raising the level of aggregate demand and with increasing the supply of basic goods and services, as opposed to raising the incomes of the poor merely to a minimum subsistence level. Actually, basic needs policies are not restricted to the eradication of absolute poverty but extend to the satisfaction of needs over and above the subsistence level as a means of eliminating relative poverty through a continuous process of economic development and social progress.[12] Another difference lies in the fact that the basic needs approach stresses effective mass participation in both the formulation and implementation of policy measures as a way of ensuring that its main objective is not lost sight of.

In defining the objectives and distinguishing features of a basic needs policy approach, recognition must be given to the fact that countries will have different requirements as a result of their varying economic, political, social, cultural, and technological characteristics. As a result, there are no objective criteria for defining the contents of a basic needs bundle. While certain minimum physiological conditions are necessary to sustain life, basic needs vary between geographical areas, cultures, and time periods. It makes little sense, therefore, to attempt to define universal standards of basic needs. Moreover, there is no single level of basic needs, but instead a hierarchy.[13] Given such a hierarchy, societies can define their own basket of basic goods and services which would, out of necessity, differ according to the society's objective. However, the basic needs approach sets priorities in production and distribution. It gives the first priority to the production of what is essential to meet human needs, and in such a way that it goes to meet the needs of the most needy. It gives a much lower priority to production of goods for other than human needs, for nonbasic needs, and for the needs of those less in need.

The basic needs approach does not call for asceticism or puritanism. All that it insists on is a certain order of priorities: first, meet the basic needs of those most in need, and then, *and only then*, go about satisfying any other needs. The basic theoretical and empirical question in connection with the basic needs approach has to do with the ordering of these pursuits in terms of time. The assumption is that the pursuit of nonbasic needs will stand in the way of meeting basic needs.

The autonomy of societies in deciding their own basket of basic goods is also consistent with the Declaration of Principles and Program of Action of the World Employment Conference of 1976. In that conference, it was declared that it is important to recognize that the concept of basic needs is a country-specific and dynamic concept and that it should be placed within a context of a nation's overall economic and social develop-ment.[14] It was further stated that basic needs "in no circumstances should be taken to mean mererly the minimum necessary for subsistence; it should be placed within a context of national independence, the dignity of individuals and peoples and their freedom to chart their destiny without hindrance."[15]

The satisfaction of basic needs in developing countries cannot be achieved without both acceleration in their economic growth and measures aimed at changing the pattern of growth and access to the use of productive resources by the lowest income groups. The redistribution factor is also important here. To be of use this redistribution must result in the production of more basic goods and services. Moreover, the provision of adequate employment opportunities is an essential ingredient in this strategy. The productive mobilization of the unemployed, the seasonally unemployed, and the underemployed, plus higher productivity by the working poor, are essential means of ensuring both a level of output high enough to meet basic needs targets, and its proper distribution.[16]

However, the basic needs approach cannot and should not be interpreted as an exclusive concern with the production of basic goods and the shift toward more labor-intensive methods. On the contrary, as well as expanding the production of basic goods using different levels of technology, it is necessary to make proper provision for adequate supplies of intermediate and capital goods.[17] The precise combination of these goods will have to be determined by the specific economic condition existing in each country and particularly the level of technology.

This, therefore, raises an important issue in the provision of many of the basic needs, and that is, the question of transfer of appropriate technology. Technology has long been recognized as an important factor in development and historical studies have demonstrated the substantial contribution of technological progress to the long-term rise in productivity of labor and output in the developed nations, and its impact on the level and structure of employment and incomes. But the role of technology in the developing nations has been subject to a great deal of controversy.

Technology can be defined as the skills, knowledge, and procedures used in the provision of goods and services for any given society. Because of the unique features of each developing economy, technology must be discussed in the context of what is appropriate. But the concept of "appropriate technology" sometimes meets with the criticism that it carries a neocolonial connotation—a connotation that the existing, modern, and efficient technology is unsuitable for the developing countries, which should be satisfied with something inferior that would result in and perpetuate a technological gap. But this is erroneous. The gap exists insofar as some countries are poor while others are rich; the task is to reduce or eliminate it. [18] If the problem is regarded as technological and similar technology is applied to the two groups of countries (developed and developing), the real economic gap will increase rather than decline, unless other measures are taken.

The concept of *appropriate technology* must be looked at only in relation to some specified historical context and in terms of demand (basic needs goals) and supply (the appropriate production processes).[19] There is an urgent need for a harmonization of these two factors to bring about the management and production techniques that are best suited to the resources and future development potential of the individual countries.[20] Such technology must contribute to greater productive employment opportunities, elimination of poverty, and the achievement of an equitable distribution of income.

Technological decisions and the pace of technical change affect all development processes and, in turn, are affected by them. The various combinations and proportions in which labor, material resources, and capital are used influence not only the type and quantity of goods and services produced, but also the distribution of their benefits and prospects for overall growth. The significance of technological choices made in the course of development extends beyond economics to social structure and political processes as well, and the growing interest in finding and implementing appropriate technologies reflects an implicit recognition of the essential role of technology in development policy.[21]

Because the use of any particular technology is not an end in itself, the criteria of appropriateness for the choice of technology must be found in the goals of the basic needs approach to development. These goals are concerned not only with the volumes of output and income generated by an economy but also with the way they are produced and distributed among the population and they include, as well, particular patterns of national political change and independence.

Technology is a powerful means of international policy. It serves as a new means of projecting national influence and power into the international arena. As a result, an increasing number of Third World countries have been advocating technology policies which promote not only development but also greater national autonomy. But a careful formulation of technology policy is as important as development planning itself. Good plans can be ineffective if technology is insufficient in quantity, inappropriate in quantity, or undisciplined in its applications.[22] As such, therefore, the acquisition and transfer of technology must be limited to appropriate technology. Significant efforts should be made by the developed countries, therefore, to give access on improved terms to modern technology and the adaptation of that technology, as appropriate, to specific economic, social, and ecological conditions and varying stages of development in developing countries.

The ability to make independent technological choices, to adapt and improve upon chosen techniques and products, and eventually to generate new technology endogenously are essential aspects of the process of development. The process may be described as the accumulation of technological capacity; it is at least as important to economic development as the accumulation of capital.

The use of appropriate technology to satisfy basic needs is a national endeavor. However, its success seems to depend crucially on the establishment of a NIEO that allows for global redistribution and transfer of technology and other resources in concert with the basic needs program. It is argued that a NIEO that is not committed to meeting basic needs is liable to transfer resources from the poor in rich nations to the rich in poor nations.[23]

Basic needs and the call for the transfer of appropriate technology are not just other fads, however. They are no more, but also no less, than a stage in the thinking and responses to the challenges presented by development over the last 20 to 25 years.[24]

To satisfy basic needs is an objective with high priority. As a development strategy, satisfying basic needs through the NIEO seems to be even of higher priority. The accomplishment of this development framework places considerable emphasis on the concept of collective self-reliance.

The required global assistance must, however, be complementary to the policies being pursued in the developing nations. Technology and resource transfers, therefore, must not only be appropriate but mandatory. This means that within the context of a NIEO, appropriate technology transfers from the rich nations to the poor nations must not depend on the uncertain generosity of the rich nations, but be based on some internationally accepted measure of needs of the poor nations.

Some skeptics may maintain that integration into any international economic order in which advanced capitalist economies dominate is inconsistent with technology transfer to meet basic needs of the poor in developing countries. They may point to the People's Republic of China as a nation which, until recently, had isolated itself from the evils of the international economic system and at the same time advocated that nations ought to shut themselves off from nefarious outside influences.

But developing countries are not in a position to isolate themselves. Moreover, any such isolation would be counterproductive to the necessary technology transfers required to implement a successful basic needs policy. Also, many developing countries are former colonies whose resources were extracted and exploited both by the colonizers and private transnational enterprises with little or no benefit to the said developing countries. Many Third World leaders, therefore, share the point of view that the transfer of resources and technology from the developed nations, within the framework of the NIEO, represents nothing more than repatriation.

This is an important issue because it is with some passion that Third World leaders share this view of repatriation. Further evidence of this feeling of Third World leaders can be gleaned from the many recent nationalizations and increased tax levies that have been placed on multinational enterprises in the Third World. Increasingly, Third World leaders have been devoting more attention to changing the terms of foreign operations within their economies—nationalizing ownership and top management; setting more precise conditions concerning participation, conservation, labor, investment, and other aspects of foreign commercial activities to prevent further economic exploitation. But despite these attempts at direct intervention in the workings of their economies, numerous Third World leaders now believe that only if there is a basic change in the international economic order will the appropriate technology and sufficient resources flow to their countries to overcome some of the chronic disabilities of their economies.[25]

So there is recognition of the need for interdependence—a new interdependence within the framework of the NIEO, and in the form of a partnership based on interlocking economic systems. And yet the interdependence should be one in which the collective cooperation of the developing countries is recognized and respected as a central emphasis in the transfer of appropriate technology to meet the basic needs of the majority of the population of the Third World.

There is also growing recognition that so long as the framework of a country's policy is appropriate—that is, the provision of basic needs is being pursued—the transfer of appropriate technology can improve resource allocation and efficiency without damage to balance of payments or national integrity. Countries that have effectively controlled technology transfers have done well. In contrast, autarkic policies have often led to slow growth and heavy dependence on aid with a concomitant impairment of independence.[26]

The NIEO is concerned with formulating a framework in institutions, processes, and rules that would correct what developing countries regard as the present, unfavorable bias of the system. The provision of basic needs and the transfer of appropriate technology are two important objectives which this framework should serve, and which, in turn, would tend to make more resources available, both domestically and possibly internationally.[27]

In the past, the transfer of technology to developing nations was facilitated primarily through transnational corporations and multilateral financial institutions. Yet, only a small proportion of projects showed any attempts to grapple with the technological problems involved.[28] Direct involvement, particularly that of the multilateral financial institutions such as the World Bank, in the formulation, implementation, supervision, and assessment of a large number and variety of projects in developing nations provides these institutions with a unique opportunity to make major contributions to the promotion of more appropriate technologies,[29] especially as it relates to basic needs. This, therefore, should be advocated as a part of their policy. A basic needs strategy that is pursued through technology that is inappropriate is doomed to failure irrespective of who finances it.

CONCLUSIONS

The provision of basic needs and the transfer of appropriate technology still remain formidable tasks, though attainable in the future. The concept of basic needs brings to any development strategy a heightened concern with meeting the consumption needs of the Third World. But, it is not a welfare concept nor is it a distinct development strategy in itself.[30] It is a major objective of development that can be achieved only if the appropriate technology exists.

A strategy of integrated development embracing appropriate technology transfer, basic needs, and the perceived NIEO focuses on increasing cooperative relations among Third World nations and reducing their collective dependence on the developed nations. Its emphasis is on selective coordination of economic activities for maximizing the provision of basic needs through the NIEO. Collective self-reliance, as will be discussed further in the next chapter, is a necessary extension of national self-reliance for almost all Third World countries, both in terms of creating interdependent relationships with similar economies and of improving the terms of economic exchange with the developed nations. However, it cannot be a substitute for national strategies of self-reliance.

The recognition of a strategy of integrated development is very important at both the macro- and microlevels. At the macrolevel the strategy must be so designed to ensure consistency between the basic needs indicators and transfers derived from the NIEO. At the microlevel, there must be analysis to identify potential alternative policies and to choose those contributing most to the unity and efficiency of providing basic needs and transferring appropriate technology in the context of the NIEO.

The NIEO deals essentially with the relations between industrialized and developing countries at the global level. It is thus a macroapproach to the problem of development. The basic needs approach, on the other hand, is a microapproach. It goes down to the level of the individual human being and, therefore, sees development in terms of the fulfillment of basic, individual needs.

The provison of basic needs and the transfer of appropriate technology are now recognized as fundamental to the development process. There is a further advocacy that this should be attempted in concert with the NIEO. However, there now seems to be general agreement that the meeting of basic needs of the poor should become the core of development planning and policy.[31] Furthermore, discussions on basic needs emphasize their dynamic nature. Basic needs development is seen as evolving over time, within or without the NIEO, in line with the growth of the economy and the aspirations of the people.

For the Caribbean economies, some of the fundamental objective factors which gave rise to the declared principles of the basic needs approach are becoming more pronounced. As will be seen in this volume, indebtedness is expanding, deteriorating terms of trade for commodity producers continue to cut into the purchasing power for imports; energy costs are increasing as productive activity deteriorates for lack of foreign exchange to purchase raw materials;[32] the necessary skills, ability, and technology to manage development programs to fruition are almost deficient; and there is a rapid deterioration in the ability of governments to provide basic public services.

NOTES

1. See UNCTAD, *Trade and Development*, p. 1; Paul Streeten, "Development Ideas in Historical Perspective," in *Toward a New Strategy for Development: A Rothko Chapel Colloquium*, ed. K.Q. Hill (New York: Pergamon Press, 1979), pp. 21–52; and Tony Killick, "Trends in Development Economics and Their Relevance to Africa," *Journal of Modern African Studies* 18, no. 3 (1980), pp. 367–86.

2. For more discussion on these three elements see UNCTAD, *Trade and Development*, pp. 8–11.

3. Johan Galtung, *The North/South Debate: Technology, Basic Human Needs and the New International Economic Order* (New York: Institute for World Order, working paper no. 12, 1980), pp. 29–30.

4. M. Abdel-Fadil et al., "A New International Economic Order," *Cambridge Journal of Economics* 1 (June 1977), p. 205.

5. UNCTAD, *Trade and Development*, p. 1.

6. Shridath S. Ramphal, "What Next? A Mandate for the Developing Countries," in *Partners in Tomorrow: Strategies for a New International Order* (New York: E.P. Dutton, 1978), p. 94.

7. Ervin Laszlo, "The Objectives of the New International Economic Order in Historical and Global Perspectives," *The Objectives of the New International Economic Order*, eds. E. Laszlo et al. (New York: Pergamon Press, 1978), p. xxv.

8. Paul Streeten, "Basic Needs: Premises and Promises," *Journal of Policy Modeling* I, no. 1 (1979), p. 136.

9. Ibid.

10. T.N. Srinivasan, "Development, Poverty, and Basic Human Needs: Some Issues," *Food Research Institute Studies* 16, no. 2 (1977), p. 18.

11. For a more elaborate discussion of these differences, see, for example, Paul Streeten and Shahid Javed Burki, "Basic Needs: Some Issues," *World Development* 6, no. 3 (1978), pp. 411–21.

12. F. Lisk, "Conventional Development," p. 186.

13. Streeten and Burki, "Basic Needs: Some Issues," p. 413.

14. International Labor Office, *Meeting Basic Needs: Strategies for Eradicating Mass Poverty and Unemployment: Conclusions of the World Employment Conference 1976* (Geneva: ILO, 1977), p. 24.

15. Ibid.

16. International Labor Office, *Employment, Growth and Basic Needs: A One-World Problem* (Geneva: ILO, 1976), p. 43.

17. S.A. Kuzmin, "An Integrated Approach to Development and Employment", *International Labour Review* 115 (May–June 1977), p. 338.

18. Hans Singer, *Technologies for Basic Needs* (Geneva: ILO, 1977), p. 9.

19. W.A. Ndongko and S.O. Anyang, "The Concept of Appropriate Technology: An Appraisal from the Third World," *Monthly Review* 32 (February 1981), pp. 35–43; A.L. Edwards et al., (eds.) *New Dimensions of Appropriate Technology* (Ann Arbor, Mich.: Graduate School of Business Administration, University of Michigan, 1980); and S. Watanabe, "Institutional Factors, Government Policies and Appropriate Technologies," *International Labour Review* 119 (March–April 1980), pp. 167–84.

20. See George McRobie, "Intermediate Technology: Small is Beautiful," *Third World Quarterly* I (Aril 1979), pp. 71–86.

21. Richard S. Eckaus, *Appropriate Technologies for Developing Countries* (Washington, D.C.: National Academy of Sciences, 1977), p. 5.

22. Denis Goulet, *The Uncertain Promise: Value Conflicts in Technology Transfer* (Washington, D.C.: Overseas Development Council, 1977), p. 167.

23. Streeten, "Basic Needs," p. 143.

24. Paul Streeten, "From Growth to Basic Needs," *Finance and Development* 16 (September 1979), p. 28.

25. W. Howard Wriggins and Gunnar Adler-Karlsson, *Reducing Global Inequities* (New York: McGraw-Hill, 1978), p. 38.

26. Helen Hughes, "Achievements and Objectives of Industrialization," in *Policies for Industrial Progress in Developing Countries*, eds. John Cody, Helen Hughes, and David Wall (New York: Oxford University Press, 1980), p. 20.

27. Kempe Ronald Hope, "Basic Needs and Technology Transfer Issues in the New International Economic Order," *American Journal of Economics and Sociology* 42 (October 1983), pp. 393–403; and Streeten, "Distinctive Features," p. 11.

28. See Harold B. Dunkerley, "The Choice of Appropriate Technologies," *Finance and Development* 14 (September 1977), pp. 36–39.

29. Ibid., p. 39.

30. See Mahbub ul Haq, "An International Perspective on Basic Needs," *Finance and Development* 17 (September 1980), pp. 11–14.

31. D.P. Ghai et al., *The Basic-Needs Approach to Development* (Geneva: ILO, 1977), p. 14.

32. Kari Levitt-Polanyi, "The Caribbean Economy and the New International Economic Order," in *Latin America and the New International Economic Order*, eds. J Lozoya and J. Estevez (New York: Pergamon Press, 1980), p. 82.

3

Self-Reliance as a Development Strategy: A Conceptual Policy Analysis

In most of the literature these days recognition is given to the fact that economic growth can only be achieved by close cooperation among the developed and developing nations with as much emphasis as possible on self-reliance, which has become one of the cornerstones of development policy. It means that the developing nations, individually, must do as much as possible for themselves on the basis of their own resources. Also, it means that the developing nations must exploit every possible advantage for maximizing the positive effects of economic development by cooperation among themselves.

Self-reliance is taken here to mean autonomy of decision making and full mobilization of a society's own resources under its own initiative and direction. It also means rejection of the principle of exploitative appropriation of others' resources.

Collective self-reliance is an extension of the concept of self-reliance so as to embrace truly cooperative relations among self-respecting mobilized societies. In other words, it is self-reliance reinforced by collective solidarity. Its concern is the enhancement of Third World productive forces, surplus generation, and the power to carry forward development strategies in its own interest and for its own benefit. For this it is necessary to break with the components of the international system which generate or strengthen dependency and strengthen links with partners who share the principle of collective effort toward the attainment of legitimate aspirations of each other and of humanity as a whole.[1]

This emphasis on self-reliance implies a striving to make relations between developed and developing nations reflect genuine interdependence and international economic justice, rather than continued dependence of the developing nations on the developed nations. To the extent that developed nations reaffirm their beliefs in the notion of interdependence, there should be no fundamental conflict between self-reliant development and increased international economic cooperation.

19

The most important element of self-reliance in the developing nations is the formulation of concepts and policies of development based on their own socioeconomic realities, rather than on ideas inherited from the North. Developing nations have much to learn from the experience of developed nations. However, imitation will prove disastrous because the development strategy will be reflecting the policies of other nations and not tailored to local conditions.

The relevance and importance of a self-reliant development policy are no longer questioned by policy-makers. A self-reliant development strategy could give a great deal of impetus to the economies of the Third World countries and, in that sense, it could constitute the most dynamic element in the global strategy for development implied in the concept of the proposed New International Economic Order.

THE CONCEPTUAL FRAMEWORK: A POLICY ANALYSIS

A strategy of development emphasizing self-reliance focuses on increasing cooperative relations among Third World nations and reducing their collective dependence on the developed nations. Its emphasis is on selective coordination of economic activities for maximizing the provision of basic needs. As inferred before, collective self-reliance is a necessary extension of national self-reliance for almost all Third World nations both in terms of creating interdependent relationships with similar economies and of improving the terms of economic exchange with the developed nations. However, it cannot be a substitute for national strategies for self-reliance.

The kind of new, internal economic order needed to ensure that development is beneficial to the majorities, rather than the elites of Third World nations, is one based on principles of self-reliant development. Basic needs and justice are most fully realized in societies committed to self-reliance.[2] Thus, self-reliant development rejects concentrating national resources on the rich in the hope that something might trickle down. Instead, self-reliant development concentrates directly on those at the bottom and their basic needs. It is a model of development that emphasizes meeting basic human needs of the masses of people in a country through strategies geared to the particular human and natural resources, values, and traditions of the country and through strategies maximizing the collective efforts of people within each country and among Third World countries.[3]

The conceptual framework of self-reliance focuses, therefore, on four elements. The first pertains to basic human needs. This means attacking poverty directly and not through the trickle-down process. In other words, it means giving priority to food, shelter, housing, education, health care, and jobs, at the least. The second element relates to maximization of the use of local resources and values through the educational system as appropriate to the needs, resources, and values of the people. It entails, therefore, the development of individuals as well as nations. Education should be used to meet the basic needs of individuals to receive a foundation of knowledge, attitudes, values, and skills on which to build a later life for the benefit of themselves and society. This element can be regarded as creative self-reliance. It is not self-reliance in the sense of cutting off links completely from the world but self-reliance in the sense of being self-confident as nations to base development on their own cultural values. It implies reliance by a nation on its own thinking and on its own value system without being defensive or apologetic.[4]

The third element deals with participation of the masses in the development thrust. Participation is regarded here as the willing and active participation of the masses in the development of the nation-state in which they reside. Such participation requires that the masses not only share in the distribution of the benefits of development, be they the material benefits of increased output or other benefits considered enhancing to the quality of life, but that they share also in the task of creating those benefits. The fourth and final element in the conceptual framework of self-reliance pertains to the issue of interdependence, or collective self-reliance. That is, technical cooperation among Third World nations for their individual as well as collective development. Undoubtedly, collective self-reliance and growing cooperation among developing nations will further strengthen their role in the NIEO. Cooperation among these countries is aimed at generating or adapting knowledge needed for a socially relevant, endogenous, self-sustained development process in order to avoid the blind or forced transfer of inadequate technology. Moreover, the expansion of the capacity of Third World nations to generate and adopt knowledge through a cooperative effort can contribute a more equitable world order where choices are greater; solutions are better adapted to the specific historical circumstances of different countries; and dependence is decreased. Furthermore, cooperation among developing nations can also contribute to a filling of the vacuum of regional and interregional links among Third World nations. This vacuum is the result of the historical colonial heritage of exclusive links which were later on maintained through a world order that has not allowed the emergence of alternative patterns more suitable to the Third World than traditional center-periphery ones. The collective self-reliance approach to development, therefore, implies a delinking from those components of the international system in which a balanced relationship cannot be established and relinking among Third World nations with whom a balanced relationship may be attained.

This puts the issue of self-reliance in conceptual perspective. Primary emphasis is placed by the Third World nations on genuine cooperation, which is regarded as an egalitarian form of partnership in which nationally based effort and the benefits of a joint undertaking in the short and long term are shared evenly among nations. Cooperation is seen as a partnership in which the parties have equal status, irrespective of their economic, political, or military strengths; efforts and benefits are shared in accordance with their abilities and needs. It is, above all, a "solidarity contract" to contribute to the fulfillment of each party's legitimate aspirations, and to unite against forces opposing these aspirations and seeking to increase dependency.[5]

Therefore, a harmonization of currently conflicting objectives and lasting solutions must be found and worked out not only within the existing political, social, economic, and value systems, but also taking into account the possible changes that may be foreseen, particularly within the context of collective self-reliance.

Collective self-reliance, by enhancing the position of the developing nations, can give real meaning to the concept of interdependence. So far it has meant dominance on one side and dependence on the other. Only structural changes resulting in the reduction of inequalities among nations and the redistribution of resources can make global interdependence useful and desirable to all partners in development for lasting development.

The emphasis of a strategy of self-reliant development is that economic activity should be geared to the satisfaction of basic needs of the masses. Moreover, the developing nations and their masses are the best arbiters of their own basic needs and their order of priority. Collectively, the interests of the various developing nations are balanced against each other so as to make it profitable for each country to accept the deal as a whole.

A self-reliant approach to economic development with central emphasis on meeting the basic needs of the majority of the population of the developing nations provides a new orientation in development strategy. It implies an unprecedented expansion in the production of foodstuffs and of simple manufactured goods, using technology appropriate to the resource endowments of the developing nations themselves. Since the pattern of basic needs in developing nations is quite different from the pattern of import demand by developed nations, the adoption of a self-reliant basic needs strategy of development would mean the emergence of a new pattern of industrialization in the developing nations.

The idea of accelerated economic development through self-reliance or collective self-reliance is not a new one. Until recently, however, that concept found expression in integration schemes of a regional or subregional character, which currently embrace about one-half of the total developing nations. Within the framework of these integration schemes, some progress has been made in expanding the mutual trade of the member countries, in developing complementary industries, and in general harmonization of their development programs. In some subregional groupings, important initiatives have been taken to improve the bargaining power of the member countries in their dealings with transnational corporations and to regulate the operations of these corporations.

The new awareness on the part of the developing nations of the need to strengthen their mutual economic relations provides a unique opportunity for building a global system of economic cooperation among Third World nations on the valuable experience gained so far on a regional and subregional basis. Thus, closer economic cooperation among developing nations on a global basis would improve their bargaining power with developed nations as well as transnational corporations. It would also provide, to a much greater extent than hitherto, the means for accelerating their own economic and social development through their own efforts.

In effect, the goal is to increase the level of interdependence within the Third World, not only to achieve immediate welfare gains from increased trade and specialization, but also to improve the quality and credibility of common bargaining positions against the industrial countries. An improved bargaining position would ultimately emerge from the fact that more collective self-reliance would gradually provide the Third World with a feasible alternative in any confrontation with the rich countries. But even apart from this, there is no doubt that efforts to increase cooperation make a great deal of sense. The immediate gains may not be huge, and the gains might not be equitably distributed, but over the long term the importance of such actions could surely be important. This is particularly true if the industrial nations remain in recession, or if they turn inward, or if they begin actively to seek substitutes for many of the Third World's exports.[6]

As such, the self-reliance model has clear and important functions. It remains an alternative development strategy that—even if it is very difficult to implement in its extreme form the delinking of the South from the North—can at least provide guidance for the kinds of change that are required to eliminate underdevelopment. As an ideal type, it can provide direction for partial strategies. Naturally, the attractiveness of this alternative increases as the negotiations about the implementation of the NIEO program remain deadlocked.[7]

Collective self-reliance has therefore become inescapable for Third World countries. It is essential to their very survival and it is very much connected to the basic notion of reducing dependency. Collective self-reliance as a development strategy can hardly be understood outside the dependency framework. Self-reliance is the antithesis of dependence.

Dependency theory, however, tends to overstate the role of external influences and consequently minimizes the internal factors affecting the development of more equitable domestic economic, social, and political systems. But a reduction of the South's dependence on the North requires not only the achievement of better international bargains but also better management of local resources and significant social and economic changes within the Third World. These changes are essential for the political viability of those Third World regimes that do not depend on force to stay in power. However, dependency theory clearly has contributed to the increased awareness of Third World leaders of the relative strengths and weaknesses of their position and has certainly heightened their desire for greater autonomy in international economic affairs. It is one of the most important factors that has contributed to the growing sense of self-reliance that is prompting Third World nations to seek more influence over their political and economic destinies.[8]

The dependency perspective assumes that the development of a national or regional unit can only be understood in connection with its historical insertion into the worldwide political-economic system which emerged with the wave of European colonizations. The global system is thought to be characterized by the unequal but the combined development of its various components. Development and underdevelopment are seen as aspects of the same phenomenon. Both are linked functionally and, therefore, interact and condition each other mutually. This results in the division of the world between industrial, or center, countries and developing, or periphery, countries. The center is viewed as capable of dynamic development responsive to internal needs, and as the main beneficiary of the global links. On the other hand, the periphery is seen as having a reflex type of development which is both constrained by its incorporation into the global system and which results from its adaptation to the requirements of the expansion of the center.[9]

Dependency theory stresses the significance of the manner in which the internal and external structural components are connected. External variables are reinforced by internal factors and it is through this interplay that the Third World would like to continue to develop as long as its members are equal partners in that process, and exploitation ceases. It means then that these nations are seeking greater equity in international economic relations and, particularly, in the decision-making process affecting their development. Just as the basic key to the politics of dependency is to tap the resources of the periphery, the key to the politics of self-reliance is to gain control over resources—that is, to evolve patterns of autonomy in the context of a highly interconnected world.

The whole theory of self-reliance hinges on one fundamental hypothesis: that resources as a whole constitute a reservoir, now partly drained away, partly misdirected, and largely underutilized, that is sufficient for the satisfaction of basic human material needs all over the world.[10] It is a complex strategy—needing both built-in dynamism and firm institutional foundations—calculated to generate and implement clusters of collective schemes. It gives the Third World an identity, not as the Third

World, but as one of three economic worlds; to lift the poor countries together from passivity to participation; to give each greater economic maneuverability. In short, self-reliance not only offers scope for national development and bargaining power vis-à-vis the North, but also endless oportunity for innovation, for exploring areas in employment, job satisfaction, and human relations generally, which have not been charted before and which are probably beyond the reach of the economically established North.

CONCLUSIONS

The concept of self-reliance has achieved prominence in the current development debate. Its primary element is that economic activity should be tailored to the basic needs of the masses. Moreover, it is also now recognized that Third World nations must conceive self-reliance, not in terms of national or social isolation, but in balanced forms of association with other national and social units, thus making it a collective effort, that is, collective self-reliance, or what has come to be known as economic cooperation among developing countries (ECDC).

The collective self-reliance approach to development got its identity through the nonaligned movement and the emergence of the Group of 77 countries (now about 122) as a functional entity at the first United Nations Conference on Trade and Development (UNCTAD) in 1964. Since its creation, the Group of 77 has taken on the responsibility of negotiating consensus among developing countries and speaking in that collective voice in negotiations with the developed world. It operates primarily within the United Nations system.

Significant to collective self-reliance is the necessary delinking from those components of the international system in which a balanced relationship cannot be established and relinking among developing nations with whom a balanced relationship may be attained. It is in the relinking aspect of collective self-reliance, based on the efforts of developing nations and social groups, that technical cooperation also becomes important.

Technical cooperation is the transfer of knowledge, skills, and experience from one country to another. It takes any of three forms: experts sent to work directly with developing country "counterparts"; fellowships provided to enable men and women from developing nations to acquire skills outside their homelands; and educational and technical institutes and research facilities in developing nations built and strengthened to enable the countries to produce skilled personnel on a continuing basis. The promotion of technical cooperation among developing nations widens the resource supply base, furthers regional cooperation, and helps to continue to build self-reliance.

Self-reliance has a major role to play in the future development of Third World nations. Collective self-reliance also assumes the same role. Current world economic trends appear to indicate that dependence on the North, if not already invalid, may not be feasible much longer. The Third World nations of the South must therefore, if not voluntarily then by necessity, develop another strategy based on development created by and based in the South. The strength of collective self-reliance and the framework of ECDC can ask for no sterner test than to meet the new challenges and use the new opportunities.[11] Collective self-reliance is of utmost necessity to the economic survival of the developing nations and the Caribbean nations are no exception. In terms of the latter, the Caribbean Community (CARICOM) provides perhaps the best institutional arrangement for achieving collective self-reliance though it has generally been regarded as being more consistent with the goals and "objectives of the operational definition of collective self-reliance than the theoretical and conceptual requirements suggested by the more comprehensive definition."[12]

However, CARICOM has encountered a number of problems in its attempt to remain a viable instrument of collective self-reliance. Primary among these are the dissatisfaction of several member states with the distribution of benefits and the attempt by some of the governments to formulate and implement policies of self-reliant development consistent with their own domestic priorities but contrary to regional goals as reflected in the CARICOM treaty.[13]

This therefore poses a dilemma for the Caribbean nations. There is a vast difference between agreement on self-reliant development goals and the implementation of the relevant collective policies to achieve them. This, of course, is a historical phenomenon in the Caribbean region which somehow must be eradicated. Leadership and statesmanship must predominate above all other selfish and insular goals so that regional policy for self-reliant development gets implemented and regressive thinking is eliminated.

NOTES

1. Enrique Oteiza and A. Rahman, "Technical Cooperation Among Third World Countries for Development," *Labour and Society* 3 (July-October 1978), pp. 445–56.

2. James B. McGinnis, *Bread and Justice: Toward a New International Economic Order* (New York: Paulist Press, 1979), p. 257.

3. Ibid., p. 261.

4. Mahbub ul Haq, *The Poverty Curtain: Choices for the Third World* (New York: Columbia University Press, 1976), pp. 71–75.

5. Oteiza and Rahman, "Technical Cooperation," p. 450.

6. Robert L. Rothstein, *The Weak in the World of the Strong* (New York: Columbia University Press, 1977), pp. 261–62.

7. Karl P. Sauvant, "The Origins of the NIEO Discussions," in *Changing Priorities on the International Agenda,* ed. K.P. Sauvant (New York: Pergamon Press, 1981), p. 19.

8. Guy F. Erb, "The Developing World's Challenge in Perspective," in *Beyond Dependency: The Developing World Speaks Out,* eds. Guy F. Erb and Valeriana Kallab (Washington, D.C.: Overseas Development Council, 1975), p. 140.

9. J. Samuel Valenzuela and A. Valenzuela, "Modernization and Dependency: Alternative Perspectives in the Study of Latin American Underdevelopment," in *From Dependency to Development: Strategies to Overcome Underdevelopment and Inequality,* ed. H. Munoz (Boulder, Colo.: Westview Press, 1981), p. 25.

10. Johan Galtung, "The Politics of Self-Reliance," in *Dependency to Development,* p. 175.

11. Gamini Seneviratne, *Economic Cooperation Among Developing Countries* (New York: United Nations, 1980), pp. 44–45; and Kempe Ronald Hope, "Self-Reliant Development in the Third World," *Transnational Perspectives* 8, no. 4 (1982), pp. 13–15.

12. See Kenneth Hall and Byron Blake, "Collective Self-Reliance: The Case of the Caribbean Community (CARICOM)," in *Dependency to Development,* p. 199.

13. Ibid., pp. 201–3.

PART II

GENERAL ECONOMIC TRENDS IN THE CARIBBEAN

4

Overview of the Caribbean Economy

The Caribbean economy has undergone very little structural change since its existence and that indicates that the character of the economic process in the region has not changed. As such, the economy remains passively responsive to metropolitan demand and metropolitan investment,[1] creating an ongoing, dependent relationship on the economies of the Western industrial nations.

In the past decade this dependent relationship has led to severe economic dislocations in the Caribbean. For example, the slowdown in economic activity and the restrictive monetary and fiscal policies in the developed countries contributed to a slackening in demand for some of the traditional export products of the region, particularly bauxite and sugar, with consequences affecting earnings. This situation was further aggravated by declines in output as a result of domestic difficulties, including adverse weather conditions and problems with national economic management.[2]

The further vulnerability of the region arises in large measure from its dependence on imports not only of food and other consumer items, but of fuel and other essential intermediate and capital goods to support its productive capacity, and on a narrow range of domestic products to generate foreign exchange earnings and, although efforts have been made to expand and diversify domestic activity, the economies have been constrained mainly by the rapidly rising price of imported goods, scarce foreign exchange, and uncertainties in the international markets.[3]

Economic development in the Caribbean, then, depends essentially on the success of these economies to cope with the vagaries of the world economy and on the development of export trade.[4] During the 1950s the region managed to respond favorably. In terms of per capita product, Jamaica and Trinidad and Tobago were among the fastest growing economies in the world. Between 1954 and 1963 the Gross Domestic Product

(GDP) per capita expanded in Jamaica at an annual average rate of more than 8.9 percent while the respective figure for Trinidad and Tobago was 11.1 percent.[5] Although the rate of growth in the other countries was less spectacular, the average rate of increase in output exceeded in most cases the annual rate of population growth.[6]

During the 1970s, as seen in Tables 4.1 and 4.2, both the absolute Gross National Product at market prices and per capita Gross National Product increased, except in Guyana, where there was a decline in 1977, and Jamaica, where there were declines in 1976, 1979, and 1980. Jamaica's decrease was attributed to a combination of factors, such as rapid deterioration in the terms of trade, the low level of savings and investment, and the uncertainty created by the policy of social change and of control over the principal economic sectors by the then government of Prime Minister Michael Manley.

Looking at Table 4.3, we can gauge the relative importance of per capita GNP by comparing real rates of growth with population growth. By doing this we are able to arrive at conclusions pertaining to increases in standard of living. That is, we are able to say something about whether the population may be better off, or not, due to growth in per capita GNP.

During the 1960–76 period all of the countries, with the exception of Guyana, had greater growth rates in real per capita GNP than for population. However, looking at the more recent period of 1970–80 we see that Barbados and Trinidad and Tobago both had higher rates of growth of per capita GNP than for population. In Guyana and Jamaica, however, growth in real per capita GNP was not only lower than that for population but it was also negative for Jamaica.

Table 4.1. GNP at Market Prices by Country, 1960–80 (Millions of U.S. Dollars)

Year	Barbados	Guyana	Jamaica	Trinidad and Tobago
1960	83	158	321	448
1965	109	199	446	624
1970	168	245	856	801
1975	360	420	2,440	2,110
1976	400	460	2,390	2,400
1977	440	450	2,410	2,650
1978	520	460	2,540	3,410
1979	660	500	2,400	4,500
1980	810	540	2,360	5,850

Sources: World Bank, World Tables 1976 (Baltimore: Johns Hopkins University Press, 1976); World Bank, World Bank Atlas (Washington, D.C.: World Bank, several years); and Inter-American Development Bank, Economic and Social Progress in Latin America (Washington, D.C.: IDB, several years).

Table 4.2. GNP per Capita by Country, 1970–80 (U.S. Dollars)

Year	Barbados	Guyana	Jamaica	Trinidad and Tobago
1970	720	360	590	776
1972	800	400	810	970
1973	1,000	410	990	970
1974	1,200	500	1,190	1,700
1975	1,470	540	1,200	1,950
1976	1,620	570	1,150	2,190
1977	1,760	560	1,150	2,380
1978	2,080	560	1,190	3,010
1979	2,680	640	1,110	3,910
1980	3,270	690	1,090	5,010

Sources: Same as for Table 4.1.

The economic downturn in Jamaica, as in most of the developing countries, began in late 1973 as a result of the oil crisis and the ensuing inflation and recession in the industrialized countries. There were also unfavorable trends in the external sector which were accompanied by a sharp contraction in private investment and by precipitous declines in the levels of economic activity and employment in the agricultural, manufacturing, construction, and mining sectors. As a result, by 1976, Jamaica was in the throes of its most severe economic crisis since independence in 1962.

A principal cause in the 1976 economic downturn was the marked deterioration in the already serious balance-of-payments situation. Jamaica's export earnings fell sharply in the wake of both dampened world demand for alumina and lower prices for agricultural products, especially sugar. In addition, adverse publicity abroad affected tourism, causing a decline in the number of arrivals as well as expenditures. As a consequence, the current-

Table 4.3. Average Annual Growth Rates of Population and GNP per Capita by Country, 1960–76 and 1970–80 (Percentages)

Country	Population		Real GNP per Capita	
	1960–76	1970–80	1960–76	1970–80
Barbados	0.4	0.5	5.1	3.2
Guyana	2.2	1.7	1.7	1.1
Jamaica	1.7	1.5	2.5	−2.8
Trinidad and Tobago	1.5	1.3	1.6	3.9

Sources: Same as for Table 4.1.

account deficit widened from US$280 million in 1975 to US$295 million in 1976, despite sharply reduced imports attributed to government restrictions. However, the main problem in the balance of payments during 1976 was the capital account, where the prevailing climate of political and economic uncertainly caused not only private capital inflows and direct foreign investment to decline but also stimulated capital flight.[7]

The second major problem that affected the economy's performance in 1976 was the overall fiscal deficit, which soared to an unprecedented 18.6 percent of GDP, significantly above the 10.8 percent for 1975. This reflected the combined effect of decreased revenues, as a result of reduced economic activity, and the continued growth of current expenditures. At the same time, though, capital expenditures also increased as the government had to absorb a number of failing enterprises to prevent further declines in both the level of economic activity and employment and also to compensate for the private sector's increasing unwillingness to invest.[8]

The economic situation became so untenable that the Jamaican government declared a state of economic emergency in January 1977 and announced the immediate adoption of major corrective measures, such as a tax package designed to yield an additional J$80 million in revenue annually, largely through higher levies on gasoline and personal incomes, a freeze on wages in the public sector, and a number of restrictions on foreign exchange. Moreover, in April 1977, an emergency production plan was prepared to deal with the problems of underutilization of installed capacity and resources in the economy and to establish realistic production and employment targets. In addition, a dual exchange rate system was introduced, consisting of a new "special rate" for all transactions with the exception of those involving essential imports, government purchases, and the bauxite and alumina sector, all of which remained at the old, or "basic" rate. Then, in August 1977, another series of measures were adopted under the aegis of a standby agreement with the International Monetary Fund. The IMF's program was designed to limit public-sector expenditures and to improve the balance-of-payments situation.

In this context, the Seaga administration elected in October 1980, and re-elected in December 1983, faced the tremendous task of reversing declining output, stimulating private investment, and restoring the fiscal balance. The achievement of these goals is constrained, at least for the near future, by the availability of foreign exchange. To bridge the gap and replenish depleted reserves, the authorities completed negotiations with the IMF and the World Bank on an economic program supported by an Extended Fund Facility arrangement and a Structural Adjustment Program covering the five-year period (1982–87).[9] Some additional relief is expected from the rescheduling of major portions of the external public debt and special financial assistance from other countries and institutions.

The deteriorating economic situation in Guyana is the direct result of poor economic management and inconsistent policy directives which have resulted in the economy showing signs of bankruptcy. To attempt to rectify this situation the government entered into negotiations on both an Extended Fund Facility arrangement with the IMF and a Structural Adjustment Program with the World Bank. Both the EFF program and the Structural Adjustment Program have as their expressed policy objectives the achievement of a certain degree of structural transformation of the Guyanese economy in the medium- and longer-term, the restoration of economic activity to at least its historical level, and more efficient use of capital investments by taking maximum advantage of existing productive capacity.

Jamaica and Guyana therefore now find themselves having to exist under the principles of conditionality. Conditionality is intended as a means to ensure the efficiency of the international adjustment process to the benefit of all the IMF's membership. It also constitutes an essential aspect of the contribution that IMF makes to assist with the balance-of-payments difficulties of member nations. But the debate over such conditionality has been intense, to say the least, and has even led to calls for international monetary reform. Such calls notwithstanding, if developing nations mismanage their economies and/or must turn to the IMF for balance-of-payments support, then they must be prepared to accept the short-term conditions imposed.

The economy of Barbados generally reflects the buoyant nature of economic activity with fairly good performance in most of the productive sectors. During the postwar period the economy became more diversified with tourism and manufacturing becoming more important foreign-exchange earners than sugar, the original export staple. However, the impact of external circumstances on the Barbados economy remains considerable. In the 1960s and 1970s economic fluctuations in Barbados mirrored the swings in the economies of the country's North Atlantic trading partners.[10] More recently, shortfalls in export earnings forced the government in October 1982 to borrow from the IMF the sum of SDR 44.5 million (US$49 million). The sum of SDR 12.6 million was advanced under the Compensatory Financing Facility with the remaining SDR 31.9 million to be drawn down under the provisions of a 20-month standby arrangement.

The situation in Trinidad and Tobago is a very peculiar one. Of course, it does represent a classic situation where an economy is rapidly growing in absolute terms but shows negative growth when inflationary effects are taken into consideration. The relative magnitude of inflation in the Caribbean can be observed from Table 4.4, which shows the annual variations in the Consumer Price Index for the period 1971–80.

What Table 4.4 indicates is that all of the Caribbean countries have had significant variations in their inflation rates. However, the situation in Trinidad and Tobago is peculiar, to the extent that the country's economic

Table 4.4. Annual Variation in the Consumer Price Index by Country, 1971–80

Country	1971–75	1976	1977	1978	1979	1980
Barbados	18.9	5.0	8.3	9.5	13.2	18.7
Guyana	7.8	9.0	8.2	15.3	17.7	14.1
Jamaica	14.1	9.6	11.4	34.9	29.1	26.8
Trinidad and Tobago	13.3	10.5	11.9	10.2	14.7	17.5

Sources: International Monetary Fund, *International Financial Statistics* (Washington, D.C.: IMF, several issues).

activity is heavily influenced by the petroleum sector's earnings. Since 1973 worldwide earnings from the petrochemical industry have been increasing at an alarming rate, due to sustained increases in prices for petroleum and petroleum-based products. Though these inflationary price increases have benefited the economy of Trinidad and Tobago in absolute terms, the real net growth effect per capita has been negative when indexed for inflation.

Other studies have attempted to explain this situation by comparing variations in the level of liquidity and changes in the level of retail prices. The conclusion has been that large changes in the level of liquidity tend to be accompanied by large changes in the level of retail prices.[11] That is, as the money supply is increased on a large scale the tendency is for retail prices also to increase on a large scale. This phenomenon was particularly true in the case of Trinidad and Tobago, especially during 1978–80, the years that inflation was most rampant in the Caribbean.

During the 1970s and early 1980s the major sources of sectoral economic growth in the Caribbean have been the capital-intensive mining sector (petroleum sector in Trinidad and Tobago) and the export sugar industry. While making a substantial contribution to the balance of payments, these industries have not provided a corresponding increase in employment. As a consequence, the economy of the Caribbean has not generated sufficient increases in employment to absorb the growing labor force and unemployment remains very high, resulting in high dependency rates and serious social and economic dislocations for the population.

NOTES

1. Kari Levitt and Lloyd Best, "Character of Caribbean Economy," in *Caribbean Economy,* ed. George Beckford (Kingston, Jamaica: Institute of Social and Economic Research, University of the West Indies, 1975), pp. 37–38.
2. Caribbean Development Bank, *Annual Report 1981* (St. Michael, Barbados: Caribbean Development Bank, 1982), p. 19.

3. Caribbean Development Bank, *Annual Report 1980,* p. 19.

4. Kempe Ronald Hope, *Recent Performance and Trends in the Caribbean Economy: A Study of Selected Caribbean Countries* (St. Augustine, Trinidad: Institute of Social and Economic Research, University of the West Indies, 1980), p. 43.

5. M.A. McIntyre, "Some Problems of Development in the West Indies Today," in *The West Indies and the Atlantic Provinces of Canada* (Halifax: Institute of Public Affairs, Dalhousie University, 1966), p. 17.

6. Ibid.

7. Inter-American Development Bank, *Economic and Social Progress in Latin America* (Washington, D.C.: IDB, 1977), p. 291.

8. Ibid., p. 292.

9. Inter-American Development Bank, *Economic and Social Progress,* 1982, p. 278.

10. DeLisle Worrell, "An Economic Survey of Barbados, 1946–1980," in *The Economy of Barbados, 1946–1980,* ed. DeLisle Worrell (Bridgetown, Barbados: Central Bank of Barbados, 1982), p. 44.

11. See Wilfred L. Whittingham, "Inflation in the Caribbean Community and Latin America," in *Inflation in the Caribbean,* ed. C. Bourne (Kingston, Jamaica: Institute of Social and Economic Research, University of the West Indies, 1977), pp. 99–111.

5

The Manufacturing Sector

The manufacturing industry's share of GDP in the Caribbean has changed unevenly, as seen in Table 5.1. It increased considerably in some years and likewise declined in some years. The generally small size of the countries has led to a broadly similar pattern of industrialization in the Caribbean, although the timing and extent of industrial development has varied.

The manufacturing sector in Barbados consists largely of the production of food, beverages, tobacco, clothing, and chemicals and the assembly of electrical components. The data suggest that real output in this sector increased by 2.1 percent a year during 1946–80.[1] The main constituents of the sector's output, measured by their relative weights in the industrial production index, are beverages and tobacco (17 percent); food (15 percent); and clothing (11 percent).

Perhaps the most significant contribution of the manufacturing sector to the economy of Barbados has been the rapid growth of exports and hence foreign-exchange earnings. Whereas domestic exports grew at an average of 9.8 percent a year during 1946–80, exports of the manufacturing sector rose by 16.2 percent.[2] The increase in supply was made possible by more efficient capacity utilization, but there was also an increase in capacity as new plants were established, and this, in turn, caused the virtual exhaustion of available industrial park space. Though there was some expansion in external demand, import restrictions imposed by Jamaica adversely affected the trade of Barbados with that country, particularly with respect to textiles.

Manufacturing in Guyana consists primarily of sugar and rice processing. There is also some light manufacturing undertaken by a large number of small operations producing mainly consumer goods which require substantial imports of raw materials and intermediate and capital goods. During 1976–80, manufacturing activity was relatively stagnant in

Table 5.1.   Contribution of Manufacturing Sector to GDP by Country, 1960-80 (Percentage of GDP)

Country	1960	1965	1970	1975	1980
Barbados[a]	8.3	10.2	10.8	11.8	10.2
Guyana[b]	10.4	13.1	12.2	11.2	16.0
Jamaica[b]	13.6	15.0	13.6	18.1	15.9
Trinidad & Tobago[b]	12.5	16.5	11.7	10.8	10.4

Sources: Inter-American Development Bank, *Economic and Social Progress in Latin America* (Washington, D.C.: IDB, several years).
[a]Includes mining.
[b]Includes processing.

Guyana, resulting from the relatively low investment in it due to a complex nexus of problems and constraints, including continued uncertainty on the part of private investors about the role of the private sector in the economy in the medium and long run, publication of the Investment Code notwithstanding; foreign exchange constraints and consequent bottlenecks in the import of machinery, equipment, spare parts, and materials; irregularity of electricity supply and absence of proper back-up systems; and inadequate project preparation, evaluation, and management capabilities.[3]

The decline in Jamaica's manufacturing sector, which began in 1976, continued into the 1980s. Almost all of the industrial branches showed declines in their value added. Since a large part of manufactures in Jamaica rely on imported raw materials and intermediate products, activities decreased when the government restricted the import of such products for balance-of-payments reasons.

Up to 1950, manufacturing in Jamaica had been largely concentrated in the processing of locally produced agricultural products. The sector is now more diversified, due in part to numerous industrial incentive measures, which offer tax and other concessions to foreign and local entrepreneurs. Diversification of manufacturing has been in the direction of consumer durables and industrial goods.

The composition of Jamaica's manufacturing sector is such that productivity varies sharply. The many small entrepreneurial activities classified as part of the sector employ extremely small amounts of capital. In contrast, the large corporations employ a substantial amount of capital and are more efficient. They dominate such operations as the production of sugar, rum, molasses, and food processing.[4]

Undoubtedly, the most important limiting factor to growth of the sector was the severe shortage of imported raw materials and spare parts. Particularly during 1977, when import restrictions were most severe, real value added for the sector as a whole declined about 10 percent, with substantially larger declines in the subsectors most dependent on imports.[5] Other developments also hindered the growth of the sector, primary among which was the decline in private investment as a result of the uncertainty over the political climate which preceded the general elections of 1980.

After averaging 4 percent growth in 1974–75, the manufacturing sector in Trinidad and Tobago contributed to GDP slightly more than 10 percent in 1980. The growth was largely a result of increased domestic demand and, until recently, of expanding markets in the CARICOM area. The assembly subsector, which had appeared to be a principal beneficiary of rising consumer demand and of relatively easy credit available in 1975–76, showed a steady increase in its contribution to manufacturing value added from 26.5 percent of the total in 1974 to 30.4 percent in 1976 but then stagnated in 1980, due to declining sales as a result of higher prices.

Barbados, Guyana, Jamaica, and Trinidad and Tobago account for approximately 94 percent of manufacturing Gross Domestic Product of the CARICOM region. Manufacturing tends to depend heavily on imported inputs. On the whole, the local value added is small and few linkages have been generated within the domestic economy. The obvious reason for this state of affairs is that neither raw materials nor intermediate industries exist locally. The small size of domestic markets inhibits the establishment of intermediate manufacturing, which, to be efficient, needs to operate on a reasonably large scale. Size also affects the sector's ability to contribute to employment of the growing labor force in the Caribbean.

NOTES

1. Winston Cox, "The Manufacturing Sector in the Economy of Barbados, 1946–1980" in Worrell, *Economy of Barbados,* p. 53.

2. Ibid., p. 70.

3. Inter-American Development Bank, *Economic and Social Progress,* 1981, p. 269.

4. Ransford W. Palmer, *The Jamaican Economy* (New York: Praeger, 1968), p. 26.

5. M.A. Ayub, *Made in Jamaica: The Development of the Manufacturing Sector* (Baltimore: Johns Hopkins University Press, 1981), p. 45.

6

The Tourism Sector

Studies of the role of tourism in the international economy are only now beginning to appear in published sources. However, tourism has always been recognized as an important activity, both nationally and internationally, because of its multiplier effect and, hence, its impact on income generation, its stimulation of investment and employment, and its impact on foreign-exchange earnings. There are also secondary spillover effects in other sectors. Through increased demand for food products, souvenirs, and other goods, it generates employment in agriculture, food processing, handicrafts, and light manufacturing.

However, the emphasis given to any one of these roles in any given economy depends on the extent to which governments perceive tourism as a sector with net social and economic benefits. In the Caribbean, it is generally accepted that tourism has contributed significantly to employment, foreign exchange, and national income. This chapter examines the recent performance and trends in the Caribbean tourism sector within the framework of its growth, impact, and future.

PATTERNS OF GROWTH AND IMPACT OF THE CARIBBEAN TOURISM SECTOR

In the early 1960s, rapid economic growth in the industrialized countries gave many people levels of income well above their everyday needs. At the same time, air travel was beginning to serve an increasing number of destinations at lower costs than before, and new social attitudes toward vacations encouraged tourism throughout much of the world. In the Caribbean, these developments led to a diversification as well as a general expansion of regional tourism. As the number of tourists grew, new areas opened up. Islands which had not previously been tourist centers began to compete for a share of the rapidly growing market and a sustained tourism boom was forecast.

Table 6.1 indicates the growth of the tourist arrivals in the Caribbean for the period 1970–80. As can be observed, the island of Jamaica consistently received the largest absolute number of tourists. However, after 1974 the growth rate of tourist arrivals in the island declined considerably. Growth in tourism has shown sensitivity to economic conditions in the North American and European markets and the perception in those markets of the tourism climate in Jamaica.

The years between 1960 and 1974 witnessed a steady growth in Jamaican tourism. Stopover visitors increased about threefold during that period. The trend began to reverse in 1975, when Jamaican and other tourist destinations in the Caribbean began to feel the effects of the recession in North America and Europe. While other Caribbean destinations showed a strong recovery in 1976, the escalation of crime and the ensuing bad publicity caused a further 17.2 percent decline in arrivals in 1976 and another 19.2 percent decline in 1977 before recovering in 1978 and declining again in 1980.

Several other reasons can be given for the decline in tourism demand in Jamaica and the rest of the Caribbean. First, there was a drastic reduction in the cost of time of travel to Europe from North America. The highly diversified structure of air fares effectively undercut the Caribbean's price advantage for scheduled flights and the generally high cost of accommodation,

Table 6.1. Tourist Arrivals in the Caribbean, 1970–80[a] (Thousands)

Year	Barbados Total	% Change	Jamaica Total	% Change	Trinidad & Tobago Total	% Change
1970	156.4	—	309.1	—	76.0	—
1971	189.1	20.9	359.3	16.2	94.6	24.5
1972	210.3	11.3	407.8	13.5	97.6	3.2
1973	222.1	5.6	418.3	2.6	110.2	12.9
1974	230.7	3.9	433.0	3.5	106.2	− 3.6
1975	221.6	− 4.0	395.3	− 8.6	111.1	4.6
1976	224.3	1.2	327.7	− 17.2	129.4	16.5
1977	269.3	20.1	265.0	− 19.2	138.5	7.0
1978	316.8	17.6	381.8	44.1	150.9	9.0
1979	370.9	14.5	426.5	11.7	190.1	26.0
1980	369.9	− 0.3	395.3	− 7.3	210.0	10.5

Sources: Barbados Statistical Service, Digest of Tourist Statistics; Barbados Board of Tourism, Annual Reports; Jamaica Tourist Board, Annual Reports; Government of Trinidad and Tobago, Central Statistical Office; and Caribbean Tourism Research and Development Center, Annual Statistical Reports.

[a]Data pertain to stopover tourists only.

food, and internal transport in the Caribbean made the total vacation package in the region less competitive than those available in Europe. Hence, North Americans found it more attractive and cheaper to spend a week or two in Europe than in the Caribbean. Also, North America became a stronger competitor for European tourists.

In addition, the popularity of Caribbean vacations has typically been affected by the existence of special concessionary air fares; by currency realignments and internal inflation rates, which have altered the ability of tourists to afford Caribbean vacations; by the directions of overseas investment flows, which have induced a mix of business and vacation travel; and by the decisions of tour wholesalers, made in an international context, about the marketability of a Caribbean vacation. These factors, which have been particularly important for European tourists, but have also affected demand from other areas, have varied sharply in strength in recent years. Fluctuations in tourism demand have been the result.

Although still unsettled, the near-term prospects for Jamaica's tourism sector appear to be good. The main reasons for the projected reversal in Jamaica's tourist traffic trends are the country's locational ability to participate in the general improvement in the tourist trade both worldwide and regionally, within the context of periods of relative social calm at home and a moderation in the negative image abroad. Furthermore, major promotional efforts are being made to attract group charters and to establish all-inclusive tours which reduce the total cost of trips to the island.

In Barbados, the number of overseas visitors grew rapidly over the last decade, even though a slight hiatus followed the fuel crisis and the longer-term recession in the economies of the principal tourism-generating countries. The same is true for Trinidad and Tobago. The impact in Barbados of the general downturn in the tourism market was relatively short-lived, however. The market began to recover in 1976, attaining a new record in 1979. The data for 1980 indicates that tourist visitors have decreased marginally by 0.3 percent over the preceding year.

The recent increase in visitors to Barbados has resulted in an increase in the country's market share of tourism in the Caribbean. During the period 1970-78, the number of stayover visitors in Barbados grew at an annual average rate of 11.3 percent, compared with 3.5 percent for the Caribbean as a whole. Over the same period, the island's market share rose from 4.2 percent to 6.7 percent.

The situation in Trinidad and Tobago was somewhat similar to that in Barbados. Tourism expanded in the island during the 1976-80 period, following a period of relatively slow growth in 1974-75. Preliminary data indicate that Trinidad and Tobago is expected to continue to experience modest gains in arrivals over the next few years.

Since the energy crisis, certain changes have occurred in the characteristics of tourist demand for Barbados, as seen in Table 6.2.

Table 6.2. Origin of Stopover Tourists in Barbados, 1970–80 (Thousands)

Year	USA Number	%	UK Number	%	Canada Number	%	Caribbean Number	%	Other Number	%	Total Number	%
1970	57.1	37	12.1	8	39.6	25	33.5	21	14.2	9	156.4	100
1972	75.5	36	14.9	29	61.9	7	39.1	19	18.9	9	210.3	100
1973	73.3	33	17.7	8	68.7	31	39.4	18	23.0	10	222.1	100
1974	66.2	28	23.8	10	77.2	33	38.1	16	25.3	11	230.7	100
1975	54.9	25	24.8	11	75.5	34	38.5	17	27.9	13	221.6	100
1976	56.0	25	25.8	12	73.0	33	38.5	17	30.9	14	224.3	100
1977	70.4	26	25.5	10	83.7	31	48.6	18	40.4	13	269.3	100
1978	85.5	27	35.7	11	91.2	29	54.3	17	50.2	16	316.9	100
1979	91.4	25	49.4	13	92.7	25	76.0	20	61.4	17	370.9	100
1980	86.0	23	56.2	15	84.9	23	84.4	23	57.4	16	369.9	100

Sources: Same as for Table 6.1.

Whereas, traditionally, the United States had been the principal tourist-generating country, this position was taken over by Canada up to 1979. In 1973, some 73,000 U.S. tourists stayed in Barbados, compared with 69,000 Canadians. By 1979, there were 91,400 U.S. visitors, while the number of Canadians had risen to approximately 93,000.

To a significant extent that situation reflected a higher proportion of Canadian-financed tourist investment in Barbados supported by the earlier introduction of air charters. With the gradual development of charter operations in the United States, along with the deregulation of the air-tariff structure in general, the rate of growth of the U.S. market is expected to be significantly higher than that of Canada's in the future.

Overall, although North America remained the chief tourist-generating market for Barbados, other secondary but increasingly important market segments have emerged recently. The United Kingdom, West Germany, and Venezuela have all increased their shares of the Barbados tourist market, with the United Kingdom showing an estimated 15 percent rise in the number of tourists during 1980. Currently, more than 56,000 British tourists stay in Barbados, making it by far the most important destination in the Caribbean. Visitors from the CARICOM countries, principally Trinidad, total some 23 percent of all arrivals with the result that their share equaled that of the United States.

Tourism demand in Barbados, therefore, is relatively buoyant, a situation not being experienced in other Eastern Caribbean countries with the probable exception of St. Lucia. Apart from the relative accessibility of the island and the overall quality of the tourism product, the strength of the industry in Barbados has been its dynamism. Unlike the majority of other tourist destinations throughout the world that have experienced some degree of retrenchment in the wake of worldwide recessions, not only has

Barbados continued to expand its overall arrivals, but it has done so in a form that is best suited to the changing pattern of demand.

For example, promotional efforts have concentrated on attracting lower-income summer tourists. This is a seasonality factor which is typically dictated by conditions in the country of tourist origin rather than destination. The year-round climate in the Caribbean without variation, results in no obvious reason for seasonality. Also, there has been very rapid expansion of apartment and cottage accommodation, reflecting the changed demand of the increasing number of tourists. But an important question that can be asked here is whether these components of supply also diversified demand, or whether they merely encroached upon a limited market. This phenomenon reflects both expectations about the growth of tourism and the limited investment options of local entrepreneurs. Local investors are more easily able to finance apartments, cottages, and guest houses than larger more complex units. The outlay on smaller, less-complex units is usually small and the financial returns are fast enough to attract local investment funds.

The situation in Jamaica and Trinidad and Tobago shows similar trends with respect to country origin of tourists. Although the number of tourists from the United States has been declining and the number of tourists from Canada increasing, the largest percentage of tourists is still from the United States. U.S. tourists have heavily influenced both the general nature of tourism development in the two islands, and the design of hotels and other accommodations.

Associated with the changing tourism pattern in the Caribbean has been a change in the average length of stay of the tourists and the hotel bed occupancy rate. The average length of stay ranged from a low of 5.5 days in Trinidad and Tobago in 1972 to a high of 9.8 days in Barbados during 1980. To a large extent, this trend reflects the larger proportion of Canadians and European visitors to the Caribbean. Both groups enjoy

Table 6.3. Origin of Stopover Tourists in Jamaica, 1972–80 (Thousands)

Year	USA Number	%	Canada Number	%	Europe Number	%	Other Number	%	Total Number	%
1972	316.2	78	38.3	9	16.9	4	36.5	9	407.8	100
1973	325.3	78	36.9	9	26.8	6	29.3	7	418.3	100
1974	339.7	78	37.4	9	28.8	7	28.8	7	433.0	100
1975	297.2	75	46.7	12	26.5	7	25.2	6	395.3	100
1976	229.3	70	48.5	15	27.5	8	24.2	7	327.7	100
1977	177.5	67	40.6	15	23.5	9	23.3	10	265.0	100
1978	253.3	66	71.9	19	35.7	9	20.9	6	381.8	100
1979	279.5	66	74.4	17	52.6	12	20.0	5	426.5	100
1980	239.7	61	70.8	18	63.7	16	21.1	5	395.3	100

Sources: Same as for Table 6.1.

longer vacation benefits than their U.S. counterparts and, in part, are at-tracted to the islands, particularly Barbados, by the relatively recent developments in partly or wholly self-catering, apartment-style accom-modation. The hotel bed occupancy rate has ranged from a low of 42.8 percent in Barbados during the recession years of 1975–76 to a high of 66 percent during 1980 in Barbados also, reflecting the higher tourism de-mand in Barbados, as mentioned earlier.

Another important factor in the tourism sector in the Caribbean is that of the average expenditure per tourist. International tourism can make a significant impact on the economic fabric of host countries, not only in terms of employment generation and foreign exchange earnings but also through the linkages with other sectors of their economies. In Table 6.4, we see the average expenditure per tourist for some of the islands for the period 1972–80.

What clearly emerges is the fact that the average expenditure per tourist has been increasing annually in both Barbados and Trinidad and Tobago. The reason for this is that the average length of stay by tourists has been increasing. Moreover, the inflationary spiral has caught up with these islands and, as such, the prices of all goods and services have increased, which in turn has increased tourism revenues. In the case of Jamaica, there was a decline in tourist expenditure during 1975 and 1976.

Tourism revenues have provided the Caribbean region with a major portion of its foreign exchange earnings. Tourist-related activities grossed an average of 14 percent of Jamaica's foreign exchange earnings in the 1970s while in Barbados such activities generated slightly more than 19 percent of the GDP and 42 percent of goods and nonfactor service export earnings. However, there is some difficulty in assessing the balance-of-payments impact of tourism because of the leakage of foreign exchange.

Table 6.4. Average Expenditure per Tourist in the Caribbean, 1972–80 (In U.S. dollars)

Year	Barbados	Jamaica	Trinidad & Tobago
1972	285	240	95
1973	308	247	101
1974	340	251	161
1975	352	232	231
1976	368	225	243
1977	414	270	252
1978	452	287	263
1979	683	304	330
1980	686	611	337[a]

Sources: Same as for Table 6.1.

[a]Estimate.

This can be measured in terms of the percentage of each dollar of revenue received from tourist expenditures that is repatriated overseas.[1]

Tourism also contributes directly to employment. The ratio of employees to rooms is the indicator normally used to measure this function. The ratio has varied somewhat in the recent past because of changes in the importance of different types of accommodation. The indirect contribution of tourism to employment is harder to measure. A number of nontourist activities also benefit from tourism, but because many interrelated services are not totally dependent on tourism, the industry's contribution to employment in them cannot be assessed with any accuracy. Table 6.5 shows the estimated numbers of those directly employed in tourist accommodation during the early 1970s.

One of the less desirable characteristics of Caribbean tourism has always been its seasonal nature, which is reflected in employment. In Barbados, for example, the seasonal variation in employment in tourism is due mainly to the luxury hotels, which are by far the largest employers. The difference between the high and low seasons approaches one employee per room in Barbados.[2]

Two categories of people appear to benefit particularly from the employment opportunities provided by tourism in the Caribbean. These are young people and women. In the Caribbean, relations between the generations are governed by strict authority patterns, underpinned by the financial dependence of youth on the older generation. The widening of employment and of earning opportunities reduces that dependence and cannot but strain intrafamilial relations. In the Caribbean, youths have experienced considerable social mobility as a direct result of tourism, while family ties have loosened and intergenerational conflicts have emerged.

The Caribbean tourism sector has provided many jobs for women and those jobs have had liberating effects, but the burden of seasonal employment also seems to be borne by female employees.[3] During the low season more women are likely to be laid off than men.

Table 6.5. Tourism Employment Estimates for the Early 1970s

Country	Total	Employee to Room Ratio	Peak to Off-season Employment Ratio
Barbados	4,069	1.83	1.59
Jamaica	9,585	1.05	1.54
Trinidad and Tobago	2,437	1.50	n.a.

Sources: Sidney Chernick et al., *The Commonwealth Caribbean: The Integration Experience* (Baltimore: Johns Hopkins University Press, 1978), p. 176; and Dawn I. Marshall, *Tourism and Employment in Barbados* (Cave Hill, Barbados: Institute of Social and Economic Research, University of the West Indies, 1978), several tables.

Although the Caribbean tourism sector has been beneficial to the island economies, it has not been cost free. The major economic costs are the inflated price of land, high wages which may attract low-wage employees from menial but essential jobs, the cost of investment in infrastructure required for tourism development, and the high bills for imports of food and hotel equipment, which make heavy demands on foreign exchange. For these reasons, tourism is often not viewed by people of the region as any kind of solution to their economic problems.

There are a variety of negative aspects of tourism development, apart from the economic ones. They range from the alienation of local culture and the corruption of moral values, to social tension, the alienation of land caused by the movement of small farmers into the tourist labor force, the frustrations engendered in the local populace by the life-styles of the tourists, and the erosion of dignity and perpetuation of servitude involved in employment in the tourist sector.[4] As such, the really crucial question facing Caribbean tourism now, for an increasing number of people, is not how but whether to attract more tourists.

The most notable impact of tourism on traditional values is that certain social and human relations are brought into the economic sphere; they become part of making a living. The arrival of large-scale tourism has meant that goods or services that used to be part and parcel of people's personal and social lives have now been commercialized and are offered as commodities to the tourists.

The changes in behavior and local values are on the whole attributable to the direct interaction of the local population and tourists resulting in demonstration effects. The effects are most easily and frequently seen in the local patterns of consumption, which change to imitate those of the tourists.[5] It is for these reasons that the ambivalent attitude of the various governments seemed to have hardened into real apprehension and resentment toward tourism. Trinidad and Tobago now places tourism very low among its development priorities. Barbados, which depends heavily on tourism, is seeking to diversify its economy in order to become less dependent on the tourist industry. Jamaica, although still seeking to attract tourists, has taken steps to encourage other forms of private investment.

THE FUTURE OF THE CARIBBEAN TOURISM SECTOR

The final paragraph in the preceding section seems to fairly well sum up the future of the Caribbean tourism sector. But despite some attempts to de-emphasize it, the tourism sector is still of great importance to the economies of the islands. So much so that both in Barbados and Jamaica the Tourists Boards are projecting significant increases in the arrivals of tourists over the next few years. All of the countries have also embarked on major campaigns of advertising and marketing of tourism. Marketing efforts are directed toward increasing nontraditional sources of tourists even more, especially Venezuela and certain European countries. This is expected to yield a twofold increase in the number of tourists to Barbados within five to ten years and, provided there is no further damage to Jamaica's image, the Jamaica Tourist Board's target of an annual average increase in stopover traffic of 15 percent would again become a reasonably attainable marketing target for the 1980s and several years thereafter. Thus arrivals of more than 650,000 stopover tourists in the 1980s are expected in Jamaica.

Based on these projections, the total expenditure by tourists in Jamaica could rise to US$500 million by 1988. This growth in tourism can be accommodated without significant new investment in room capacity over the next few years, because of the rapid expansion that took place in the late 1960s and early 1970s. New investment might be considered subsequently when a clearer perspective on traffic trends develops.

To achieve this growth, however, solutions need to be found to those problem areas that either constrain the future developments of tourism in the Caribbean or may lead to suboptimal growth and possibly deleterious social impacts. To a large extent, the nature and scale of future tourist development must depend on how the Caribbean governments interpret the impact that tourism makes on the economic and social structure of their economies and the role this industry can play in assisting governments to achieve their objectives.

There is no doubt that, carefully planned and regulated, tourism can be a major positive factor in the future development of the Caribbean. Yet, given a laissez-faire approach, much of the economic benefits may be dissipated and the impact on the Caribbean socially disruptive. Unlike other industries, the tourism product is consumed at the point of production and brings the consumer into direct contact with the producer. In order, therefore, to minimize possible negative social aspects while at the same time maximizing the likely benefits, the tourism industry should be under regular governmental scrutiny and appraisal.[6]

Over the longer term, the Caribbean's superb resort assets, its warm climate throughout the year, its location reasonably close to such important sources of tourists as the United States and Canada—together with the growth of incomes and scarcity of beaches in those North American countries—will ensure the eventual recovery of demand for tourism in the Caribbean region. In fact, over the longer term, demand seems likely to meet a physical constraint before it can be satisfied, although the relatively small size of the industry in the Caribbean makes it unlikely that such a growth constraint will arise over the next five years.

Of course, variation of tourist flows among nations will continue. In general, the Caribbean countries see tourism as expanding, though a number of factors, both domestic and external, are seen to have a significant potential impact on tourism demand. Unprecedented worldwide inflation, recession, and unemployment have made the task of forecasting future demand even more difficult. Moreover, it is not certain whether tourism should be regarded as an integral part of consumer expenditures or as a part of discretionary income. If it is the latter, adverse economic circumstances which reduce discretionary income are likely to hamper tourism prospects.

CONCLUSIONS

The Caribbean governments hold the key to the area's tourism future. In the past they have allowed the tourism sector much too free a run, and to some considerable extent they must blame themselves for many of the present problems. The tourism sector will probably always remain controversial, but the greater the linkages to other sectors, the greater the compatibility between tourism and local culture, and the more equitable the distribution of benefits from tourism, the more acceptable and effective the sector will become as a development tool in the Caribbean. Tourism development in the Caribbean should be undertaken consciously and methodically, and be carefully planned as part of the national development effort. It should capitalize on the unique features of the countries in order to make maximum use of local resources, to ensure a marketable product, and to reduce the risk of competition from other destinations.

The greatest single need in the region is to improve the links between the tourism sector and the rest of the economy. This type of increased economic benefit from tourism can only come about, however, if the tourism sector is guided by plans and strategies geared to national objectives. This requires careful planning and an appropriate mix of policies. In particular, there must be integration of tourism planning with the development planning mechanism. Moreover, steps must be taken to ensure that all sections of the population in as many regions as possible benefit from tourism. This is particularly important, given the now accepted fact that in developing countries, such as the Caribbean islands, tourism is largely an economic activity with social consequences.

NOTES

1. It has been estimated that the leakage from one dollar of tourist expenditure in Barbados is 42 cents and in Jamaica 34 cents. See Sidney Chernick et al., *The Commonwealth Caribbean: The Integration Experience* (Baltimore: Johns Hopkins University Press, 1978), p. 175.

2. Dawn I. Marshall, *Tourism and Employment in Barbados* (Cave Hill, Barbados: Institute of Social and Economic Research, University of the West Indies, 1978), p. 36.

3. John M. Bryden, *Tourism and Development: A Case Study of the Commonwealth Caribbean* (New York: Cambridge University Press, 1973), p. 131.

4. See Irene Hawkins, *The Changing Face of the Caribbean* (Bridgetown, Barbados: Cedar Press, 1976), pp. 136–37.

5. Emanuel de Kadt, ed., *Tourism: Passport to Development* (New York: Oxford University Press, 1979), pp. 64–65.

6. Similar arguments have been made elsewhere. See, for example, C.L. Jenkins, "Tourism Policies in Developing Countries: A Critique," *International Journal of Tourism Management* 1, no. 1 (March 1980), pp. 22–29.

7

The Agricultural Sector and Economic Development in the Caribbean

Debates over development strategy have often swirled around the relative importance to be assigned to agriculture versus industry. Historical evidence suggests that this dichotomy is frequently overstated. Specifically, the notion that rapid industrialization entails a total neglect of agriculture is erroneous; it underestimates the importance of the mutually beneficial links between agricultural and industrial development and indeed, in most developing nations successful industrialization has been supported by sustained and broadly based agricultural growth.

It would seem, therefore, that the major issues in agricultural development in the developing countries are how to sustain a rate of growth that allows for a balanced expansion of all parts of the economy, and how to ensure that the pattern of agricultural growth is such as to make a strong and direct impact on rural poverty and, indirectly, on the reduction of migration of the poor to urban areas.

In the struggle toward industrialization, it has been relatively easy to overlook the importance of the agricultural sector in development and to neglect the necessary harmony between policies to encourage the growth of industry and the performance of agriculture. But, despite the recent rapid rise of industry and the growing urbanization, the agricultural sector still looms large in the developing nations since it is the sector which provides employment for the bulk of the labor force, contains the majority of poor people, and is the birthplace of many of the urban poor. Food and fiber, the products of the agricultural sector, are, moreover, prominent among those which poor people demand in greater quantities as their incomes rise. Furthermore, it is generally the foreign-exchange earnings from the agricultural sector which tend to permit or constrain the expansion of industrial output and employment.

This chapter examines and reviews the role of agriculture in the economic development of the Caribbean countries, with emphasis on the recent performance and current trends of that role.

GROWTH, STRUCTURE, AND CHANGE IN THE AGRICULTURAL SECTOR

Table 7.1 reveals that, with the exception of Jamaica and Guyana, agriculture's share of total value added to Gross Domestic Product has been diminishing steadily. In Guyana, value added by agriculture increased considerably in 1975 and then declined again after then showing a marginal increase in 1980. The 1975 increase was the result of an increase in agricultural production and the collection of windfall revenues from a sugar levy imposed in 1974. In Jamaica, there was an increase in 1977 and 1978 reflecting the strong performance of crops for domestic consumption boosted by the restriction imposed on the import of food products. However, the data for 1980 indicate that Jamaican agricultural value added fell by 8.6 percent in real terms because of continued structural problems.

Despite the declining importance of agriculture in Barbados, along with fishing, it continues to be the largest productive sector in the country. The agricultural sector in Barbados consists mainly of sugar cane production, but it also produces significant amounts of foodstuffs for local consumption, mainly vegetables, livestock, and fish. In 1980 the relative share of the sugar cane subsector was 69 percent, compared with a fairly stable average of 59 percent in 1976–79. Acreage under sugar cane (reaped) increased in 1980 and so did productivity. However, the overall performance of the nonsugar agricultural subsector was rather poor in 1980, with the result that, although value added in the sugar cane subsector increased by 18.8 percent, output in the sector as a whole grew by only 5.2 percent.

Table 7.1. Contribution of Agricultural Sector to GDP by Country, 1960–80 (Percentages)

Country	1960	1965	1970	1975	1976	1977	1978	1979	1980
Barbados	28.0	26.0	15.0	13.3	12.0	11.3	10.9	10.8	10.8
Guyana	26.2	24.0	19.3	32.0	28.0	20.8	18.3	17.7	18.6
Jamaica	12.3	11.6	8.1	7.4	7.3	8.8	9.5	9.3	8.6
Trinidad and Tobago	11.9	7.9	5.2	4.5	3.6	3.4	3.1	3.1	2.4

Sources: United Nations, Yearbooks of National Account Statistics;and Inter-American Development Bank, Economic and Social Progress in Latin America (Washington, D.C., 1981); and World Bank, World Tables 1980 (Baltimore: Johns Hopkins University Press, 1980).

In Guyana, the weak performance of its productive sectors in the 1970s caused a decline in the share of agriculture in current price Gross Domestic Product. The declining contribution of the agricultural sector continued through 1979, mainly as a result of an extended strike in the sugar industry, adverse weather, and a decline in cultivated acreage.

The sugar subsector continues to dominate Guyana's agriculture. It accounted for 14.5 percent of GDP in 1976–80. The rest of the agricultural sector is accounted for by paddy rice, other crops, livestock, forestry, and fisheries, in descending order of magnitude. Paddy production and milling contributed, on the average, another 4 percent to GDP in 1976–80; rice production increased 19 percent in 1980 compared with an average decline of 18 percent per year in 1978–79 from the peak performance in 1977 when production reached 213,000 metric tons.

The relatively poor performance since 1976 of the traditional subsectors of sugar and rice can be attributed to a number of complex factors, including poor labor relations resulting in work stoppages, especially in the sugar subsector; adverse weather patterns, which negatively affect agricultural production; inadequate flood control and irrigation, especially in the rice subsector; problems associated with pest and disease control, particularly in the sugar subsector; and the lack of key agricultural inputs, such as fertilizers, agricultural chemicals, equipment, and spare parts.

In contrast to the uneven growth of crops, the dairy products and livestock industry has grown satisfactorily since 1970. Much of the growth is attributable to the significant increase in pork and poultry production. Guyana is self-sufficient in poultry and egg production at the present time. Much of the livestock production is concentrated on the coast and is carried out by small farmers. Most beef is produced on mixed cattle-crop farms along the coast, largely as a supplementary enterprise and managed extensively.

Jamaica's agricultural sector has traditionally been divided into export-oriented medium- and large-size plantations (producing primarily sugar and bananas) and small farmers producing largely for domestic consumption. Over the years, this structure has contributed to the emergence of a highly unequal distribution of agricultural land and income, mostly in favor of the export-oriented sector.

Given this structure as well as mounting problems posed by unemployment and food imports, the government in its long-term development strategy has given high priority to the modernization of the agricultural sector, with emphasis on more efficient use of available land resources, greater production of food for domestic consumption and creation of employment opportunities. To achieve this, the government initiated, in 1973, Project Land Lease, which by 1977 had benefited more than 23,000 small farmers through leasing land from private as well as government properties. Similar projects such as Project Food Farms and

Project Self-Help were launched in 1973 also and, subsequently, in 1975 the First Rural Development Project was also formulated with international technical and financial assistance. The government restated the need for restructuring the agricultural sector in its 1977 Emergency Production Plan. Among the recommendations of the plan was the immediate cultivation of 50,000 acres of land and the adoption of measures to strengthen infrastructure and credit.

Between 1977–78, the agricultural sector performed favorably, growing at 9.3 percent, in real terms, compared with a decrease of 4.1 percent in 1976. This reflected significant production increases in some of Jamaica's domestic consumption crops, primarily root crops and vegetables. These increases were large enough to offset the moderate expansion in export crops, mainly sugar and bananas.

In 1980, agriculture continued to be beset by structural problems, particularly those affecting sugar and bananas, as well as by poor weather and a volatile labor situation. Value added in the sector fell an estimated 8.6 percent—following a 6.8 percent drop in 1979. This disappointing overall performance in Jamaican agriculture is rather unfortunate since the sector generated over US$85 million in foreign exchange in 1980.

In Trinidad and Tobago, the role of the agricultural sector has been steadily declining for several years. In 1980, it accounted for only 2.4 percent of GDP, whereas in 1975 it accounted for 4.5 percent. One aspect of the problem has been the decline in local fertilizer sales in most years since 1973, so that by 1980 they were at about the same level as 1972, despite the substantial growth in domestic fertilizer production and exports. Moreover, sugar production was down 21 percent in 1980 or less than one-half the level recorded in 1972, after declines averaging 3.2 percent annually in 1976–79. Exports, of course, were down even more; 31.6 percent in 1980 and an average of 4.1 percent annually in 1976–79 in terms of volume. As a result, Trinidad and Tobago has not even been able to fill its export quota under the Lomé Convention. Problems exist on both the agricultural and industrial fronts, and include shortages of factory equipment, declining yields, labor shortages, and unplanned cane fires.

The food processing industry, which is expected to create linkages with the agricultural sector and contribute to a reduction in the food import bill, has been having only moderate success. However, in 1979, the food production index grew by 11.5 percent. The most dynamic of the food-processing industries have been fruit and vegetables, which have attracted a large number of small operators and provided a basis for a sound cottage industry. Nevertheless a number of factors, including insufficient agricultural services; a widening urban-rural wage differential; rising production costs; and a weak marketing system for domestic food crops, have all contributed to a general decline in the agricultural sector in the past decade in Trinidad and Tobago.

Along with the declining share of agriculture in GDP in the Caribbean has been the uneven decline of per capita food production since 1976. As shown in Table 7.2 the per capita food production level in all of the countries during 1971–79 was below that of the base period 1961–65.

Declining per capita food production, apart from indicating the general state of the agricultural sector, also points out the dilemma of economic development in the Caribbean. One of the fundamental roles that agriculture has to play in economic development is the expansion of local food supplies. This becomes important because as economic development proceeds there is a substantial increase in the demand for agricultural products. A failure to expand food supplies might impede economic development, as it results in either an increase in imports and loss of foreign reserves or increases in food prices. Spending scarce foreign exchange on food means that less is available to import capital, technology, and other factors of production. Poor agricultural performance, in other words, hinders the growth of the rest of the economy and limits the resources available to promote growth.

Another important aspect of food production is its contribution to the formation of human capital. Until quite recently, economists regarded food strictly as a consumption good. It is now recognized, however, that part of food utilization really should be considered an investment which improves the quality of the labor force. Malnutrition causes both mental and physical retardation, and poor diets also affect general health. Hence, it is absolutely essential, for the continued promotion of economic development, that the levels of per capita food production increase rather than decline.

Table 7.2. **Indexes of per Capita Food Production by Country,[a]**
1971–79 (1961–65 = 100)

Year	Guyana	Jamaica	Trinidad & Tobago
1971	87	78	79
1972	74	77	81
1973	65	73	70
1974	86	75	74
1975	85	69	63
1976	75	71	75
1977	77	67	72
1978	83	67	71
1979	74	65	74
% Growth			
1977–78	9.1	0.0	0.8
1978–79	– 11.9	– 3.0	2.8

Sources: Same as for Table 7.1.
[a]No data available for Barbados.

Also of importance is the role of agriculture's contribution to employment in the Caribbean. In Table 7.3 the proportion of the Caribbean labor force in the agricultural sector is exhibited. From that table it can be gleaned that the percentage of the labor force employed in agriculture has been declining. In 1980, there was some leveling off with the 1979 figures in Trinidad and Tobago, but it was insufficient to reverse the trend which began in the 1950s and which, after 1970, has resulted in the services sector in all four countries being the major employer, accounting for more than 40 percent of the labor force. The primary employer in the Caribbean services sector is the government.

Though the rapid growth of services sector activity is a new phenomenon in the Caribbean economy, it can be stated that one of the primary reasons that the supply of labor has shifted from agriculture to the service and industry sectors has been the greater possible opportunities for employment in the urban areas where those two latter sectors exist.

Now, let's move to the issue of agricultural trade and its contribution to the overall trade of the Caribbean nations. With the exception of Guyana, all of the countries experienced deficits in their balance of agricultural trade during the 1970s. In 1975, however, Barbados and Jamaica joined Guyana as countries with a surplus in their balance of agricultural trade. That surplus was due primarily to increases in the volume of sugar production and the resultant increase in the value of sugar exports which was aided by increases of world prices.

The Caribbean region as a whole, and the smaller islands in particular, depend heavily on food imports. The relationship between agricultural trade and the total trade of each of the four nations indicates that the volume of agricultural imports in relationship to total imports of goods and services has been changing unevenly during the 1970s while at the same time the volume of agricultural exports has shown a decreasing tendency.

Table 7.3. Caribbean Labor Force Employed in Agriculture, 1950–80 (Percentages)

Country	1950	1960	1970	1977	1980
Barbados	28.6	26	19.9	9.6	9.6[a]
Guyana	43.7	34	32.0	30.9	28.6[a]
Jamaica	51.6	39	29.4	24.0	21.0
Trinidad and Tobago	24.8	22	18.5	13.0	16.0

Sources: Same as for Table 7.1; World Bank, World Development Report 1980 (Washington, D.C.: World Bank, August 1980); and ILO, Yearbook of Labour Statistics (Geneva: ILO, several years).

[a]Most recent estimate.

The composition of the import bill for the Caribbean nations gives an indication of the major food deficiencies of the region. The most important items are animal proteins—meat, dairy and fish products, and animal feed—which made up more than 50 percent of the total value of food imports while fruits and vegetables account for about 8 percent.

In terms of intraregional trade of agricultural products, Barbados and Guyana are responsible for approximately 30 percent of the imports while Guyana and Trinidad and Tobago are responsible for approximately 44 percent of the exports.[1] The regional integration effort in the Caribbean has hardly affected agriculture. This is so primarily because agricultural exports from the Caribbean go to destinations outside the region rather than to other countries within it. Moreover, the countries of the region have broadly similar weather, topography, and soils, leading to a high degree of intraregional competition, rather than to complementarity in the crops produced.[2] The major agricultural products traded within the region are rice, which comes primarily from Guyana, coconut products, vegetables, processed food, and fruits.

ASSESSMENT OF AGRICULTURAL DEVELOPMENT

Agricultural development in the Caribbean seems to suffer from some basic problems that are associated with the structure of the industry as a whole, together with technical and institutional weaknesses. However, the overall decline and transformation of Caribbean agriculture seems consistent with the notion of what is expected to occur during economic development. That is, the decreasing importance of the agricultural sector in the national economy and the growing importance of the industry and service sectors.

But, it is desirable that this be accompanied by increased productivity in the agricultural sector and increased food production capacity to supply the growing share of the population not employed in agriculture. This process has not yet taken place in the Caribbean. The relatively low productivity of Caribbean agriculture has given rise to a very severe problem. That is the problem of feeding the expanding population of the Caribbean over the long term.

Accelerated growth in the agricultural production of developing nations is of primary importance. It not only increases a nation's chances of feeding its populace but it also can sharply increase the transfer of resources between agriculture and other sectors of the economy. Such changes affect relative rates of capital formation and income growth in various sectors, the structure of growth, and overall rates of growth.

Sustained agricultural production, however, requires major policy decisions and some steps have been taken in that direction. A Regional

Food Plan (RFP) was designed by the Caribbean governments and was approved in 1975. The RFP was designed specifically to reduce the region's rapidly rising food import bill through the implementation of projects to supply the region with vital agricultural inputs. Additionally, a Caribbean Food Corporation (CFC) was established in 1976 as the primary regional institution for implementing the RFP. Shares in the CFC are held by all the member governments of the Caribbean Community (CARICOM). Moreover, as mentioned before, in 1977 Jamaica established its own Emergency Production Plan which had as its primary goal the restructuring of the agricultural sector.

The CFC grew out of efforts toward implementing an improved trade regime in the agricultural sector through the establishment of joint regional projects. The RFP's largest component is the regional livestock program and its ambitious overall scope is indicated by its projected achievements. By the end of 1985, when the RFP was to be fully implemented, it was expected to result in the production of 23 million pounds of beef per year; 77 million hatching eggs per year; 7.5 million pounds of mutton and lamb per year; 427.6 pounds of liquid milk; 33.5 million pounds of soya beans; 2 million pounds of red kidney beans; and 2 million pounds of black-eyed peas.[3] However, these targets had not been realized.

Though some progress has been made with respect to the RFP, the regional governments need to place renewed emphasis and interest in its implementation. The CFC, the implementing agency for the RFP, was established in 1976, but it was not until 1979 that some CARICOM countries took legislative action to give the CFC an operational status. In the near future, all CARICOM countries are expected to enact the necessary legislation to enable the CFC to act effectively as the implementing agency for the RFP, as was originally planned.

The CFC is currently endeavoring to find financial and managerial resources for regional food and agricultural projects. The authorized capital of the corporation is $100 million, divided into shares of $1,000 each which may be increased by the board of governors on the recommendation of the board of directors.

Additionally, in Trinidad and Tobago, the government is determined to reverse the trend in the decline of agricultural production and greater dependence on food imports and, to that end, has adopted a system of subsidies and price supports as well as a priority program of investment in the agricultural sector, including land settlements, mixed farming with tree crops for hillside areas, the establishment of extensive acreages of fruit crops, and the rehabilitation of old cocoa plantations, where possible.

However, in any attempt to increase Caribbean agricultural production, consideration must be given to two factors: increasing the acreage available for agricultural production, and increasing the crop yield. In the first case, the issue is one of expanding crop area through new land development. Jamaica, for example, has made some progress in that direction and land is now made available to small farmers under Project Land Lease and Project Self-Help, which were initiated in 1973. But, with the exception of Guyana, where there are government-owned and controlled estates, land holdings in the Caribbean has taken the form either of very large estates involved in commercial, export-oriented agriculture, or very small, owner-operated farms. In both situations there are significant inefficiencies that result.

On the large estates inefficiencies in land use occur primarily because of the amount of land that remains uncultivated. Estates usually cultivate one crop on the most suitable sections of their total holding so that while output per acre of cultivated lands might be high, output per acre of land owned is typically much lower. Moreover, the crop that is produced for export usually tends to be related to the needs of the parent company and is not necessarily the most appropriate crop for the land. Estates are also plagued by a chronic shortage of labor. This is caused by three main factors: the social stigma attached to plantation work, the high wages paid to the small section of the labor force working in modern capital-intensive activities, and the comparatively strenuous nature of agricultural work.[4]

On the small farms inefficiencies exist because of poor cultivation practices, poor and inadequate use of inputs such as fertilizer, the absence of proper soil conservation and irrigation methods, and the sporadic provision of complementary services. The combined effect of all these factors is that small landholders are one of the poorest groups in the region.

Land reform, therefore, seems necessary in the Caribbean. Land reform can be regarded as a systematic, policy-directed change in the terms under which the agricultural population holds and uses land. The objectives are, generally, to improve the farming population's economic performance as well as its economic and social situation. Essentially, land reform seeks to redistribute rights in land for the benefit of small farmers and agricultural laborers.[5] Since land reform, in the sense of redistribution of land, involves a conflict of interest between haves and have-nots, it is also a political question. Guyana's nationalization of the country's sugar estates is a prime example. The government's commitment to ownership and control of the country's major resources dictated such an outcome.

However, the scope of the land reform effort in the rest of the Caribbean, to date, has been marginal. Jamaica has experimented with state farms and also, along with Guyana, with cooperatives. But those programs have not been successful so far. It is, therefore, necessary that a major program of land reform be implemented in the Caribbean.

The benefits of any vigorous land reform program are many. First, the transfer of land from large properties into small ownership can be expected to lead to some increase in agricultural production, as a result of higher inputs of labor, due to its higher marginal productivity. An essential reason for the continued success of agricultural development after land reform is, as generally recognized, in the production incentive it gives small-scale, own-account workers.

Also, when production goes up in the wake of land reform, more of it is likely to stay in the rural area as farmers' incomes. The whole incentive theory of land reform as a factor causing production to increase assumes that this happens, and so the agricultural population ought to become better off. At least in the short run, this should also mean better off in relation to the people in other sectors. This characteristic is one that leads to increased distributive equity in agriculture, which may carry over into other sectors, and could conceivably be one of the more important, as yet overlooked, aspects of land reform.[6]

Given this normal level of expectation pertaining to incomes and production, reform can be compatible with development, though the change in structure in itself is not likely to generate a higher rate of growth. In the Caribbean, it is essential that attempts be made to derive some of these advantages.

Essentially, land reform provides the landless rural classes and small owners with new opportunities to better their lot. Higher incomes will result in their being able to have more food, better housing and clothing, and a greater chance to educate themselves and remove themselves from the poverty rolls. The experience in countries that have undertaken land reform is encouraging in this respect, even in those where land reform has been the result of a violent change in the agrarian structure and without the benefit of careful planning and execution, as happened in the early stages of land reform in Mexico.

Related to the issue of agricultural productivity and income, resulting from land reform, is their dependence on credit, infrastructure, extension services, and research activities. However, all four of these factors are grossly inadequate in the Caribbean. In 1974, the Caribbean Agricultural Research and Development Institute (CARDI) was established. But CARDI has been terribly ineffective to date, primarily because of the lack of financial support it currently receives from member governments. This situation, of course, needs to be changed if agricultural research in the Caribbean is going to contribute to increased agricultural productivity and development.[7]

A fundamental problem affecting agricultural activity in the Caribbean is that of the lack of agricultural credit. However, as is the case in most economic activities, some marginal steps have been taken to alleviate the problem in recent times. Guyana, for example, established two cooperative banks. One of them, the Guyana National Cooperative Bank (GNCB), was established in 1970 primarily to mobilize the savings of the nation and to act as the government's financial agent in the promotion and financing of all types of cooperatives. The GNCB is a full-fledged commercial bank operating on sound development banking principles.[8] The second bank created was the Guyana Agricultural Cooperative Bank (GACB). The main purpose of the GACB is that of mobilizing the savings and the financing of agricultural cooperatives and other rural development projects.

Agricultural credit plays an important role in development of the agricultural sector. Although the magnitude of agricultural credit has been increasing in most Caribbean nations, it is still limited. A primary issue seems to be unequal access. It was found that, in Guyana, the major constraint in the use of credit came from inadequate demand, which was the result of the low incomes and backwardness of the farmers.[9] This, therefore, means that access to credit must be equalized.

An agricultural credit system in the Caribbean must allow free transfer of resources between sectors, between regions, and across income classes so as to bring about an efficient allocation of a country's scarce resources. It must finance the needs arising from the use of appropriate technology in agriculture. It must encourage and mobilize savings from the incomes generated by the expanding agricultural production. As an important factor of production, credit must foster an equitable distribution of the increasing agricultural income.[10] The extent to which agricultural credit can perform these various diverse functions effectively rests, on the one hand, on the commitment of the Caribbean governments and, on the other hand, on the organizational abilities and skilled human resources required to create and nurture an appropriate institutional infrastructure.

One interesting feature of Caribbean agriculture, particularly in Trinidad and Tobago, is its considerable and growing mechanization. This in turn has resulted in a decrease in the number of people employed in the agricultural sector and further rural out-migration, as will be seen in Part III of this book.

But, can migration to Caribbean cities be discouraged? It can be argued that so little has been done to make rural farm life desirable compared with urban life that it is only to be expected that anyone who can will move to the city. On the other hand, a strong argument can be made that agriculture cannot be expected to absorb all of the rural labor force in the Caribbean unless there are major increases in the demand for agricultural products. What is needed, therefore, is a comprehensive, integrated rural development program which is not only employment-oriented but one which provides infrastructure, as well as fiscal and other services befitting rural areas.

Rural development is taken here to mean the far-reaching transformation of social and economic institutions, structures, relationships, and processes in any rural area. The cardinal aim of rural development is viewed not simply as agricultural and economic growth in the narrow sense, but as balanced social and economic development, including the generation of new employment; the equitable distribution of income; widespread improvement in health, nutrition, and housing; greatly broadened opportunities for all individuals to realize their full potential through education; and a strong voice for all rural people in shaping the decisions and actions that affect their lives.[11]

All of the four countries in this study do have some type of rural development program. However, they have met with marginal success. In Guyana, for example, the program is aimed at development of rural cooperatives and agricultural land settlement with the expected result being a contribution to the growth of agriculture, which in turn is expected to provide considerable indirect support for the growth of rural nonfarm activities and employment.[12]

In Jamaica, as mentioned before, the First Rural Development Project, aided by international technical and financial assistance, was formulated in 1975. But what is needed in the Caribbean is a rural development strategy which shows clear, annual, and attainable targets for the share of public expenditure and public investment in agriculture, and for the share benefiting rural activities. This means, of course, that the strategy must be integrated into their development plans.

A rural development strategy may enter into the planning process at some or all of the following levels: the aggregate level, the sectoral level, the project level, and at the level of special measures loosely linked with the main structure of the plan. The Caribbean countries have acquired a great deal of experience in formulating development plans and, as such, the inclusion of a rural development strategy in these plans should pose no major problem.

Realization of the objectives of a broad-based rural development strategy, however, hinges on national commitment and on the translation of that commitment into three sections of action. First, there must be the necessary policy changes, including more equitable distribution of land rights and incentive pricing for crops produced by subsistence farmers, in particular for food crops. Second, resources must be allocated on a priority basis to increase the productivity of the subsistence rural sector—in order to develop agricultural technology, effective extension, and transportation networks. Third, an adequate effort must be geared to developing institutional capability, not only in the organized public sector but also in the rural agricultural sector to use to the maximum the existing resources and thus ensure effective implementation of the policies and plans directed at the unemployed.

Fundamental to any process of planned rural development is participation of the rural poor in that process. This refers to the active and willing participation of rural peoples in development of the area in which they reside.[13] Such participation requires that these people not only share in the distribution of the benefits of development, be they the material benefits of increased output or other benefits considered enhancing to the quality of life, but that they share also in the task of creating these benefits. Participation has been regarded as a substitute for political mobilization and it is, in that sense, therefore, the antithesis of politicization by providing, optimally, political legitimization for institutional programs without significant conflict.[14] This serves then to enhance the viability and success of the program or programs.

CONCLUSIONS

The importance of the agricultural sector and its contribution to economic development in the Caribbean has been on the decline during the past two decades. As a result, the role of the sector in generating the necessary employment and foreign exchange earnings has been a very disappointing one.

Several structural problems exist. There are also many technical and institutional weaknesses coupled with the characteristic of dualism resulting from the contrast between small farms and estates. Dualism is shown not only in such areas as resource availability and use, but also in the ecological and social impacts of the technological options chosen within the two types of farms. As such, any survey of Caribbean agriculture would conclude that the technology applied at both ends of the spectrum of agricultural enterprises results in varying degrees of technological dysfunctionality.[15]

Many of the structural problems plaguing Caribbean agriculture are historical in origin, although they might have been reinforced by government policies during the past two decades. What is, therefore, essential is the establishment of individual agricultural-development programs in each of the countries based upon their needs and available resources. Within this context, distributive land reform becomes important, particularly in Barbados, Jamaica, and Trinidad and Tobago.

Both historical and empirical evidence suggests that egalitarian farm systems have been compatible with the reduction of poverty. Japan and Taiwan are good examples. Land reform also leads to increased productivity. Compared with large farms, small farms have higher employment and crop yields per unit of land, a higher capital/land ratio but lower capital/labor ratio, and income distribution in small farm systems tends to be more egalitarian.[16] Even with an initial fall in production, the share of income of the rural poor tended to increase the redistribution of land meant the redistribution of income from property.

However, apart from land reform, the agricultural-development program must contain elements which address the issues of infrastructure, extension services, credit, marketing policies, price policy, migration, employment, and rural cooperatives. It must involve a more integrated form of development based on changing the social relations of production in the rural areas of the Caribbean. It ultimately means, therefore, the development of rural communities equipped with the necessary infrastructure and productive organization to make them economically and socially viable.[17]

But what are the prospects for the immediate future? The shifting political situation in the region inevitably will have a major impact both in terms of what policy decisions are made and in the implementation of those decisions. The 1980 elections in Jamaica, for example, resulted in the removal of Michael Manley's government, which had espoused socialism and major land reforms, and the installation of a government sympathetic to capitalism. Under this new government future major land reform and further distribution of cultivable land may not be possible.[18] As such, the large private plantation system in Jamaica may regain its prominence.

Land reform is one of the most relevant institutional factors in agricultural development. Without land reform in the Caribbean, small farmers would be left with two alternatives. These are (1) to migrate temporarily to other rural areas or (2) to move to the urban areas. The option is usually for the second alternative, which then results in increases in the urban rate of unemployment, because although the rate of growth and the demand for labor are greater there than in the rural areas, they are not sufficient to absorb both the cities' own natural increase in population and the flow of migrants from the rural areas.

Inevitably, all of this leads to friction—a friction which has its roots in the rural areas. But despite this friction there still does not exist integrated rural development programs in the Caribbean.[19] Instead, the agrarian-reform strategies have as their objectives: to increase production and supply levels; reduce the rural exodus to the urban areas; and enlarge the rural markets for goods and services coming from the branches of the economy. Though these objectives are commendable, until the agricultural development strategy becomes an integrated one, its potential impact is bound to remain marginal.

NOTES

1. See Kempe Ronald Hope, "CARIFTA and Caribbean Trade: An Overview," *Caribbean Studies* 14 (April 1974), pp. 169–79; Kempe Ronald Hope, "The Post-War External Trade of Guyana," *Economia Internazionale* 28 (February–May 1975), pp. 139–56; and Chapter 11 of this volume.

2. Chernick et al., *Commonwealth Caribbean*, p. 125.

3. Caribbean Development Bank, *Annual Report 1976*, p. 20.

4. For more on this issue, see George Beckford, *Persistent Poverty: Underdevelopment in Plantation Economies of the Third World* (New York: Oxford University Press, 1972), p. 86; and

P. Foster and P. Creyke, *The Structure of Plantation Agriculture in Jamaica* (College Park, Md.: University of Maryland, Agricultural Experiment Station, 1968), pp. 7–8.

5. See Doreen Warriner, *Land Reform in Principle and Practice* (London: Clarendon Press, 1969).

6. Folke Dovring, *Economic Results of Land Reform* (Washington, D.C.: U.S. Agency for International Development, Spring Review of Land Reform, June 1970), p. 23.

7. For a good critical review of agricultural research in the Caribbean see L.B. Coke and P.I. Gomes, "Critical Analysis of Agricultural Research and Development Institutions and Their Activities," *Social and Economic Studies* 28 (March 1979), pp. 97–138.

8. For a thorough discussion of the role of the GNCB in Guyana, see Kempe Ronald Hope, "National Cooperative Commercial Banking and Development Strategy in Guyana," *American Journal of Economics and Sociology* 34 (July 1975), pp. 309–22.

9. Gladstone Lewars, *Small Farm Financing in Guyana 1968–1970* (Kingston, Jamaica: Institute of Social and Economic Research, University of the West Indies, 1977), p. 74.

10. See Uma J. Lele, "The Role of Credit and Marketing Functions in Agricultural Development." Paper presented at the International Economic Association Conference, in Bad Godesberg, Germany, August 26–September 4, 1972, p. 1.

11. P. Coombs and M. Ahmed, *Attacking Rural Poverty: How Nonformal Education Can Help* (Baltimore: Johns Hopkins University Press, 1974), pp. 13–14.

12. See Kempe Ronald Hope, "Problems of Rural Cooperatives in Guyana," *Review of International Cooperation* 72, no. 2 (1979), pp. 75–82.

13. See David J. King, *Land Reform and Participation of the Rural Poor in the Development Process* (Washington, D.C.: World Bank Conference Papers on Land Reform, 1973).

14. Charles Harvey et al., *Rural Employment and Administration in the Third World: Development Methods and Alternative Strategies* (Geneva: ILO/Saxon House, 1979), pp. 23–25.

15. Coke and Gomes, "Critical Analysis," p. 97.

16. Dharam Ghai et al., *Overcoming Rural Underdevelopment* (Geneva: ILO, 1979), p. 27.

17. For further, thorough arguments in support of these points of view see the chapter entitled "The Role of Agriculture in Economic Development" in William Murdoch's book, *The Poverty of Nations: The Political Economy of Hunger and Population* (Baltimore: Johns Hopkins University Press, 1980), pp. 169–201; and Nevin S. Scrimshaw and Lance Taylor, "Food" in *Economic Development*, eds. Gerard Peil et al. (San Francisco: W.H. Freeman, 1980), pp. 26–36.

18. See "Jamaica Veers to the Right," *South: The Third World Magazine* (December 1980), pp. 12–15.

19. See E.S. Liboreiro, "The Small Farmer in the Context of Agrarian Reform and Rural Development in Latin America and the Caribbean," *Land Reform: Land Settlement and Cooperatives*, no. 1 (Rome: FAO, 1979), pp. 80–97; International Labor Office, *Growth, Employment and Basic Needs in Latin America and the Caribbean* (Geneva: ILO, 1979); and Frank Long, "The Food Crisis in the Caribbean," *Third World Quarterly* 4 (October 1982), pp. 758–70.

PART III

POPULATION, LABOR FORCE, AND EMPLOYMENT

8

Urban Population Growth in the Caribbean: Trends, Consequences, and Policies

One of the most significant changes of recent times, and one that seems to be of even greater importance in the future, is the rapid growth of the urban population in developing nations. This phenomenal growth of urban populations is fueled by two primary forces. These are (1) natural increase, and (2) migration. Both forces have resulted in a growing urbanization trend in the developing nations. Urbanization is conventionally defined as the process of growth in the urban population, rather than growth in the urban population per se.[1] At high levels of urbanization the task of socioeconomic development can become complicated and appropriate national urbanization policies would need to be implemented.

In this chapter, an analysis is made of the trends and consequences of rapid urban population growth in the Caribbean with primary emphasis on the impact of such growth on socioeconomic development and the resulting policy implications.

TRENDS IN URBAN POPULATION GROWTH

Table 8.1 indicates the rapid pace of urban population growth in the entire Caribbean. Between 1950 and 1970 urban populations in the Caribbean grew at more than twice the rate of the rural populations while during the period 1970–80 the growth rate of the urban population was more than four times that of the rural population and that increasing trend is expected to continue into the future. By the year 2000, it is expected that more than 64 percent of the entire Caribbean's population will reside in urban areas, compared with 38 percent in 1960. This growing rate of urbanization can be further verified by looking at the data for the individual countries, as shown in Table 8.2.

Table 8.1. Average Annual Percentage of Growth in Urban and Rural Populations in the Caribbean 1950–60, 1970–75, 1980–90

Urban Growth Rate			Rural Growth Rate		
1950–60	1970–75	1980–90	1950–60	1970–75	1980–90
2.93	3.31	3.18	1.35	0.73	0.71

Sources: United Nations, *Trends and Prospects in Urban and Rural Population, 1950–2000* (New York: United Nations, 1975), Tables C1 and C2; and United Nations, *Patterns of Urban and Rural Population Growth* (New York: United Nations, Population Studies, No. 68, 1980), Annex II.

During the period 1960–80 three of the four Caribbean nations (the exception was Barbados) had urban population growth rates of more than 4 percent. The low growth rate of the urban population in Barbados reflects the considerable success of the island's family planning program, as well as a slower rate of rural-to-urban migration.

In Table 8.3, we see the share of the urban growth due to migration for the entire Caribbean region. If the projections and data are correct, it would seem that during the 1980s, rural-urban transfers as a percent of urban growth would decline marginally. But a more accurate picture of internal migration as a source of urban growth can be gleaned from Table 8.4, which provides data on the individual countries.

Migrants from the rural areas contribute—at a rate varying from 42 percent in Trinidad and Tobago to 52 percent in Jamaica—to the annual growth of the urban population in the Caribbean. The vast majority of the migrants are young adults. In all of the countries, the majority of the population made at least two major moves.[2] The original move was from a

Table 8.2. Urban Population as a Percentage of Total Population and Growth Rates of Urban Population (1960–80), by Country

Country	Percentage Urban			Growth Rates of Urban Pop. (1960–80) %
	1960	1970	1980	
Barbados	40.8	43.5	46.3	1.0
Guyana	28.9	31.7	46.6	4.2
Jamaica	34.0	41.6	69.3	7.3
Trinidad & Tobago	39.2	53.0	63.9	4.2
Caribbean	38.2	45.1	52.2	—

Sources: Same as for Table 8.1; *World Tables 1980* (Baltimore: Johns Hopkins University Press, 1980), pp. 438–39; and Inter-American Development Bank, *Economic and Social Progress in Latin America 1980–81* (Washington, D.C.: 1981), statistical appendix.

Table 8.3. Average Annual Rate of Rural-Urban Transfer and Rural-Urban Transfer as a Percentage of Urban Growth in the Caribbean, 1950-60, 1970-75, 1980-90

Rural-Urban Transfers Per 1,000 Urban Population			Rural-Urban Transfers as A Percent of Urban Growth		
1950-60	1970-75	1980-90	1950-60	1970-75	1980-90
5.7	9.4	8.9	19.5	28.4	28.0

Sources: Same as for Table 8.1; and Sally Findley, *Planning for Internal Migration: A Review of Issues and Policies in Developing Countries* (Washington, D.C.: U.S. Department of Commerce, Bureau of the Census, ISP-RD-4, 1977), p. 36.

rural to an urban area with subsequent moves to other urban areas. In both Guyana and Trinidad and Tobago, the great majority made three moves. Also, with the exception of Guyana, women moved more than men. The greater internal movement of women can be accounted for, to some extent, by the increasing number of women entering the labor force. The relatively low female labor-force participation rate in Guyana can be explained by the age composition of the population. About 55 percent of Guyana's population is below the age of 20.

CONSEQUENCES OF URBAN POPULATION GROWTH

From all of the data presented in the last section there seems to be an obvious conclusion. For the four countries in this study, urban population growth and urbanization occur primarily because of net rural-urban migration. Without such migration, the growth rate of the urban population would decline by more than one-half in some countries and by slightly less in others.

Table 8.4. Internal Migration as a Source of Urban Growth, 1970-75 (Percentages)

Country/Region	Urban Population Growth Rate	Share of Growth Due to Migration
Caribbean	3.3	29.4
Guyana[a]	6.8	51.0
Jamaica	3.8	52.6
Trinidad and Tobago	2.0	42.1

Sources: Inter-American Development Bank, *Economic and Social Progress in Latin America* (Washington, D.C.: IDB, several years); and Bertrand Renaud, *National Urbanization Policies in Developing Countries* (Washington, D.C.: World Bank Staff Working Paper No. 347, July 1979), p. 187.
[a]1970-76.

One of the major consequences of this rapid rural-urban migration and the process of urbanization in the Caribbean in the last two decades has been the buoyant supply of urban job-seekers, which has resulted in further increases in the rates of urban employment and underemployment.

Only a few years ago, rural-urban migration was viewed favorably in the economic development literature. Internal migration was thought to be a natural process in which surplus labor was gradually withdrawn from the rural agricultural sector to provide needed manpower for urban industrial growth. The process was deemed socially beneficial since human resources were being shifted from locations where their social marginal products were often assumed to be zero to places where this marginal product was not only positive but also rapidly growing as a result of capital accumulation and technological progress.

However, in contrast to this viewpoint, it is now persuasively clear that rates of rural-urban migration continue to exceed rates of job creation and to surpass greatly the capacity of both urban industry and services to absorb this labor effectively. In the Caribbean, relatively large-scale rural-urban migration in recent years is also causing urban congestion and, from the experience of the developing world, rural-urban migration will continue as long as the urban expected real income is greater than the average real agricultural product. This flow is motivated, however, not only by the expected income differential between the rural agricultural sector and the modern urban sector but also by the expected income differential between the rural sector and the informal urban sector.[3] In Barbados, for example, wages in the rural agricultural sector average approximately 42 percent less than in the nonagricultural sector.

It seems clear, however, that expectations about employment and income differentials in Caribbean urban areas are not the only factors that encourage rural-urban population flows. Expectations about social and cultural amenities, housing, social services, and quality of life in the urban areas seem also to play a role in motivating the rural-urban flow. As such, high urban unemployment does not appear to deter migration.

But no longer is migration viewed by economists as a beneficent process necessary to solve problems of growing urban labor demand. On the contrary, migration today is seen as the major contributing factor to the ubiquitous phenomenon of urban surplus labor and a force that continues to aggravate already serious urban unemployment problems caused by growing economic and structural imbalances between urban and rural areas. Overurbanization, therefore, is not a comfortable concept among economists and planners. One reason is that it was not supposed to happen. Planned industrialization did not result in the expected returns over the long term and the economic incentive to move into the cities remains high.[4]

It is in this context of slowly growing urban employment opportunities accompanied by a disproportionately high rate of rural-urban migration that the chronic urban unemployment and underemployment problem has emerged in the Caribbean. Migration in excess of job opportunities is therefore both a symptom of and contributing factor to the slow rate of economic growth in the Caribbean since unemployment and underemployment result in a loss of productive capacity for each economy.

A further consequence of rapid urban population growth as a result of rural-urban transfers is that of the fertility factor. The vast majority of Caribbean migrants tends to be in the peak reproductive age groups. They are young adults whose fertility is higher than that of the urban population as a whole. They are concentrated in the 15–30 age range and are primarily women. Their departure from the rural areas not only reduces the size of the rural population directly but has the potential of an even greater effect because the children born to them are likely to go with them and future births will also occur in the urban destinations. This raises the issue of the migration demographic multiplier. There is a migration demographic multiplier because migrants are generally young, usually under 30, and move to the urban areas during their most fertile years. The effect of the demographic multiplier is longer lasting than that of the employment multiplier. Its magnitude is related to patterns of family formation and is rather country specific.[5] Furthermore, the effects of the demographic multiplier guarantee that the population of the urban areas will continue to grow naturally by large absolute numbers for quite a while. This in turn guarantees further upward pressure on the absorptive capacity of the urban areas. That is, the ability of the urban economy and society to employ growing numbers of new labor-force entrants productively and to provide basic social services to accommodate them.

Social services are currently unable to keep pace with the demand. Caribbean hospitals and schools are overcrowded in the urban centers. Major traffic congestion occurs during most of the working hours. Housing, already too expensive for the majority of urban dwellers, is becoming almost unavailable and squatter settlements are becoming prevalent. Urban food supplies, which once came from the rural areas, now have to be imported, due to the declining agricultural sector in the Caribbean which, in turn, has resulted in declining per capita food production.[6]

In essence then, the consequences of rapid urban population growth in the Caribbean lead to diseconomies of scale and negative externalities. The size and rate of growth of the urban population is excessive in relationship to the absorptive capacity of the urban areas. That is, the urban economy lacks the ability to employ growing numbers of new labor-force entrants productively and to provide basic social services to accommodate them. Yet, because development planning is geared to the urban economies with the resultant effects of severe imbalances in job opportunities and wage scales, and an education system geared toward urban residents, rural residents assume that their economic future can only be achieved by moving to the towns, however narrow their chances of success.

The social and economic consequences of rapid urban population growth are therefore interdependent. In the Caribbean, there is no clear line dividing social from economic factors, but social consequences are defined here as changes in the network, pattern, and attitude toward social relationships. These may include changes in the roles within the family structure and relations, patterns of informal social contacts, and even the pattern of participation in formal associations. For the rural-urban migrants the most dramatic social changes are those involved in shifting from a rural to urban life-style. The majority of the migrants, for reasons of insecurity, their lack of familiarity with the cities, and the expense of locating and acquiring housing, reside with their relatives or close friends and this condemns them to accept the established norms and customs of that household.

However, apart from that adjustment, migrants who reside with relatives or friends tend to be better off than those who do not. Those without kin or friends to help them are at a severe disadvantage in finding jobs and building adequate lives for themselves. Whereas friends and kin in the urban areas facilitate migrant adjustment to the urban areas by providing loans of cash or kind to tide the migrants over until they find their own source of income; help them become involved in the city's social life, easing the transition from rural to urban customs; and perhaps most importantly, help the migrants find jobs. Also of importance here is the role changes of female migrants in the Caribbean. Women in the Caribbean have generally been regarded as subordinate to men.[7] However, as migrants, they are predominantly single; they tend to be between the ages of 15 and 30; and they tend to have an average of two dependents. These factors necessitate the need for them to seek employment and better incomes in the urban areas and, in that respect, the reasons for departing from the rural areas are similar to those of the Caribbean men. But even in cases where women are married, they may also have to work for additional income to supply family necessities previously derived from farming or relatives.

In addition to the social and economic consequences there are also some political consequences. Political activity, like most other activities in the Caribbean, is centered around the urban areas. As such, and except during national election campaigns, rural residents tend to show little interest in issues of politics. Rural migrants therefore exhibit no desire to get involved in urban politics during their initial period of residence in the urban areas. In other words, they attempt to remain politically aloof.[8] However, they soon find themselves actively involved, having been influenced by their friends and relatives. In the Caribbean, this influence is transmitted and reinforced through the racial and ethnic cleavages that exist. The rural migrant soon realizes that some type of political affiliation is necessary in the urban areas and that it is useful that such affiliation be along racial/ethnic lines. As such, the rural migrant, having been recruited and influenced, quietly adapts to urban political behavior. They become earnest participants in the political process with representative membership in institutionalized political groupings that can be mobilized or tapped for political support by astute politicians with the hope of some future individual or group benefit.

POLICY IMPLICATIONS AND CONCLUSIONS

Rapid urban population growth seems entrenched in the Caribbean. Along with such growth comes the social, economic, and political consequences discussed in the foregoing section. The Caribbean has been found to be characterized by acute inequality of income between the urban and rural populations and between different categories of workers and socioeconomic classes, with a chronically high level of urban unemployment and rural underemployment.

The declining agricultural sector as well as the implementation of development strategies with an urban bias have resulted in rapid rural-urban migration, which is currently responsible for the growing urbanization, which in turn is responsible for the serious socioeconomic dislocations occurring in the urban centers of the Caribbean.

Although continued and even accelerated rural-urban migration is inevitable in the Caribbean, there has been a tendency to do very little about it. This has tended to create distortions and imbalances in both economic and social opportunities between the rural and urban areas. However, any concern with socioeconomic development must focus attention on the relationship between the migration/employment dilemma and development. This means the discouraging of rural-urban migration through policies which emphasize the development of the rural sector in the Caribbean. Yet, there is very little information on the relationship of migration to rural development or on the relationship of policy to migration. Most of the effort has been concentrated on family planning programs, that is, on fertility control. However, any complete evaluation of the dynamics of population change, of the interrelation between population and development, and of potential policies for coping with problem conditions in urban and rural locations cannot rest on attention to one component of population change alone (fertility) but must focus as well on the other major component (migration) and on the interaction between both.

The fertility factor will, however, remain important in the Caribbean. Interrelations between migration and fertility are complex and relate both to whether those leaving rural areas have higher or lower fertility than those remaining behind; whether, in turn, rural-to-urban migrants differ in their fertility behavior from the natives of the cities; and whether the migrants are in fact contributing more than their share of children to the natural increase of the cities.

A solution to the rural-urban migration and urbanization problems would be difficult enough if it were just a matter of more jobs. However, the kinds of jobs, the increases in output, and other factors are all important if the Caribbean labor force is to be productive. Hence, a population policy that is integrated into the national development plans is most desirable. It must be a policy that takes into consideration a rural development strategy to reverse the flow of population out of the rural areas and stimulate development of the more traditional agricultural sector to increase the number of available jobs.

But the expansion of job opportunities is not a naturally occurring phenomenon. The problem exists now and will remain until the end of the century. Increasing the number of jobs now would, of course, help raise income but the problem will reoccur unless there is a continued effort to expand employment opportunities in order to match the steady growth of the labor force, particularly in the urban areas.

The problem of unemployment in the Caribbean is in reality a range of related problems, some more serious, some less serious, most extending well beyond the groups directly affected by open unemployment. While the urban population growth causes increases in the labor force and rural-urban migration continues, there is an immediate need for expanded employment opportunities and a viable population planning policy.

The low absorption capacity of the urbanized manufacturing sector in the Caribbean is particularly striking in this regard because the reduction of the agricultural labor force has been accompanied not only by very high rates of unemployment but also by a substantial reduction, by 12 percent, of the ratio of employment to working-age population.[9] Women and young people are mainly affected by this unemployment.

What is needed then, are dispersed appropriate national urbanization policies for the individual Caribbean nations. The dispersed urbanization strategy combines the integrated rural development approach with an explicit focus on developing rural service centers, market towns, and small cities. Instead of focusing solely on rural development, this strategy recognizes that rural development is linked to a network of central places serving rural areas. The smaller cities and towns within rural regions serve rural development needs, improving rural employment and reducing rural outmigration.

This type of urbanization policy lies in creating industrialization from the ground up simultaneously with investments in agriculture. It is, in other words, a policy of complementarity between the rural and urban sectors and directed at diversification of the entire economy. However, its progress must stay in balance and the benefits must be shared reasonably between the two sectors. In the past, the distribution of the benefits associated with modernization have been consistently directed toward the urban areas and rural residents, quite sensibly, flocked to them. If, however, rural incomes approximate parity with urban ones, the element of economic coercion in rural-urban migration will be largely removed. If rural standards of living can be generally raised then the rural exodus can be stemmed. The growth of the urban population in the Caribbean will not, however, cease. But with a concerned retreat from urban bias and a serious commitment to complementary urban and rural development, urban population growth could proceed in a manageable manner.

Finally, something must be briefly said about the role of technology in the national urbanization policies advocated in this chapter. Technology will obviously play an important part in the accomplishment of the goals set forth. Moreover, it has been argued also that the challenge to technology for the Caribbean is the modernization of the region.[10]

Technology has been defined as the skills, knowledge, and procedures used in the provision of goods and services for any given society.[11] Due to the unique features of each Caribbean economy, technology must be seen in the context of what is appropriate for each of them. That is, each nation must establish technology as a variable in the process of socioeconomic change and modernization. However, the appropriateness of technological application can only be determined by technology assessment. Therefore, there need be no dichotomy between technology transfer and technology assessment, either at the conceptual or at the operational level.

Technology assessment is indispensable in the search for relevant methods to satisfy national goals and policies with respect to urbanization. Technology assessment provides the most convenient way of evaluating technologies, and this in turn provides a nation with stronger arguments, based on fact, when bargaining with suppliers of technology. Moreover, at the regional level, technology assessment provides some insurance against unscrupulous vendors of technology playing off one developing nation against another.[12]

The role of technology in national urbanization policies is that of providing linkages which imply flows between the urban and rural sector. The experience of Japan is a good example of the positive aspects of intersectoral technology transfers. For the Caribbean nations, appropriate technology must not only be sought but also developed indigenously and employed to deal with the problems of urban growth and urbanization. Urban problems in the Caribbean can be solved only within the context of increased national employment, increased productivity, and increased effective investment, including investment in human resources. This can only be accomplished within the framework of the application of technology that is appropriate.

NOTES

1. United Nations, *Patterns of Urban and Rural Population Growth* (New York: United Nations Population Studies no. 68, 1980), pp. 33–34.

2. Kempe Ronald Hope and Terry Ruefli, "Rural-Urban Migration and the Development Process: A Caribbean Case Study," *Labour and Society* 6 (June 1981), pp. 145–46.

3. Michael P. Todaro, "Internal Migration, Urban Population Growth and Unemployment in Developing Nations: Issues and Controversies," *Journal of Economic Development* 5 (July 1980), pp. 8–11.

4. Michael P. Todaro, *City Bias and Rural Neglect: The Dilemma of Urban Development* (New York: Population Council, 1981), pp. 6–7.

5. Bertrand Renaud, *National Urbanization Policies in Developing Countries* (New York: Oxford University Press, 1981), p. 88.

6. Kempe Ronald Hope, "Agriculture and Economic Development in the Caribbean," *Food Policy* 6 (November 1981), pp. 256–57.

7. Frances Henry and Pamela Wilson, "The Status of Women in Caribbean Societies: An Overview of Their Social, Economic and Sexual Roles," *Social and Economic Studies* 24 (June 1975), pp. 168–69.

8. Joan M. Nelson, *Access to Power: Politics and the Urban Poor in Developing Nations* (Princeton, N.J.: Princeton University Press, 1979), pp. 112–16.

9. International Labor Organization, *Growth, Employment*, p. 34.

10. J. Dellimore, "Intermediate Technology and the Modernization of Anglophone Caribbean States," in *Integration of Science and Technology with Development: Caribbean and Latin American Problems in the Context of the United Nations Conference on Science and Technology for Development*, eds. D.B. Thomas and M.S. Wionczek (New York: Pergamon Press, 1979), pp. 81–84.

11. See Chapter 2 in this volume.

12. United Nations, *Technology Assessment for Development* (New York: United Nations, 1979), p. 6.

9

The Unemployment Problem in the Caribbean

Primary source data on the labor force, employment, unemployment, and internal migration in the Caribbean are either scarce or obsolete. However, one of the economic problems that seems to be most prevalent there is that of the high level of unemployment, as shown in Table 9.1.

This chapter deals with the unemployment dilemma in the Caribbean, within the context of Caribbean socioeconomic development, providing some basic information on the salient unemployment/employment characteristics and highlighting the likely implications given those characteristics.

In Barbados the period from 1970 to 1980 witnessed an 18-percent increase in the labor force, largely due to a substantial rise in the female participation rate and population increase. Consequently, although employment expanded over the period, the overall unemployment rate jumped from 9 percent in 1970 to 13.7 percent in 1980.

In Guyana, the unemployment rate increased from roughly 16 percent in 1970 to an estimated 20 percent in 1980. The labor force in 1980 was 34 percent of the total population. The participation rate of females was approximately 15 percent, that of males approximately 46 percent. A striking feature of Guyana's labor force is its age composition. About 35 percent is between the ages of 14 and 24 and of that total about 42 percent are unemployed.

With respect to Jamaica, the curtailment of imports in the 1970s provoked acute shortages of raw materials and intermediate goods, thereby further reducing the level of economic activity in the manufacturing, construction, and distributive trade sectors. Consequently, unemployment, which had averaged 21 percent of the labor force in 1974–75, rose to an estimated 30 percent in 1980 for the second consecutive year.

Table 9.1. Unemployment Rates in the Caribbean, 1960–80 (Percentages)

Country	1960	1970	1980
Barbados	8.0	9.0	13.7
Guyana	8.0	16.0	20.0
Jamaica	13.0	18.0	30.0
Trinidad & Tobago	12.0	12.5	8.7

Sources: World Bank, World Tables 1976 (Baltimore: Johns Hopkins University Press, 1976), pp. 514–17; K. Ruddle and M. Hamour, Statistical Abstract of Latin America 1970 (Los Angeles: UCLA Latin America Center, December 1971), pp. 92–93; and Inter-American Development Bank, Social and Economic Progress in Latin America (Washington, D.C.: IDB, 1981).

In Trinidad and Tobago, which like Jamaica and Barbados has officially adopted family planning as a matter of national policy, the 1980 unemployment rate was approximately 8.7 percent.

Unemployment and underemployment in the Caribbean means a loss of productive activity for the economy as a whole, but to the unemployed it means loss of income, less food, poorer shelter, less of all the basic elements needed to satisfy human needs, and a general perpetuation of their state of poverty. For all of the countries the unemployment rate is higher than in the United States and other industrial countries at any time in this century, including the depression. Thus, the problem of unemployment is on the one hand a sterile statistic used by economists, but on the other hand to millions of Caribbean citizens it signifies hunger, poverty, poor health, frustration, and idleness.[1]

From Table 9.2, it can be seen that the labor force is expected to grow twofold from 1960 to 2000. Currently, the labor force of the Caribbean is estimated at about 30 percent of the total population. The number of workers in the labor force is dependent on both the pool of existing

Table 9.2. Caribbean Labor Force, 1960–2000[a] (Thousands)

Country	1960	1965	1970	1975	1980	1985	1990	1995	2000
Barbados	91	89	90	98	107	115	125	133	143
Guyana	173	187	204	242	288	341	391	442	493
Jamaica	608	630	636	672	749	858	966	1071	1171
Trinidad & Tobago	281	285	314	354	403	453	495	533	568
Total	1153	1191	1244	1366	1547	1767	1977	2179	2375

Sources: International Labor Office, Labor Force Estimates and Projections, 1950–2000 (Geneva: ILO, 1977).

[a]Data are midyear medium variant projections.

workers and those entering the labor force. The growth rate is contingent upon population increase, net migration, and social and economic factors. The two primary socioeconomic factors are education and socialization. These two factors are interrelated. For example, since more and more Caribbean women are seeking higher education and entering the labor force, not only could their fertility rate tend to decline in the future but also the population growth rate could fall.

In examining the growth rates of the total labor force in each of the four countries as well as its male and female components several conclusions may be drawn. First, in the decade and a half preceding 1970, the growth of the labor force in each country was modest and, with the exception of Guyana, all of the countries had periods of negative growth. Second, with the exception of Jamaica, the rate of growth of the female sex in the labor force was greater than that of the male sex after 1970. This reflects a trend which is becoming more pronounced, namely, the increase of women in the labor force. Even though their total number has remained relatively small in comparison with men, the increase has been enough to influence the average growth of the labor force as a whole.

This brings us to the labor force participation rates in the four countries. The participation rates were not substantially different from what obtained in other regions. The major difference is that, until recently, the number of women entering the labor force of the Caribbean countries was small. In 1980 the female labor force participation rate in the Caribbean was approximately 19.5 percent.

Where country differences in participation rates exist, they are only partly due to differences in the age and sex composition of the populations. The differences narrow down in the case of males when the rates are standardized for differences in age distribution, but actually increase in the case of females. Thus, the relatively low female participation rate in Guyana can be explained by the age composition of the population. About 55 percent of Guyana's population is below the age of 20. However, the relatively high female participation rates of Barbados cannot be attributed to the island's particular age structure. Although, as would be expected, the chief differences in age- and sex-specific participation rates are found among the relatively younger and older ages, they are also plainly present among workers in the intermediate age groups.[2]

In general, work rates tend to be significantly lower among the younger age groups of the working population than those of older workers. Similarly, females typically have lower work rates than males of corresponding age. Differences in age- and sex-specific work rates in the Caribbean region conform to this general pattern, but the relative magnitudes of the differences appear to be atypically large.[3]

In the four countries in this study as in many other parts of the world, the type of work done by those employed is strongly linked to their sex. It was found that working women were twice as likely to hold a white-collar job as men. For the four countries as a whole 27.6 percent of the working women had white-collar jobs compared with 12.8 percent of working men. However, there are some striking differences within each country. For example, 36.8 percent of working women in Trinidad and Tobago had a white-collar job, compared with only 23.4 percent of working women in Jamaica.

Opportunities clearly exist for women to hold good jobs in the Caribbean. The education system prepares them as fully as it prepares the men. In Guyana, for example, education is free, up to the university level. As such, excess demand for skilled workers and managerial talent may have favored educated women who chose not to emigrate.

The sectoral component of the labor force is shown in Table 9.3. As can be seen, the patterns of change of sectoral activity between 1970 and 1980 has been quite similar. The services sector had a higher proportion of the labor force than either agriculture or industry. It is clear therefore that the shift taking place in the labor force is away from agriculture and into services as the main sector in the Caribbean. It should be noted also that industry has replaced agriculture in importance in the Caribbean. Though the rapid growth of service sector activity is a new phenomenon in the Caribbean economy, it can be stated that one of the reasons the supply of labor has shifted from agriculture to the service and industry sectors has been the greater opportunities for employment in that modern sector.

However, how effectively and efficiently the service and industry sectors can continue to absorb such a large influx of workers remains to be seen. This, of course, will be dependent on the extent to which the traditional agriculture sector is left behind the more modern industrial and

Table 9.3. Sectoral Distribution of Caribbean Labor Force, 1970 and 1980[a] (Percentages)

Year/Sector	Barbados	Guyana	Jamaica	Trinidad & Tobago
1970				
Agriculture	19.9	32.0	29.4	18.5
Industry	31.6	32.7	25.6	35.1
Service	48.5	35.0	45.0	46.4
1980				
Agriculture	9.6[b]	28.6[b]	22.0	16.0
Industry	25.3[b]	32.9[b]	25.0	36.0
Service	65.1[b]	38.5[b]	53.0	48.0

Sources: Same as for Table 9.1.
[a]The data are midyear estimates.
[b]Most recent estimate.

service sectors. Since the modern sector is often characterized by relatively higher wage rates, there is usually a supply of labor available to this sector. Therefore, the growth of employment in the modern sector is primarily determined by the growth in the demand for labor. The traditional sector, on the other hand, is characterized by personalized economic relationships which permit the absorption of labor into economic activities even at very low levels of productivity. Thus the growth of employment in this sector is determined not only by the demand for labor, but also by the supply in the economy as a whole.[4]

Perhaps the primary concern with the unemployment problem in the Caribbean is that it includes a pool of persons who, because they are not employed, are not contributing to their own well-being and the gross national output.[5] This results not only in socioeconomic problems for the unemployed but it also influences unsuccessful job-seekers to abandon their search, thus creating a cadre of discouraged individuals, and further reducing the national productivity effort. Although estimates of unemployment in the Caribbean, whether or not inclusive of discouraged job-seekers and visible underemployment, fail to indicate the existence of sectoral differences in marginal productivity, the evidence indicates that high rates of unemployment in the Caribbean are the direct result of population and labor force growth rates, which have tended to exceed the increase in the availability of jobs.

Some studies have found that rapid population growth retards the transformation of the sectoral structure of the labor force.[6] Oberai, for example, has shown that if the labor force increases at 3 percent, the share of modern sector employment in the total labor force decreases by 1 percent, and the share of the labor force in other sectors and in unemployment increases by 4 percent.[7] The available evidence therefore indicates quite clearly that population growth has significant implications for employment and wage rates. As such, for policy-making, at least in the short run, the labor force can be treated as independent of population growth and should be so recognized in the Caribbean.

CONCLUSIONS

High unemployment seems destined to remain a phenomenon in the Caribbean, given the current structural deficiencies that exist in those economies, as well as the existence of external economic dependence which constrains the earnings capacity and hence the finance for job-creating development projects. The problems with unemployment in the Caribbean, therefore, derive partly from the nations' small size, partly from economic fragmentation, and partly from the fact that they have not had well-coordinated development strategies.

What then should be done? Given the constraints on government expenditure in the Caribbean, the respective governments need to develop incentive packages and concessional terms that would encourage private investment, whether it is foreign or domestic in nature, in order that excess capacity may be utilized and the necessary impetus provided for economic growth. This recommendation (now a matter of policy in Jamaica) has proved unpopular in the past. However, and as proclaimed by the government of Prime Minister Seaga of Jamaica, there is a growing recognition that as long as the framework of a country's policy is appropriate, the establishment of foreign, as well as indigenously owned firms, and associated technology can improve resource allocation and efficiency without damage to national integrity. Countries that have effectively provided a wise mix of monetary, trade, taxation, and other policies, augmented by direct controls, where appropriate, have done well. In contrast, autarkic policies have often led to slow growth, high unemployment, and heavy dependence on aid with a concomitant impairment of independence,[8] as currently exists in the Caribbean region. Also, of course, attention needs to be directed at national urbanization policies as advocated in the previous chapter.

NOTES

1. Kempe Ronald Hope, "Population, Labor and Employment in Caribbean Socio-Economic Development," in *Caribbean Issues of Emergence: Socio-Economic and Political Perspectives*, ed. V. McDonald (Washington, D.C.: University Press of America, 1980), p. 270.

2. Sidney Chernick et al., *Commonwealth Caribbean*, p. 66.

3. Ibid., p. 74.

4. A.S. Oberai, *Changes in the Structure of Employment with Economic Development* (Geneva: International Labor Office, 1978), p. 20.

5. Jack Harewood, *Unemployment and Related Problems in the Commonwealth Caribbean* (St. Augustine, Trinidad: Institute of Social and Economic Research, University of the West Indies, 1978), pp. 56–57.

6. Lyn Squire, *Employment Policy in Developing Countries: A Survey of Issues and Evidence* (New York: Oxford University Press, 1981), p. 184.

7. A.S. Oberai, *Changes in the Structure*, pp. 20–22.

8. Hughes, "Achievements," p. 20.

PART IV

EXTERNAL TRADE

10

Import-Substitution Strategies in Developing Countries: A Critical Appraisal with Reference to Jamaica

This chapter examines the strategy of import-substitution in developing countries, from a critical standpoint, using Jamaica as a reference and case study. The argument is that strategies of import-substitution in developing countries have not been successful and could only prove to be successful when accompanied by other policies such as export promotion. Before moving on to examine the thesis, we will first briefly review some of the important literature pertaining to import-substitution in developing countries.

BRIEF OVERVIEW OF THE LITERATURE

Development planners, up until the late 1960s, used as the pillar of all their efforts the import-substitution strategy. This strategy is based on industrialization through the establishment of, or the boosting of, existing enterprises producing goods which were formerly imported.

There are two prerequisites to this strategy of development. First, a country must have a substantial amount of imports and secondly, there should be protection for the new manufacturing industries that are to produce the types of goods that were formerly brought in from abroad.[1]

However, although it was easy enough to reduce imports of the goods immediately affected, it was not always realized that the process would lead to increased imports of different types of imports—of inputs for the newly stimulated home industries. And to the extent that the policy was successful in creating higher incomes, more imports were also induced. This occurrence forced many authors to conclude that import-substitution at one stage of production leads to its being attempted at another. The result, as pointed out by Little, Scitovsky, and Scott, is to provide "too much capacity at the final and too little at the intermediate stages of production.''[2] This, of course, leads to more imports of inputs than had been anticipated, which in turn leads to balance-of-payments problems and to underutilization of capacity at the final stages of production. Hence, it was not surprising that Rawle Farley declared that "import-substitution does not guarantee any lessening of dependence on the external sector. The development of one industry necessarily generates new interindustry requirements, particularly in terms of intermediate products. This in turn generates new import requirements and leads to an elevation, not a lessening of import coefficients."[3]

Import-substitution as a strategy seemed to have gone too far, in the sense that the real contribution of industry to a nation's development was less than it appeared because protection, through distorting prices, raised the prices of stimulated manufactures in relation to the prices of outputs from other sectors. In some cases, the contribution to value added of a particular industry was actually negative.

An import-substitution bias means a balance-of-payments policy that favors import control or restriction over export encouragement. This, in turn, implies a lower value for foreign exchange than that appropriate to a policy of equal encouragement to exports and import-substitution. If market prices were given and could be taken to represent unit costs and utilities at the margin, the resulting resource allocation would require a greater value of resources to save an additional unit of foreign exchange through export expansion.

Since this kind of welfare loss is generally well understood, the persistence of this direction of bias in balance-of-payments policies suggests either that considerations other than economic efficiency are held to be more important, or that the assumptions underlying this type of welfare judgment are considered to be invalid.

A further argument, as made by John Power, can be applied to the import-substitution bias with respect to development planning. Power makes a strong case with respect to effects upon potential saving. He is concerned with the decline in profits due to high prices, lack of political control of consumption, and the demonstration effect associated with "consumption liberalization," all of which make the task of raising the portion of gross product saved a more difficult one.[4]

Similarly, as Peter Clark points out, the structure of the import bill has implications for the rate of saving needed to execute a desired program of investment. Further, he noted, as with the components of the import bill, the selection of a set of import-substitution industries will determine the saving requirement in the present as well as the future that will be necessary to maintain a particular target rate of growth.[5]

Nicholas Kaldor argues that the establishment of most industries in developing countries suppresses the capacity to export. He explains that the protection provided the infant industries forces domestic costs above the world level, causing factors to shift out of export production. The process becomes self-reinforcing, leading to increased import requirements relative to the export capacity and, hence, as stated before, chronic balance-of-payments problems. The incentive to expand exports is removed because of the penalty rendered on export producers by the deflation of foreign exchange associated with protected import-substitutions.

IMPORT-SUBSTITUTION STRATEGIES IN DEVELOPING COUNTRIES

Given the thrust of this overview of the literature, the leading question to be answered is why the developing countries continue to pursue import-substitution as a development strategy. There are several reasons, but the primary reason for the widespread pursuit of import-substitution in the developing countries has been based on objectives of industrialization and balance-of-payments support.

A typical argument put forward for industrialization through import-substitution is that the developing countries' demand for industrial imports increases at a faster rate than does the foreign demand for their exports, particularly when attempts are made by the countries to implement development plans. Because of this, it is argued that the developing countries should endeavor to produce those industrial products which they cannot purchase because of foreign exchange constraints. This can be accomplished by encouraging foreign investment and the reallocation of existing resources toward the development of those industries.

In general this is a reasonable argument for import-substitution. However, there are problems when the size of the countries is taken into consideration. No doubt, it would be valid in large nations such as India, Pakistan, and Brazil, but it is certainly not valid for small ones such as Jamaica and other Caribbean countries. Those countries do not have access to large enough resources to permit reallocation for industrialization purposes. Moreover, foreign investors find the larger developing countries more attractive for investment in manufacturing and other industrial activities. Finally, even if it is possible to reallocate some resources for industrialization, those countries would also create demand for a variety of new imports, such as the plant and equipment, raw materials, and even other imported consumer goods. They may even have to import foreign technicians and other experts not available locally.

There are several consequences of this tendency of import-substitution policies to generate demand for new imports. Firstly, it tends to increase the countries' dependence on imports rather than reducing it, especially when the availability of those imports is important for economic stability. Secondly, it gives rise to the possibility for further import-substitution. This becomes possible if the established industries are required to produce some of their inputs. This might be a difficult and slow process. Thirdly, if the import-substitution strategy results in a higher per capita income, then there is the likelihood that this could result in increased demand for other consumer goods. All of these factors, in one way or another, will create foreign exchange problems as has been aptly described in the following terms:

> the chronic foreign-exchange shortages of many developing countries is partly due to an underestimation of the tendency of import-substitution to generate demand for imports and consequent over-optimism about its ability to reduce the economy's dependence on imports.[6]

Another peculiar argument put forward in support of the import-substitution strategy in developing countries is related to the historical experiences and development process of the industrialized countries. The argument is based on the conclusions of some historical studies of the developed countries which indicated that a large proportion of the growth of their industries can be attributed to strategies of import-substitution.[7] We need not go into any detailed discussion of how different the economic history of those countries is from the history of the developing countries. It should suffice to point out, however, that the latter, particularly the smaller ones, do not have access to the economic resources and military prowess, which the developed countries had, to generate the industrialization process and to support their import-substitution strategy. Moreover, the small countries should never entertain the thought of repeating that type of industrialization process.

A more interesting argument which is usually put forward in support of import-substitution is that the import-substituting industries will provide increased employment opportunities and thus reduce the strains of high urban unemployment. Since the wage rates tend to be much higher in the urban centers than in the rural areas, the import-substitution strategy, it has been argued, would help to remove such labor-market distortions by increasing the price of the domestic substitutes. With increased prices for these goods the higher wages in the cities could be more easily met. But there are certain problems with this argument. It should be pointed out that in the initial stage of the import-substitution strategy the domestic import-substituting industries would most likely be "final touches" industries with very little local value added. Consequently, the employment opportunities would be minimal. In addition, the import-substitution policies would shift "the distribution of income in favor of the urban sector and higher income groups, whose expenditure pattern typically has the highest component of imports."[8]

The developing countries generally emphasize the import-substitution strategy to encourage industrialization, balance-of-payments support, and self-sufficiency. In the 1970s, the Jamaican government adopted an import-substitution strategy. It is not very clear whether this strategy was arrived at as part of overall development planning or whether it was chosen simply by default, because of acute foreign exchange problems. Several pronouncements by government ministers would seem to indicate that there was no carefully planned approach.

Even if we assume that the government did examine a number of alternative strategies, the import-substitution strategy was most likely to be selected, because it apparently called merely for restrictions on imported consumer goods, a process achievable without much trouble. Also, the country's balance-of-payments problem could have reinforced the attractiveness of this strategy. Now, let us leave for a moment the question of why import-substitution was adopted and examine how it was implemented in Jamaica.

Beginning in the 1970s, the government imposed restrictions on several consumer goods, such as nonessential consumer durables as well as on raw materials and capital goods. The restrictions took the form of higher tariffs, prescribed quotas, and administrative controls and they were regulated through the Ministry of Trade.

The higher tariffs and stipulated quotas by themselves created serious distortions but there were other problems as well.[9] There is no doubt that Jamaica had the potential to produce economically some of those goods but one would expect import restrictions to come into effect after steps have been taken to initiate and expand domestic production. However, this was not the case and the result was severe shortages of those goods and resultant higher prices.

Further distortions were created when those goods were imported from CARICOM countries. Since those goods were not restricted in CARICOM countries they were imported from regular suppliers and then re-exported to Jamaica duty-free, thus providing exorbitant profits for businessmen in such countries as Barbados and Trinidad and Tobago. This indicates that the import-substitution strategy was being undermined by existing CARICOM arrangements.

The import-substitution strategy should be conceived as a process, beginning first with the replacement of consumer goods, then moving on to the production of intermediate goods, and finally the production of industrial goods. Any country considering import-substitution should carefully examine the other alternatives available for industrialization. An import-substitution strategy should not be adopted merely as a method to generate foreign exchange savings in the initial stage. Such an approach would only result in the implementation of policies which will inhibit economic growth and deter the initiation of the second stage. As John H. Power pointed out,

It is a simple matter to formulate and implement a policy of protection
for the first stage. . . . But the crude policies of protection that may
serve adequately in the first stage, and the economic structure that they
encourage are likely . . . to become barriers to growth in subsequent
stages.[10]

If the Jamaican government was genuinely preoccupied with foreign
exchange savings when it adopted the import-substitution policy, then it
was bound to restrict nonessential consumer goods. But the replacement
of such goods with domestic products would naturally result in the production of unnecessary goods and the creation of an unsuitable industrial
structure for the country's development.

The Jamaican government's preoccupation with foreign-exchange
savings was evident in its imposition and rigid enforcement of foreign exchange controls. In the 1970s there were several adjustments in the exchange rate of the Jamaican dollar. However, there is no direct evidence of
any deliberate overvaluation of the Jamaican dollar but one can infer from
the requests by the IMF for a devaluation that it was somewhat overvalued.
According to the IMF regulations, devaluation of a country's currency will
be permitted only to correct for a "fundamental disequilibrium" in
balance of payments. A quick glance at Table 10.1 would indicate that
Jamaica has had an adverse trade balance for a prolonged period of time
and that trend continued into the 1980s.

We can use a simple partial-equilibrium analysis to illustrate how
import-substitution leads to an overvaluation of the domestic currency.

In Figure 10.1, let the DD and SS curves represent the demand and
supply of foreign exchange respectively, assuming, for simplicity, that all
demand for foreign exchange derives directly from the demand for imports, and the supply of all foreign exchange comes directly from exports.

Under conditions of a floating exchange rate, the equilibrium price of
foreign exchange would be OP_e with OQ_e units of foreign exchange

Table 10.1. Balance of Payments of Jamaica, 1970–80 (Millions of U.S. Dollars)

Item	1970	1973	1975	1976	1977	1978	1979	1980
Exports (f.o.b.)	342.1	392.9	810	632	734	738	770	1,088.9
Imports (c.i.f.)	449.0[a]	676.2	1,119	912	747	865	1,012	1,173.0[a]
Trade deficit	– 106.9	– 283.3	– 309	– 280	– 13	– 127	– 242	– 84.1
Current account balance	– 152.9	– 181.0	– 283	– 331	– 92	– 114	– 228	– 186.5
Decrease (+) or increase (–) in reserves	– 21.2	+ 25.5	+ 79	+ 244	+ 88	+ 107	+ 133	– 39.2

Sources: Bank of Jamaica, *Annual Reports;* and Inter-American Development Bank, *Economic and Social Progress in Latin America* (Washington, D.C.: IDB, several years).
[a](f.o.b.).

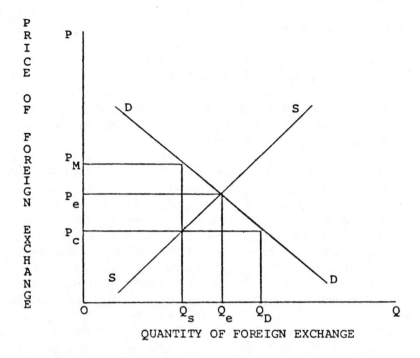

QUANTITY OF FOREIGN EXCHANGE

Figure 10.1. Illustration of how the import-substitution strategy leads to an overevaluation of domestic currency.

supplied and demanded. However, with an effective import-substitution strategy in force, the price of foreign exchange in terms of domestic currency would necessarily be lower. This should be obvious since there is always an excess demand for foreign exchange. In the diagram this can be reflected by a price such as OP_c with quantity supplied equal to OQ_s and quantity demanded equal to OQ_D. Thus we have an excess demand equal to the difference between OQ_D and OQ_s.

If the available quantity of foreign exchange OQ_s were auctioned in the money market then the importers would be prepared to pay as much as OP_M units of domestic currency for a unit of foreign exchange. On the other hand, if import controls are used and the available foreign exchange offered to importers at the same exchange rate applicable to exporters, then the importers are only required to pay OP_C units of domestic currency for a unit of foreign currency.

This undervaluation of foreign currency or overvaluation of domestic currency tends to discourage the earning of foreign exchange through increased exports and would require rigid foreign exchange and import controls to deal with the excess demand for foreign exchange. The overvaluation of the domestic currency effectively undervalues the price of the imports and thus underestimates the real social cost of the country's imports. Such a situation only misleads the public into purchasing more imports than can be financed with the available foreign exchange.

In order to provide a rough estimate of the overvaluation of the Jamaican dollar, the relative version of the Purchasing-Power Parity Hypothesis was used. It was found that the dollar was overvalued by approximately 37 percent. The method used to calculate this overvaluation was as follows: A base period was picked in the country's recent past when conditions were normal and economically stable and then the exchange rate of that period was multiplied by the ratio of the change in the domestic price level to that of its major trading partners. In the case of Jamaica, 1968 was selected as the base period of tranquillity. The exchange rate of the U.S. dollar in terms of Jamaica's currency was then J$0.83. The relative change in the domestic price level since this base period was then calculated. It was observed that from 1968 to 1977 the domestic inflation rates were, on average, about 50 percent above the rates of Jamaica's major trading partners—the U.S., U.K., and Canada—in the industrialized world. The potential current equilibrium exchange rate was then calculated by multiplying the exchange rate by the ratio of the change in the domestic price level to that of the trading partners, that is, multiplying J$0.83 by 1.50 (the relative price index). This gives us an approximate equilibrium exchange rate of J$1.25. With the official exchange rate being only J$0.91 in 1977 we have a 37 percent overvaluation. Thus, to the extent that the Purchasing-Power Parity Hypothesis is theoretically sound, we can conclude that the Jamaican dollar was overvalued.

Currency overvaluation imposes an extra burden on export-oriented industries and to a large extent inhibits their growth in small developing countries. A lower valued currency in those countries would encourage more export-oriented or "outward-looking" policies and thus support the exporting industries in their efforts to enter world markets and become more competitive in the long run. It would also discourage the importation of certain commodities and make some domestic industries more competitive.

The overvaluation of currency also allows for a distortion in the capital/labor ratio in production activities. Since imported goods are made cheaper, production processes with high import content would be selected. Such a situation would tend to reduce the employment effects of an import-substitution strategy, as pointed out by Henry J. Bruton.

> The overvalued local currency may encourage investment, but it has other characteristics much less likely to facilitate growth. It makes for capital intensity in production higher (due either to choice of technique or choice of product) than would be the case if foreign exchange were

priced right. It thereby dampens the employment effects of the IS activities. It also creates a level of import intensity of production that is incompatible with foreign-exchange-earning power, i.e. it penalizes export competing and increases the need for imports.[11]

Another limitation is related to the choice of new or existing activities on which to base the import-substitution strategy. The choice of consumer goods seems to be arbitrary and thus much would depend on rational judgment of the policy-makers and their particular interests. This is a serious problem in the Caribbean. Some of the restricted foodstuffs and consumer goods are essential items in the diet of low-income groups and the few domestic substitutes available are priced much higher than they can afford, thus creating severe hardships for the group that can least afford to bear them.

The high tariffs and quotas needed to implement the import-substitution strategy result in an inefficient utilization of economic resources. The small countries have domestic markets which are too small to justify the setting up of industries of efficient scale. Therefore these industries have to be protected by very high nominal tariffs. Usually the high tariffs on consumer goods are followed by a reduction in the tariffs imposed on intermediate goods and raw materials required for the domestic production of those consumer goods. This would mean that those industries enjoy effective rates of tariff that are much higher than the nominal tariff rates would indicate.

The effective tariff rate takes into consideration the protection afforded to the intermediate inputs as well as the nominal tariff rate imposed on the final goods. This makes the effective rate more economically relevant since it provides a more accurate measure of the degree of protection provided to those industries.

The very high effective rates tend to discourage the production of intermediate goods and raw materials in developing countries. In other words, they inhibit "backward linkages." In addition, the high effective rates encourage industries with a small proportion of domestic value added to the final goods. This seems to be the case in the Caribbean. There has been a large increase in the importation of intermediate goods in recent years.

Import-substitution policies also have adverse effects on savings and investments. The various technical and economic inefficiencies which the import-substitution policies create mean lower incomes, and especially lower profits, which would cause savings to fall. Further, the administering of the import controls results in serious bureaucratic delays in the processing of import permit applications and other related documents. Such delays have adverse effects on the planning and undertaking of investment.

CONCLUSIONS

The impact of import-substitution policies go beyond simple resource misallocation to adverse effects on technical efficiency, innovations, and saving. What is needed, however, are rational policies for export expansion.

From the analysis presented in this chapter we can conclude that past trading strategies pursued by the Jamaican government created costly economic distortions. They resulted in severe economic and technical inefficiencies in the economy and would have continued to retard the development process unless efforts were made to improve them.[12] The Jamaican government should continue to adopt a much more prudent use of the marketplace in allocating available foreign exchange and thus some of the dangers of a pure import-substitution strategy could be avoided and more satisfactory economic results attained.

Every effort should be directed toward the developing of "outward-looking" trading strategies. A system of export promotion coupled with a process of import liberalization would contribute to a more efficient resource allocation by permitting specialization according to the country's comparative advantage. Such "outward-looking" policies would also enable the country to achieve all possible economies of scale that are associated with practically all forms of industrial activity and which are denied to small countries establishing industries solely to supply the limited home market.

NOTES

1. See Robert J. Alexander, "The Import-Substitution Strategy of Economic Development," *Journal of Economic Issues* I (December 1967), pp. 297–308.

2. Ian Little, Tibor Scitovsky, and Maurice Scott, *Industry and Trade in Some Developing Countries* (London: Oxford University Press, 1970), p. 62.

3. Rawle Farley, *The Economics of Latin America: Development Problems in Perspective* (New York: Harper and Row, 1972), p. 219.

4. John H. Power, "Industrialisation in Pakistan: A Case of Frustrated Take-Off?" *Pakistan Development Review* 3 (Summer 1963), p. 26.

5. Peter B. Clark, *Planning Import Substitution* (Amsterdam: North-Holland, 1970), p. 24.

6. Little, Scitovsky, and Scott, *Industry and Trade,* p. 63.

7. H.B. Chenery, "Patterns of Industrial Growth," *American Economic Review* 50 (September 1960), pp. 639–41, 651.

8. Little, Scitovsky, and Scott, *Industry and Trade* p. 63.

9. For a detailed discussion of economic and technical inefficiencies of high tariff rates, see John H. Power, "Import-Substitution as an Industrialization Strategy," *The Philippine Economic Journal* 5, no. 2 (1966).

10. John H. Power, "Limitations of Import-Substitution" in *Leading Issues in Economic Development,* ed. G. Meier (New York: Oxford University Press, 1975), pp. 520–21.

11. Henry J. Bruton, "The Import-Substitution Strategy of Economic Development: A Survey," *Pakistan Development Review* 10 (Summer 1970), p. 131.

12. Recent steps have been taken toward such improvement. After a series of currency realignments in 1977, and a 54-percent devaluation in 1978, as part of an IMF stabilization program, and the creation of a system of monthly devaluations which totaled 15 percent by May 1979, the exchange rate was amended in January 1983 and based on a two-tier system, including both an official bank rate and a legalized, freely floating parallel market rate for trade in certain types of goods. In November 1983 the dual exchange-rate system was abolished, the Jamaican dollar was devalued by 77 percent, and an auction system was put into effect for bids on available foreign exchange through the Bank of Jamaica. By the end of 1985, the official exchange rate fluctuated between J$5.20 and J$6.40 = US$1.00.

11

A Macroeconomic Overview of the Trade Impact of CARICOM

This chapter examines the impact of the Caribbean Community (CARICOM) on the trade of the Commonwealth countries in the Caribbean.[1] The integration movement among the Commonwealth Caribbean states can be viewed as an attempt to overcome the handicaps of small size, economic fragmentation, and extensive dependence on extraregional markets and suppliers of resources of all kinds. The principal idea behind integration is that a pooling of local resources and markets will yield a higher level of economic and social benefits than could be attained by the countries individually.[2] On the expectations that mechanisms can be designed which will lead to this end, or will at least give them a stronger bargaining position in relation to the outside world, the Commonwealth Caribbean states consider the integration option worthwhile. Since each of the alternatives available to them involves some degree of dependence, it is understandable that they would want to choose that course which provides the best combination of economic viability and political autonomy.[3] The Caribbean Community represents the closest approximation to that ideal and was created in August 1973.

PURPOSE AND OBJECTIVES OF CARICOM

CARICOM has been established to achieve two broad central purposes.[4] The first is the economic development of each member country and of the region as a whole. The second is the enhancement of the effective sovereignty of the member states of the region and the self-determination of their people.

To achieve these two central purposes, CARICOM embraces three broad areas of cooperation which, taken together, extend far beyond the purely economic. These three areas are the following:

1. Economic integration, as represented by the Caribbean Common Market, which replaced the Caribbean Free Trade Association (CARIFTA).[5]
2. Cooperation in noneconomic fields and in the establishment and operation of common services such as health, education, school examinations, shipping, air transport, scientific research, meteorology, and so on.
3. The coordination of the foreign policies of the independent member states of the region.

CARICOM is unique in that it explicitly provides for the coordination of the foreign policies of its independent member states. It also represents the highest point of economic integration and general cooperation ever achieved in the history of the English-speaking Caribbean and has a-chieved such objectives as the establishment of a common external tariff, a harmonized system of fiscal incentives for industry, double-taxation and tax-sparing agreements, and the formation of the Caribbean Investment Corporation (CIC), designed to channel equity funds to the developing member countries.

Moreover, particularly in order to achieve its purpose of enhancing the effective sovereignty of the region and its member states, CARICOM has "international legal personality," that is, the capacity to negotiate and conclude treaties and agreements with third countries, groups of third countries, and international organizations. In addition to this, decisions of the organs and institutions of CARICOM have more binding force and are in some cases made by majority and not unanimous vote. The organs and institutions often have their own independent source of revenue. Also, even though the final decision-making bodies are composed of delegates of national governments, there is sometimes a Parliamentary Assembly whose functions range from the purely deliberative to those of voting money for the conduct of affairs of the group.

THE TRADE OF THE CARIBBEAN
ECONOMIES BEFORE CARICOM

The overall annual growth rate of the Caribbean countries' exports averaged 8 percent for the period 1950–69. Table 11.1 shows that for Trinidad and Tobago, Jamaica, and Guyana the rate of increase was higher from 1950–52 to 1960–62, then it declined, while for Barbados it was very low in the earlier period and improved in the latter.

The high growth rate experienced by Jamaica during the 1950s was due primarily to the rapid development in bauxite output which considerably altered the distribution of exports and gave great impetus to the export sector. In the case of Trinidad and Tobago, the export growth rate was determined by the increased production of petroleum and petroleum products which were exported to a ready market in Latin America and the

TABLE 11.1. Average Value of Total Exports by Country, 1950–69 (Millions of U.S. Dollars)

Period	Barbados	Guyana	Jamaica	Trinidad & Tobago	Total
1950–52	20	37	49	121	227
1960–62	26	86	176	326	614
1967–69	39	115	237	458	849
% Increase					
1950–52 1960–62	2.6	8.8	13.7	10.4	10.5
1960–62 1967–69	5.9	4.2	4.3	5.0	4.7
1950–52 1967–69	4.0	6.9	9.7	8.1	8.0

Source: Kempe R. Hope, "CARIFTA and Caribbean Trade: An Overview," *Caribbean Studies* 14 (April 1974), pp. 169–79.

Caribbean. In Guyana, the rate was due to increases in the production of rice, sugar, and bauxite. During the period 1962–68, exports of rice, sugar, and bauxite increased a good deal more slowly, with the results that the growth rate of total exports was lower than in the preceding ten years.

The growth in imports of the Caribbean countries between 1950–69 showed the same trend as that of exports. The fastest growing periods for Jamaica, Guyana, and Trinidad and Tobago were from 1950–52 to 1960–62, while Barbados's imports showed rapid growth between 1960–62 and 1967–69.

In general, all the Caribbean countries experienced some deficits on their trade accounts, in real money terms, before the formation of CARIFTA in 1968. Barbados had a deficit on her balance of trade between 1950–69; Guyana fared somewhat better by recording surpluses during 1961–64 and also in 1968; Jamaica's fate was similar to that of Barbados; and Trinidad and Tobago was only able to obtain surpluses in 1967 and 1968 after a spell of deficits since 1956.

Economic integration provides a wider market and a more diversified range of natural resources and so helps to bring about a relatively more self-contained pattern of economic development. CARIFTA boosted reciprocal trade among the Caribbean countries and was certainly an important factor in the growth of the intra-Caribbean trade, but it was more beneficial to Barbados, Guyana, Jamaica, and Trinidad and Tobago, the more-developed Caribbean countries.[6] From 1967 through 1970, exports

TABLE 11.2. Average Value of Total Imports by Country, 1950–69 (Millions of U.S. Dollars)

Period	Barbados	Guyana	Jamaica	Trinidad & Tobago	Total
1950–52	28	40	84	123	275
1960–62	49	82	217	329	677
1967–69	87	120	392	468	1067
% Increase					
1950–52 1960–62	5.8	7.5	10.0	10.4	9.4
1960–62 1967–69	8.5	5.6	8.8	4.2	6.3
1960–62 1967–69	6.9	6.6	9.5	7.8	6.3

Source: Kempe R. Hope, "CARIFTA and Caribbean Trade: An Overview," Caribbean Studies 14 (April 1974), pp. 169–79.

by CARIFTA area markets increased some 74 percent, from US$48 million in 1967 to US$83.6 million in 1970, as seen in Table 11.3. These figures represent a growth in intra-area exports by the four more-developed countries of 77 percent over the four years as compared with only 35 percent for the smaller Caribbean countries.

In examining the growth of member countries' total trade, it was found that food and industrial products were the major items in intra-CARIFTA trade. In Guyana rice and molasses accounted for about three-fourths of the intra-area exports. In Trinidad and Tobago, petroleum products were predominant, and accounted for half of the country's intra-area exports. For Jamaica, chemicals accounted for about half of the intra-CARIFTA exports.

On the whole, Trinidad and Tobago was the largest exporter in the region, with slightly more than 50 percent of total regional exports, while Barbados, Jamaica, and Guyana together accounted for some 38 percent of the total, and the smaller countries about 10 percent. Trinidad and Tobago and Guyana provided the largest markets for CARIFTA exports, with a combined average of about 40 percent of the total.

Table 11.4 reveals that in terms of world trade, CARIFTA area trade also grew significantly. Total imports of the more-developed countries increased from US$972 million in 1967 to US$1,254 million in 1972, of which 3.2 percent was imported from CARIFTA sources in 1967, rising to

TABLE 11.3.   Intra-CARIFTA Trade 1967–70[a] (In Thousands of U.S. Dollars)

Imported By	Year	Exported By					
		Barbados	Guyana	Jamaica	Trinidad & Tobago	Smaller Caribbean Countries	Total CARIFTA
Barbados	1967	—	1,504	529	3,675	818	6,526
	1968	—	1,497	1,102	4,938	875	8,412
	1969	—	1,747	1,443	6,648	711	10,549
	1970	—	2,304	1,998	8,460	613	13,375
Guyana	1967	406	—	958	10,985	468	12,817
	1968	398	—	1,301	12,840	169	14,708
	1969	482	—	1,832	13,844	68	16,226
	1970	464	—	1,514	16,155	356	18,489
Jamaica	1967	19	2,706	—	1,701	6	3,802
	1968	19	1,303	—	2,347	31	3,700
	1969	118	1,532	—	4,168	37	5,855
	1970	311	2,838	—	5,573	68	8,790
Trinidad	1967	742	4,966	1,055	—	1,069	7,832
	1968	669	4,906	1,346	—	926	7,847
	1969	985	5,537	3,031	—	1,370	10,923
	1970	1,330	5,731	4,550[a]	—	1,775	13,386
Smaller	1967	3,923	1,685	1,051	9,332	997	16,988
Countries	1968	4,647	1,788	1,384	10,922	966	19,707
	1969	5,288	2,238	2,039	13,372	1,397	24,334
	1970	6,381	2,330	2,217	16,950	1,719	29,597
Total	1967	5,090	10,231	3,593	25,693	3,358	47,965
CARIFTA	1968	5,733	9,494	5,133	31,047	2,967	54,374
	1969	6,873	11,054	8,345	38,032	3,583	67,887
	1970	8,486	13,203	10,279	47,138	4,531	83,637

Source: Same as for Table 11.1.

[a]Based on import figures (c.i.f.) as reported by the importing country, except the smaller-country group, for which export figures (f.o.b.), as reported by the exporting country, are used with 10-percent upward conversion to approximate c.i.f. valuation.

TABLE 11.4.   CARIFTA Trade as a Ratio of Total Trade of Member Countries, 1967–72 (In Millions of U.S. Dollars and Percentages)

Country	Year	Imports			Exports		
		CARIFTA	Total	Percentage	CARIFTA	Total	Percentage
Barbados	1967	6.5	79.9	8.1	5.1	42.4	12.0
	1968	8.4	83.3	10.1	5.7	36.6	15.6
	1969	10.5	76.5	13.7	6.9	26.1	26.4
	1970	13.4	93.4	14.2	8.5	27.6	30.8
	1971	11.8	95.6	12.3	5.1	20.9	24.6
	1972	14.3	106.1	13.5	6.9	24.7	28.1
Guyana	1967	12.8	132.5	9.7	10.2	112.3	9.1
	1968	14.7	106.1	13.9	9.5	108.8	8.7
	1969	16.2	118.2	13.7	11.1	120.1	9.2
	1970	18.5	126.7	14.6	13.2	141.5	9.3
	1971	15.9	104.9	15.1	12.5	112.8	11.1
	1972	18.6	107.6	17.3	13.6	108.3	12.6
Jamaica	1967	3.8	348.4	1.1	3.6	222.1	1.6
	1968	3.7	383.0	1.0	5.1	219.2	2.5
	1969	5.9	442.1	1.3	8.3	280.7	2.3
	1970	8.8	537.3	1.6	10.3	405.3	2.5
	1971	10.4	432.7	2.4	12.2	259.0	4.7
	1972	25.0	464.1	5.4	16.1	275.8	5.9
Trinidad	1967	7.8	411.2	1.9	25.7	441.5	5.8
	1968	7.8	420.0	1.9	31.0	459.9	6.7
	1969	10.9	484.4	2.3	38.0	464.9	8.2
	1970	13.4	560.5	2.4	47.1	456.4	10.3
	1971	12.6	521.3	2.4	39.3	392.9	10.0
	1972	16.1	576.9	2.8	44.8	412.7	10.9
Total	1967	31.0	972.0	3.2	44.6	818.3	5.4
More-	1968	34.7	992.4	3.5	51.4	824.5	6.2
Developed	1969	43.6	1,121.2	3.9	64.3	891.8	7.2
Countries	1970	54.0	1,317.9	4.1	79.1	1,030.8	7.7
	1971	50.7	1,154.5	4.4	69.1	785.6	8.8
	1972	74.0	1,254.7	5.9	81.4	821.5	9.9

Sources: Same as for Table 11.1; and Sidney Chernick et al., *The Commonwealth Caribbean: The Integration Experience* (Baltimore: Johns Hopkins University Press, 1978), statistical appendix.

5.9 percent in 1972. Their total exports to all countries rose unevenly from US$818.3 million in 1967 to US$821.5 million in 1972, of which 5.4 percent went to CARIFTA markets in 1967, rising to 9.9 percent in 1972.

THE TRADE OF THE MORE-DEVELOPED COUNTRIES SINCE CARICOM's ESTABLISHMENT

As seen in Table 11.5, the more-developed countries increased the absolute value of their intrazonal exports from US$142.8 million in 1973 to

TABLE 11.5. CARICOM: Intrazonal Trade, 1973–79 (Milions of Dollars)

Countries	1973	1974	1975	1976	1977	1978	1979
Barbados							
Exports	14.6	18.4	19.6	23.2	23.2	31.9	33.6
Imports	19.2	31.5	31.2	35.6	39.6	35.6	52.3
Balance	−4.6	−13.1	−11.6	−12.4	−16.4	−3.7	−18.7
Guyana							
Exports	27.4	37.1	50.4	43.1	41.2	41.3	43.6
Imports	32.0	57.2	63.9	80.9	69.6	56.6	79.2
Balance	−4.6	−20.1	−13.5	−37.8	−28.5	−15.3	−35.6
Jamaica							
Exports	24.5	32.3	34.4	43.9	34.7	36.4	58.6
Imports	30.7	61.1	82.1	47.9	41.7	30.8	54.2
Balance	−6.2	−28.8	−47.7	−4.0	−7.0	5.6	4.4
Trinidad & Tobago							
Exports	76.3	141.1	163.3	162.8	152.7	148.1	213.4
Imports	27.6	35.4	41.4	50.4	50.4	64.3	74.3
Balance	48.7	105.7	121.9	112.4	102.3	83.8	139.1
Total More-Developed Countries							
Exports	142.8	228.9	267.7	273.0	251.8	257.7	349.2
Imports	109.5	185.2	218.6	214.8	201.3	187.3	260.0
Balance	33.3	43.7	49.1	58.2	50.5	70.4	189.2

Source: Inter-American Development Bank, *Economic and Social Progress in Latin America 1980–81* (Washington, D.C.: IDB, 1981), p. 123.

US$349.2 million in 1979. In percentage terms, the increase was 140 percent or an average of 20 percent per year. The value of the exports of each of the more-developed countries to the CARICOM region is also shown in Table 11.5, which reveals some interesting data about the idividual countries.

In the case of Barbados, the absolute value of the 1979 exports to CARICOM was significantly higher than it was in 1973. However, in 1973, whereas exports to CARICOM amounted to 10.2 percent of the more-developed countries' total exports to CARICOM, this figure had declined to 9.6 percent in 1979. The value of Guyana's exports also decreased significantly over the same period and the percentage of exports to CARICOM vis-à-vis total CARICOM more-developed country exports declined to 12.5 percent in 1979 from 19.2 percent in 1973. For Jamaica, there were decreases also in the percentage of exports to CARICOM. Exports to these countries dropped from 17.2 percent in 1973 to 16.8 percent in 1979 after having shown slight fluctuations in the intervening years. Trinidad and Tobago registered increases in the value of its total exports and there was also a relative percentage increase in exports to CARICOM more-developed countries from 53.4 percent in 1973 to 61.1 percent in 1979.

Looking at the data in terms of the relative share of each country in exports to all of CARICOM, it is seen in Table 11.6 that the country with the greatest share of intrazonal exports has consistently been Trinidad and Tobago, with more than 50 percent of the more-developed countries exports to CARICOM throughout the period. In contrast to Trinidad and Tobago, Barbados has consistently had the smallest percentage share of the trade, ranging from 7.3 percent to 12.2 percent. Over the entire period, Guyana has increased her share of the trade (from 16.7 percent in 1972 to a high of 19.0 percent in 1973 and then back down to 12.2 percent in 1979). Jamaica's share had declined abruptly from 19.8 percent in 1972 to 12.8 in 1975 and back up to 16.4 percent in 1979.

TABLE 11.6. **Share of Each Developed Country in Intrazonal Exports, 1972–79 (Percentages)**

Year	Barbados	Guyana	Jamaica	Trinidad & Tobago
1972	8.5	16.7	19.8	55.0
1973	10.0	19.0	17.1	53.1
1974	8.1	16.2	14.1	61.5
1975	7.3	18.7	12.8	60.5
1976	8.4	15.6	15.9	58.9
1977	9.1	16.2	13.7	60.2
1978	12.2	15.8	13.9	56.6
1979	9.4	12.2	16.4	59.8

Source: Same as for Table 11.5.

The value of imports by the more-developed countries is also shown in Table 11.5. Between 1973–79 there continued to be an inconsistent increase in the total value of imports from the world and from the CARICOM region. The imports from the non-CARICOM world grew annually, except in the cases of Jamaica in 1976 compared with 1975, and Trinidad and Tobago in 1973 compared with 1972. At the level of combined more-developed-country imports there is again an inconsistent increase in the value of total imports and in imports from CARICOM.

SUMMARY AND CONCLUSIONS

On the basis of the data presented in this chapter, several observations can be made. First, in relation to the pre-CARICOM period, the value of combined more-developed countries exports has increased in the post-CARICOM period, both for intrazonal and extrazonal exports. Extrazonal exports have continued to gain more rapidly than intrazonal exports. However, the sharper increases in the absolute value of the exports of Trinidad and Tobago, particularly since 1974, were the result of that country's increasing importance as an oil exporter. Both Guyana and Jamaica, which have been experiencing serious balance-of-payments problems, have imposed limitations on the quantity of imports from other CARICOM members. Such restrictions are permissible under Articles 28 and 29 of the Caribbean Community Treaty.

In terms of imports, the slight increase in the relative positions between the value of imports by the more-developed countries from CARICOM with respect to imports from the world suggests that modest gains have occurred in the deepening and strengthening of the CARICOM trading arrangements over the period. However, the relatively low percentage of intrazonal imports continues to indicate the region's overwhelming dependence on world sources to supply its basic needs.

During 1977 the more-developed countries introduced new measures designed to facilitate the determination of origin of raw materials imported for use in manufacturing or processing. The new rates, known as the Process List, replaced the earlier Basic Materials List for the more-developed countries only. Under the new Process List, the basic consideration is that when a product is processed from imported materials there must be a change of classification of the item under the Brussels Tariff Nomenclature (BTN), between the imported raw materials and the finished product.

A definite advantage which emerges from member countries participation in CARICOM is the ability to combine their resources in such a way as to make them more meaningful to the development of the region as a whole and the individual members. When countries get together, in this manner, in the interest of their own development, then the possibility is that regional industries will be set up and these will make use of the resources of these territories. These regional industries will be expected to take advantage of the economies of the large-scale production and will avoid the waste of scarce resources, while at the same time achieving an adequate balance among the member countries with respect to industrial location. A good example of such an industry in the case of CARICOM is an aluminum smelter. Instead of exporting all the bauxite and alumina from the area for smelting in other parts of the world, the Caribbean commodity can be smelted at some central spot in the area. This might provide the base for the establishment of subsidiary bauxite-based industries. Such examples could be multiplied. The establishment of a number of integrated industries will increase the value added to the economies concerned and thus enhance their growth potential.

The larger the market the greater is the scope for specialization. The traditional theory of economic integration suggests two ways of increasing growth: (1) trade creation and (2) trade diversion. In the first case the integration leads to a greater degree of division of labor between the partner countries, each specializing in those commodities in which it is at a comparative advantage, and substituting imports for those domestic goods in the production of which it is relatively inefficient. In the case of trade diversion, the discriminatory reduction of tariffs encourages the member countries to buy, from each other, goods they hitherto purchased from countries outside the community. What this means is that we see the effectiveness of integration by being able to ascertain how far trade is diverted because the members of the association now buy goods from one another instead of their former suppliers.

Given this framework, a case can be made for an extension of CARICOM to include such countries as Haiti, Cuba, the Netherlands Antilles, and any Latin American countries that show a desire to become members. Or better still, CARICOM can be integrated with one or more of the other economic blocs such as the Latin American Free Trade Association (LAFTA), the Central American Common Market (CACM), or the Eastern Caribbean Common Market (ECCM). The benefits to be derived from any such extension or integration are obvious. There would be an extension of the free trade market and a further diversion of trade.[7] Many of the Caribbean countries have little or no trade relations with most of the other economic blocs. As an example, Jamaica has no economic contact whatsoever with the Central American bloc.[8]

In 1980 CARICOM celebrated the seventh anniversary of its establishment. Since 1973, several significant problems relating to its objectives and efficient functioning came to the fore. In order to rectify those problems CARICOM decided in March 1980 to appoint a group of experts to prepare a new strategy for the integration movement during the decade of the

1980s. The group issued its report in 1981 and among its findings and recommendations was that CARICOM countries as a community should seek to expand their trade and economic relations with the outside world.[9] This is known to economists as export expansion or promotion and has been recommended before. Additionally, a litany of other measures has been put forward to increase the effectiveness of CARICOM. They include such bankrupt ideas as import-substitution to more contemporary development strategies emphasizing common policies on foreign direct investment and technology transfer. However, on balance and as argued by Frank Long, whilst the report has identified areas aimed at strengthening the integration process, it has failed to provide a worthwhile analysis of the socioeconomic and political factors inducing the present state of organic weakness of CARICOM. Furthermore, the report did not address itself to the economic constraints of the integration process, given the present levels of development of CARICOM member states, and the prevailing levels of dependency.[10]

More recently, in November 1982, the heads of governments of CARICOM countries met in Jamaica. It was only their third meeting in nine years and they managed to reaffirm their strong conviction and belief in CARICOM as the only viable option available for the optimal development of all human and natural resources of the region.[11] The heads of governments met again in Trinidad in July 1983, on the tenth anniversary of the Caribbean Community, where they were able to agree on some of the issues left standing from the previous conference. Another summit was held in the Bahamas in July 1984, and there was agreement to take steps to remove trade barriers.

NOTES

1. The other members of CARICOM are Grenada, Dominica, St. Lucia, St. Vincent, Antigua, Montserrat, St. Kitts-Nevis, Bahamas, and Belize.

2. Hope, "CARIFTA," pp. 169–79; and Hope, "Post-War," pp. 139–56.

3. Chernick et al., Commonwealth Caribbean, p. 5.

4. See William G. Demas, Essays on Caribbean Integration and Development (Kingston, Jamaica: Institute of Social and Economic Research, University of the West Indies, 1976), pp. 117–21. This section is partly derived from this publication.

5. Caribbean Free Trade Association (CARIFTA) was in existence since May 1968.

6. Hope, "CARIFTA," pp. 169–79.

7. Hope, "Post-War," p. 148.

8. Fuat Andic, Suphan Andic, and Douglas Dosser, A Theory of Economic Integration for Developing Countries (London: Allen and Unwin, 1971), p. 117.

9. See The Caribbean Community in the 1980's: Report by a Group of Caribbean Experts (Georgetown: CARICOM Secretariat, 1981), pp. 102–25.

10. See Frank Long, "Review of the Caribbean Community in the 1980's: Report by a Group of Caribbean Experts," *Third World Quarterly* 4 (October 1982), pp. 827–30.

11. See "The Ocho Rios Declaration of the Third Meeting of the Conference of Heads of Government of the Caribbean Community, November 16–18, 1982," as reported in *Caribbean Contact* 10, no. 8 (December 1982), pp. 8–9.

PART V

DEVELOPMENT PLANNING AND RESOURCE ALLOCATION

12

Development Planning in Guyana: Promise and Performance

The concept of development planning has several connotations and forms. In some instances, it has been used to denote a wide range of activities from the central management of the economies in communist countries to government-sponsored forecasts by private groups in countries such as Sweden. Most authorities, however, agree that planning refers to the formulation and execution of a consistent set of interrelated measures designed to achieve certain specific economic and social goals. Or, as former Prime Minister Jawaharlal Nehru of India defined it, more simply and pragmatically: "Planning is the exercise of intelligence to deal with facts and situations as they are and find a way to solve problems."[1]

Albert Waterston concludes that

> countries were considered to be engaged in development planning if their governments were making a conscious and continuing attempt to increase their rate of economic and social progress and to alter those institutional arrangements which were considered to be obstacles to the achievement of this aim.[2]

To plan economically, one need not have a moral purpose; one need only be prudent in the use of scarce resources.[3] Just as economic planning eschews moral judgments, it has no one approach to all problems. It does not, for example, necessarily involve regimentation, collectivization, or industrialization.[4] Nor is its use limited to a particular kind of economy or society. It exists under a variety of political systems.

Despite the great variety of forms which it may take, all planning has certain common attributes. These include looking ahead, making choices, and, where possible, arranging that future actions for attaining objectives follow fixed paths; or, where this is impossible, setting limits to the consequences which may arise from such action.[5]

This chapter has as its objective a macroeconomic analysis of development planning in Guyana with particular reference to how it has performed as an instrument of development policy and some suggestions and recommendations for future planning.

THE PHILOSOPHY OF DEVELOPMENT PLANNING IN GUYANA

Planning in Guyana, as in most Caribbean and developing countries, has been mainly a postwar phenomenon.[6] It developed as part of the process which evolved after World War II, whereby a large measure of responsibility for purely internal affairs was conceded to the inhabitants of these territories through their elected representatives. With the granting of universal adult suffrage and the formation of nationalistic political parties, urgent attention had to be given to the devising of the best means for bringing about economic development. It was realized that complete reliance on market forces could not be expected to bring about the desired level of economic development, and that elected governments would have to play a more positive role in the development process.

Development planning is, therefore, seen in Guyana as a technocratic conception for the fulfilment of specific development goals.[7] Plan enforcement requires that the market judgment and the decisions reached by individuals and interest groups be more or less superseded by considerations of public interest as expressed in the plan. Arguments in favor of plan enforcement are thus based on two sets of propositions: namely that free enterprise resource allocation is inefficient or, to be more precise, that it is less efficient than planned allocation, and that there is a lack of congruence between private interest, expressed in the free enterprise system, and public interest. As a consequence, in the absence of the planned channeling of investment, the period of structural and technological backwardness would be prolonged needlessly.

Finally, it is alleged that the market test is very much incomplete in that it fails to reflect important national goals, and may even result in a pattern of allocation directly opposed to such goals. For example, it is argued that the pursuit of individual profit may result in a socially unacceptable distribution of the gains from growth, or in a socially unacceptable spatial pattern of development. As such, the case for development planning in Guyana rests on the assumption that the planning calculus is superior to the imperfect calculus of the market.[8]

DEVELOPMENT PLANNING, 1945–81

The beginnings of development planning in Guyana can be traced to 1945, when an allocation of G$12 million was received under the Colonial

Development Welfare Act of 1945. But the first rudimentary attempt at planning was made in 1947 when the Ten-Year Development Plan 1947–56 was drawn up. Expenditure in this plan was broadly allocated under three main heads as shown in Table 12.1.

TABLE 12.1 Ten-Year Development Plan 1947–56: Allocation of Expenditure

Head	Allocation (Millions of Guyana dollars)
Three Major Drainage and Irrigation Projects	6.5
Social Welfare, Justice, and Public Buildings	11.2
Economic Services, including agriculture, forestry, transport surveys and research	10.3

Source: British Guiana Ten-Year Development Plan 1947–56 (British Guiana: Legislative Council Sessional Paper, 1947).

The program was phased in such a way that around G$20 million or about two-thirds of the total planned expenditure was to be disbursed during the first five years and another G$6 million later. However, the planned target set for these years was not realized; and between 1947 and 1950, only G$2 million was spent. There were also a number of new projects advanced for consideration after the plan was launched; and in 1950, a revision was necessary so that some of these new projects might be included.

In 1953, after the first five years of the ten-year plan, an economic survey mission organized by the International Bank for Reconstruction and Development (IBRD) visited the country at the request of the government, and submitted a report on economic development in which a five-year development program was recommended.[9] The investment program recommended for 1954–58 aimed at increasing national income by 20 percent and income per capita by 6 percent, in five years.

The IBRD mission estimated that gross investment prior to 1954 had been running at a rate of more than 20 percent of national income; and for the five-year program it assumed a rate of 24 percent, the extra amount to be supplied mainly from government sources, with private investment maintained at the existing level.

Of a total investment program of G$66 million, G$25 million was to be spent on projects such as drainage and irrigation, land settlements, etc., which were for the benefit of the agricultural sector, and G$22 million for transport and communications. This transport program was closely tied to agricultural development, aiming mostly at reducing costs of transport of agricultural products and opening new areas on the coast for agricultural development. It is evident that this expenditure pattern followed closely that which had already commenced under previous development and welfare schemes. Thus, it could be claimed that the IBRD report and plan served mainly to consolidate and justify the pattern of expenditure already committed. In particular, it emphasized the prevailing tendency to concentrate development on the improvement and expansion of coastal lands. The immediate objectives with regard to the interior were seen to be in the form of more surveys of agricultural and mineral possibilities rather than actual investment. The IBRD report, therefore, tended to draw a sharp line of distinction between the "interior" and the "coast." In this light, it can be argued that more attention could have been given to the development of access to the interior with resultant spillover effects on riverine lands.

However, the rationale behind the IBRD plan was the emphasis on projects which promised the most returns to the country in view of the financial, human, and other resources available at that time. Although cognizance was taken of the urgent need for agricultural diversification, agricultural improvement projects were concentrated mainly in the rice sector.

The government of the day considered that a larger program than the one recommended by the mission was necessary and an initial program for 1954–55 was drawn up, to be subsequently absorbed in a long-term development plan. A total of G$44 million was allocated for this purpose, with G$33 million of this amount to be expended on economic development and the remainder for social services.[10] However, from the very outset, it was realized that expenditure of this magnitude, which was more than three times the average for the preceding three years, was unlikely to be achieved in the opening period of the long-term program. In fact, the plan was not completed until March 1954, and financial sanction of the Legislative Council was not obtained until the end of May. New departments of housing, land settlement, drainage and irrigation, and the organization of the Credit Corporation had to be established, and staff recruited and trained. Time had to be spent in carrying out preliminary investigations, preparing plans, and obtaining machinery and equipment. Thus, the year 1954 was one of preparation; and it was not until 1955 that the program began to gain momentum. However, certain difficulties encountered at the outset continued; the lack of qualified and experienced technicians in certain fields continued to prove an important bottleneck. Nevertheless, a total of G$26 million was spent for two years.

In accordance with its original intention that initial programs for the years 1954–55 should be later absorbed in a long-term plan, the government decided to prepare a five-year development program framed on the recommendations of the World Bank but with the addition of a number of new projects. Thus, a new set of allocations for 1956–60 were put together. Unexpected balances from the 1954–55 program were incorporated into these new allocations.

The allocations envisaged a total expenditure of G$91 million, G$61 million for economic development, and the remainder for social development.[11] But toward the end of 1958, it was decided to shorten the plan by one year; that is, to the end of 1959. Thereafter, it was intended that development would continue under a new five-year program, 1960–64, which has expected to provide for the continuation of projects not completed at the end of 1959.

The 1960–64 plan was drawn up by Cambridge economist Kenneth Berrill. The plan proposed a minimum investment program of G$110 million, but the actual expenditure was reduced to G$78.5 million as seen in Table 12.2. This reduction had to be effected because the authorities failed to raise the requisite proportion of foreign funds for financing the development plan.

The Berrill Plan attracted much criticism. It stressed maintaining a high level of employment and suggested that rice production, which was always profitable and employment generating, be continued. Peter Newman, in his criticism of the plan, pointed out that the long-run effect of raising income per capita is more important that the short-run objectives of maintaining full employment, and suggested the need for diversification of agricultural output and the introduction of heavy industry backed up by light industry.[12] He argued further that such a strategy would enable the country to enjoy a high growth rate in the long run and avoid the social problems accompanying an economy with a high dependence on a few stable exports.

However, experience teaches us that any program which concentrates on diversifying agricultural output and encourages industrial production calls for a large injection of capital. In such a case, foreign aid would have had to supplement the low level of domestic savings; but the Guyanese people have always been wary of the implications of any injection of foreign capital and the concomitant risk of increasing foreign control of the means of production.

The comments of Thorne, Cumper, and Boulding were, however, supportive of Newman with regard to the principles of planning and the long-run economic future of Guyana.[13] They all argued that a policy which encouraged diversified agricultural output and the establishment of light and heavy industry was to be preferred to the policy of giving further encouragement to rice production; and further, that the aim of raising

Table 12.2. Guyana: Allocation and Actual Development Expenditure, 1960-64 (Millions of Guyana Dollars and Percentages)

	Allocations		Expenditures	
	$	%	$	%
Drainage and Irrigation	28.4	25.7	23.6	30.1
Land Development	4.3	3.9	1.9	2.4
Sea Defenses	7.4	6.7	7.6	9.7
Other	4.9	4.4	3.5	4.5
Total	45.0	40.7	36.6	46.7
Forest, Lands, and Mines	3.9	3.5	1.5	1.9
Transport and Communication	12.5	11.3	8.1	10.3
Roads	14.5	13.1	8.8	11.2
Public Buildings	2.8	2.5	1.5	1.9
Miscellaneous Public Works	0.6	0.5	0.7	0.9
Education	4.1	3.7	3.3	4.2
Health	1.9	1.7	1.8	2.3
Housing	5.5	5.0	2.8	3.6
Other Social Services	2.2	2.0	1.5	1.9
Power	2.6	2.4	2.7	3.4
Water	2.9	2.6	1.9	2.4
Credits	11.5	10.4	5.3	6.7
Miscellaneous	0.7	0.6	2.0	2.6
Totals	110.7	100.0	78.5	100.0

Source: British Guiana Legislative Council, *Development Estimates, 1964.*

income per capita was more important to development than that of maintaining full employment.

Any trained economist knows that any developing economy that is primarily an agricultural one would have to depend a great deal on its agriculture for its long-term development. Diversification of agriculture would, therefore, be a sine qua non for economic development of any such economy. In the case of Guyana, the arguments against diversification of agriculture have been that such a program would result in further foreign control of Guyana's resources, since foreign aid would be necessary to implement the program.

But, Guyana has a long history of dependence on foreign capital and has never been able to achieve full employment; and further investments in the rice industry have resulted in very poor yield returns. The rate of unemployment in Guyana, as stated before, is estimated to be between 15 and 20 percent, depending on the seasonal adjustments. The magnitude of the unemployment situation will undoubtedly remain one of Guyana's major economic problems. The reasons underlying such a high and sustained rate of unemployment lie in the fact that the labor force increases annually at a much more rapid rate than the increase in jobs. During the period 1960–65, the slow rate of increase in jobs was due primarily to increased mechanization in most of the industries, including rice. Those who were part of the annual increases in the labor force during that period, therefore, became the victims of the pressure of mechanization. Employment, under the pressure of mechanization, showed a tendency to decline at a rate above the rate of increase of the labor force. Another interesting feature of the unemployment situation was that the increase and the ratio of unemployment have been faster and higher among females than males.

The rationale behind the Berrill Plan was a somewhat misguided one. The most significant feature was the high percentage of funds allocated for sea defenses, and drainage and irrigation. The provision of sea defenses, and drainage and irrigation facilities has always presented one of the most intractable problems to the government. The emphasis arose because the coastal area is below sea level and flood control had the highest priority.

The defects of the 1960–64 development program can also be examined within the context of the entire planning effort between 1954 and 1964. In this respect, a comparison can be made between development expenditure realized during the period of the 1954–59 plan and that of the 1960–64 plan. The actual development expenditure for the 1954–59 plan amounted to G$105.8 million, and although the planned expenditure for the 1960–64 plan was slightly higher (G$110 million), actual expenditure amounted to G$78.5 million or just about 74 percent of the expenditure realized for 1954–59.

The period 1945–64 can be regarded as one of piecemeal, rather than national planning. Although it is quite clear that the government was in many instances thinking in national terms, the "plans" were simply statements of how the government proposed to spend its financial resources and lacked any conscious efforts at coordinated economic development.

In 1964, when the 1960–64 plan was coming to an end, a new government took office. As there was neither time nor available data to prepare a new plan starting in 1965, capital expenditure in this year was devoted primarily to the completion of certain projects, and the rehabilitation of coastal roads and public buildings. Under these circumstances, a new development plan for the period 1966–72 was formulated.

The main objective of the 1966–72 plan and the development strategy underlying it was to raise the real income and standard of living of the population, reduce the high level of existing unemployment, and build up the infrastructure.[14] The plan proposed a government expenditure program totaling G$294.25 million at 1966 prices for the seven-year period. The planned expenditure was more than three times that of the actual total expenditures of the previous plan. The bulk of the expenditure was allocated to sea defenses, drainage and irrigation, and transportation. The sectoral allocation of expenditure was, to a certain extent, of the same pattern as the previous plan; but it could be claimed that the plan placed more emphasis on the diversification of agricultural output, the promotion of industry, and the carrying out of the basic mineral and forest surveys than the previous plan.

The financing was intended to be derived from two main sources. It was estimated that G$50 million would be obtained from internal borrowing, and the other G$245 million was expected from external sources in the form of grants, soft loans, and hard loans. Once again, plan financing showed a heavy dependence on foreign capital. The justification for this has been discussed earlier in terms of the low rate of domestic savings.

Though the plan made mention of the contribution of the private sector, it did not in any way project or quantify the expected contribution of this sector. Private enterprise was expected to help willingly so that the economy would flourish and expand. No attempt was made to show what kind of help was required or desired from private enterprise in order that the goals be realized. Moreover, the plan advocated the establishment of an efficient infrastructural framework within which private enterprise could function. But no consideration was given to the expected returns of such projects over the long run.

In essence, the plan was primarily one for the public sector only.[15] It simply showed how the government planned to spend funds, if acquired, over a seven-year period. The macroeconomic growth targets were too optimistic, especially in view of the limited possibilities for export growth. The objectives, with the exception of its intent to diversify agriculture, were not clearly stated. The sectoral programs were a diverse, incongruous collection of projects. In contrast, a good plan involves an overall look at each sector; and on the basis of the findings, all the factors which help determine a rational approach to development of each sector are laid down and linked to each other to form an integrated total, consistent with an overall analytical framework covering the availability of resources and an assumed rate of growth.

The illogical structure of the plan, its ambiguity in terms of stated objectives, and, to a certain extent, the existence of a new concept of development based on cooperativism, influenced the Guyana government to abandon the plan during the 1970–71 period. The government intended to formulate a ten-year plan covering the period 1971–80 with detailed project priorities and public investment recommendations at five-year intervals. However, a draft five-year plan for 1972–76 was released, instead, in 1973.

The objectives of the 1972–76 plan can be identified as the creation of employment opportunities for all Guyanese, the attainment of an equitable distribution of income, the achievement of an equitable geographical distribution of economic activities, and the establishment of the foundation for the attainment of self-sustained economic growth.[16] The plan gave paramount importance to people and the society. The Guyana government, therefore, determined to eschew the conventional approaches to the formulation of economic-development plans and considered first the nature of the society.

The plan envisaged a total expenditure of G$1,150 million over the five-year period as shown in Table 12.3. Of this total expenditure, government and public enterprises were to spend about G$650 million, and cooperatives and private enterprise about G$500 million. Given that these targets were realized, it was expected that Gross Domestic Product would increase on an average by 8.5 percent annually; unemployment would be reduced to 2.9 percent; and per capita income would increase by approximately 6 percent annually. Sixty-five percent of the financing was expected from domestic savings and the other 35 percent from capital inflows.

From currently available data, it is found that the economy of Guyana, in terms of GDP, had an annual average growth rate of approximately 2.4 percent, in real terms, during 1972–76. This, of course, falls way short of the plan projections of 8.5 percent annually which was achieved only in 1974 with a rate of 8.8 percent. However, this situation in

Table 12.3. Development Plan 1972–76: Sectoral Allocation of Planned Expenditure (Millions of Guyana Dollars)

Sector	1972	1973	1974	1975	1976	1972–76 Total
Agriculture	24.0	38.2	35.9	33.7	33.2	165.0
Fishing	2.5	5.3	11.3	4.7	3.2	27.0
Forestry	2.0	6.9	20.2	21.2	14.2	64.5
Mining & Quarrying	6.0	13.0	14.0	17.0	12.0	62.0
Manufacturing	24.2	49.7	42.0	42.7	28.4	187.0
Engineering & Construction	1.0	2.0	3.0	2.0	2.0	10.0
Distribution	9.1	12.0	10.4	2.5	3.0	37.0
Transport & Communication	24.8	32.1	34.1	55.6	61.3	207.9
Housing	18.0	25.0	50.0	67.0	90.0	250.0
Buildings for Financial Agencies	1.0	1.0	2.0	1.0	1.0	6.0
Public Buildings & Equipment	16.1	25.6	28.2	26.4	33.7	130.0
Other	0.5	0.5	1.0	1.0	2.0	5.0
Total	129.2	211.3	252.1	274.8	284.0	1151.4

Source: Government of Guyana, *Draft Second Development Plan, 1972–76* (Georgetown: Ministry of Economic Development, 1973).

1974 was brought about by unusually favorable weather that resulted in large increases in the production of rice and sugar, coupled with a significant increase in the world price of sugar.

But despite the sluggish growth rate, the government achieved its investment target and even surpassed it considerably. The actual gross domestic investment and its financing is shown in Table 12.4. However, assuming the data are accurate, to accept this as some great measure of success of a development plan could be misleading. In examining the impact of gross investment during 1972–76 one finds the Guyana economy continues to be severely affected by the low productivity of investment. An indication of this is provided by the fact that the assumed overall incremental capital/output ratio in the 1972–76 development plan was 3.8, whereas the actual figure for that period was 8.0.[17] Hence, there seems to be a great need for reorienting investment toward projects with shorter gestation periods.

Table 12.4. Actual Gross Domestic Investment and Its Financing, 1972–76 (Millions of Guyana Dollars)

Investment and Financing	1972	1973	1974	1975	1976	Total
Gross Domestic Fixed Investment	118.9	175.5	252.1	380.0	479.1	1405.6
Financed from Gross National Savings	106.1	51.9	221.4	325.7	139.5	844.6
Capital Inflow and Use of International Reserves	12.8	123.6	30.7	54.3	339.6	561.0

Sources: Bank of Guyana, *Annual Reports*; and Government of Guyana, Ministry of Economic Development, Statistical Bureau.

Moreover, although the overall gross domestic investment was more than the planned investment, gross national savings, which financed about 60 percent of the total investment, averaged just less than 18 percent of GDP rather than the 27 percent estimated in the plan. If the government is to continue its ambitious investment program in the future, it is crucial to increase this figure to between 20 and 25 percent of GDP. Savings performance of this magnitude will depend on careful budgetary management by the central government, and the pursuit of management and pricing policies by public corporations which will generate adequate funds for financing their capital-investment programs without undue reliance on transfers from the central government.

Further, the plan failed to reduce unemployment to 4.9 percent in 1976. Unemployment continues to be above 15 percent. This is not surprising, however, since due account was not taken of the manpower constraints of the economy when the plan was formulated.

In macroeconomic terms, the 1972–76 plan competently analyzed some of the major constraints and opportunities facing the Guyana economy and set some appropriate priorities and policies. But, it was, obviously, overly optimistic in its target.

In 1978, a new development plan covering the period 1978–81 was released by the government. The goals and objectives of the plan were basically similar to those of the 1972–76 plan. The main targets were a real GDP growth rate of 17 percent for the four-year period (compared with 9.9 percent in 1974–77), significant growth in employment in agriculture and construction, increased labor productivity through the introduction of surplus-sharing projects and training programs, a higher domestic savings rate (from the equivalent of 5 percent of GDP in 1977 to an average of 16 percent in 1980–81), and maintenance of a tax revenue/GDP ratio of more than 30 percent. The planned total public sector investments for 1978–81 was G$1,122 million and almost half of it was expected to be financed with external resources.[18] No formal development plan beyond that period was prepared. However, a capital expenditure and investment program of over G$1.3 billion was outlined for 1981–83 with emphasis on agriculture, forestry, and fishing.

AN ANALYTICAL APPRAISAL

Development planning in Guyana to date has had little impact on the country's economy. The plans were more concerned with being consistent, and represented documents which were loaded with misconceptions and misguided macroeconomic growth targets. Most of the plans neglected private sector participation in the economy, although the private sector constitutes an indispensable potential asset for national development. The private sector constitutes the economic decision making and activity that occur outside the ministries, public corporations, and other agencies of the government. In Guyana, there was a substantial enough private sector. Consequently, the role that the private sector played in the development process was of great importance even though much of its potential for growth may have not yet been realized. Private sector participation in development planning is probably the major means by which the interests of private individuals and particularistic groups can be harmonized in voluntaristic ways with those of the society as a whole.

Development planning must deal with the real-life problems and limitations — social, political, and administrative, as well as economic — if it is to amount to something more than a test of economic virtuosity. The rather disappointing experience in Guyana during the last two decades reflected the fact that the planners were more concerned with constructing a plan for publication. As a result, the plans have been statements of aspiration rather than reasonable expectations.

All of the development plans during that period gave little or no consideration to overall rural development. Rural areas were totally neglected as the plans emphasized urban growth. Rural areas should be conceived, for purposes of planning economic development, to be the rural people and the geographical segments in which they live, taken in conjunction with those urban areas and people with whom they share close economic and social interdependence. Planning within a framework of such functional economic areas would have potentials (in addition to those of facilitating the location in the area of more investment and economic activity) for bringing about the use of such areas as loci for adaptive planning. In Guyana, 90 percent of the population lives on 4 percent of the land. The majority of this population is located on the coastal plain, which is predominantly rural. It would seem quite obvious, therefore, that the development strategy must be geared also to alleviating rural poverty and to promoting the growth potential of the vast rural areas.

It must be a strategy of integrated rural development which contains elements of serious attempts by the government to involve rural cooperatives in the national development plans. Though overall emphasis has been placed on the cooperative order in Guyana and the need to be self-sufficient in food production, no particular mention has ever been made, in any of the plans, of an all-embracing program for total involvement of the rural cooperatives.

Government policy must be directed to build a strong agriculture through strong rural cooperatives — able to withstand the impacts of economic, social, and political forces. This is an agriculture with a rural cooperative system that has developed a leadership capable of taking the initiative in formulating policies that reflect the needs and interests of the rural poor. With such conditions prevailing, the government will find it rather advantageous to continue to support and encourage further development of rural cooperatives as a most effective way of implementing agricultural policies.[19]

The most obvious and probably the most important function of planning consists of the coordination and rationalization of government policies. Planning should, therefore, encourage authorities to think in terms of opportunity costs and to explore direct as well as indirect effects of policies. With this in mind, it can be advocated that the central government should have developed a number of institutional arrangements whereby a particular agency or group of agencies exercised a coordinating role over the related functions of other government departments. This would have served to uncomplicate the formulation of a clear policy for government expenditure in Guyana, which has been complicated by the division of functions within the executive branches, and has resulted in great delays and increased costs in policy implementation.

A prime example of this problem can be found in the bauxite industry, which has been completely nationalized by the government and now operates as a government corporation. The end result has been chronic supply constraints, particularly with respect to water management, and institutional and human resource problems, which appear to be escaping adequate attention and resolution. As such, the linkage effects between planning and one of Guyana's major industries has yet to take effect.

Planning strategy, as noted before, must consider first the roots of the development problem. One of the most important aspects of the development problem in Guyana is that of the low level of domestic savings. If domestic savings are low, then the acquisition of foreign funds becomes very significant to the development process. Planning, therefore, should be used as a tool of increasing savings and hence increasing the growth potential.

Development planning is basically an effort to specify and to control the paths along which economic growth will occur; the fundamental assumptions and preconceptions underlying such planning are, therefore, of extreme importance. It must be spelled out whether the development planning process should proceed from the top down or the bottom up and must include the broadest possible participation by both government and business groups which, unfortunately, was not the case in the development plans in Guyana during the past two decades.

Planning for development has many dimensions; and, as such, planners should always be looking for significant linkages that will help progress toward the specified goals. Particularly, planners should exercise caution in conception but boldness in execution.

The disenchantment with planning in Guyana during the postwar era results largely from the failures of the plans to take account of the real developmental problems in the economy of Guyana. Planners during that period never understood the society, and the result was an irrational application of macroeconomic policy instruments for unjustified growth targets. This may explain, in part, the high degree of abandonment of these plans and the common tendency of failure to achieve targets as specified therein. The visiting economists, or so-called foreign experts, who prepared the majority of Guyana's development plans during 1945–76 were academic economists who had enormous visions of rising, real, per capita income during the tenure of the plans. However, they failed to realize that they must first find out how the economy works. The visiting economist has to be able to build up a complete picture of a society that is quite novel to him. It is clearly rather optimistic, however, to expect someone to be able to do this for a foreign country, given the expert's short period of stay. The training economists receive does not prepare them for such tasks and, in some ways, makes it more difficult. What usually happens is that the model that the economist — consciously or unconsciously — uses turns out to be the sort of model suitable for a developed country.

It can be readily seen, therefore, that the visitor who stays for only a few weeks (a fortiori, the person who works on a country's problems without visiting it) will be unable to make the necessary appraisal of the socioeconomic structure and the capacity of the administration. Visiting economists, consequently, however experienced and eminent, are very unlikely to be a success.[20] They may even make the rather grotesque error of handing out quite sweeping recommendations that derive rather from ideological bias than from study of the local problem — recommendations such as "balance the budget," "control imports," or "unify the exchange rates." Some peripatetic economists prescribe the same medicine for all countries, whatever the symptoms.

CONCLUDING COMMENTS

There is no doubt that planning is a growth industry. In Guyana, it has become legitimized, even though it has been previously suspect and failed miserably as an instrument of development policy during the postwar period, when the "seven sins of development planners" were committed.[21] But as the blush of enthusiasm gives way to sober consideration of sticky problems, the practical issues of refinement and implementation should take precedence within an indigenous framework.

Developing countries have much to learn from each others' planning techniques. The failure of one set of techniques and the success of another set must ultimately lead to a reassessment of the entire planning effort.

Discussion of planning engages man's heart as well as his mind. A quintessential problem in analyzing planning has been that at its very core are great moral and political issues, and thus it can never be judged solely on technical considerations. Like other all-encompassing concerns, the discussion of development planning impinges on sensitive and troubled areas. The problems are always multidimensional.[22]

But behind the controversies, technical and otherwise, the forces of convergence must slowly take hold. Economies which seem different in all important respects — stage of development, ideological orientation, economic structure — must evolve toward the use of broad methods to govern their resource allocation decisions. Partly, this should reflect processes of choice and adaptation, the transfer of technique and knowledge, and the emulation of successful experimentation.

The future, therefore, should not emerge as a pale carbon copy of this or that system now existing. The point is that there must be much borrowing and innovating by all. The less-developed economies will have to undergo a process analogous to selective absorption. The future is likely to reverse our present modes of thought. Today we emphasize the differences among nations in their economic policies, although we recognize some similarities. The common need and basis of planning, no matter what formal differences persist, will compel us to adopt a new perspective.

As stated before, planning in Guyana, in terms of the primary economic indicators, has not been terribly successful. There seems to be, however, an overwhelming desire to continue to plan the economy. Understandably, this desire has emerged from the perceived sense that the case for planning reduces to the simple argument that explicit targets are better than implicit targets; that bringing to light hidden, and often imperfectly understood, approaches to policy is necessary for a correct evaluation of the alternatives; that taking into consideration the mutual interdependence of economic phenomena is a more efficient procedure than duplication and overlapping of isolated efforts. Classical economic theory attributes the function of efficient allocation of resources, between sectors and over time, to the market. However, because of the scarcity of resources in developing countries and the presence of indivisibilities and externalities, then some means of ensuring consistency and coordination of allocative and investment decisions must be undertaken. Planning provides some of those means.

As such, the issue to be resolved, in countries such as Guyana, is not whether to plan but how to plan and plan effectively within the context of the constraints placed upon less-developed economies. For such planning to be effective it must be of a short-term nature and be synchronized with the budget process.

NOTES

1. J. Nehru, "Strategy of the Third Plan," in *Problems of the Third Plan* (New Delhi: Government of India, 1961), pp. 33–34.

2. A Waterston, *Development Planning: Lessons of Experience* (Baltimore: Johns Hopkins University Press, 1965), p. 27.

3. Ibid., p. 9.

4. J. Friedmann, "Introduction (to) the Study and Practice of Planning," *International Social Science Journal* 11, no. 3 (1959), p. 329.

5. Waterston, *Development Planning*, p. 9.

6. Kempe Ronald Hope and W. David, "Planning for Development in Guyana: The Experience from 1945 to 1973," *Inter-American Economic Affairs* 27, no. 4 (Spring 1974), pp. 27–46.

7. Hope, *Post-War Planning*, p. 2.

8. Ibid.

9. See IBRD, *The Economic Development of British Guiana* (Baltimore: Johns Hopkins University Press, 1953).

10. British Guiana Legislative Council, *Sessional Paper*, no. 5 (1959), p. 7.

11. British Guiana Legislative Council, British Guiana Development Programme 1956-60, paper no. 8, (1956), pp. 2-3.

12. P. Newman, "The Economic Future of British Guiana," Social and Economic Studies, 9, no. 3 (September 1960), pp. 263-96.

13. See A.P. Thorne, "British Guiana's Development Programme," Social and Economic Studies 10, no. 1 (March 1961), pp. 6-17; G. E. Cumper, "Investment Criteria: A Comment," Social and Economic Studies 10, no. 1 (March 1961), pp. 18-24; and K.E. Boulding, "Social Dynamics in West Indian Society," Social and Economic Studies 10, no. 1 (March 1961), pp. 25-34.

14. Government of Guyana, Development Programme 1966-72 (Georgetown: Government Printery, 1966), pp. II.1 - II.15.

15. This point has been stressed by many. See, for example, Havelock Brewster, "Planning and Economic Development in Guyana," in Readings in the Political Economy of the Caribbean, eds N. Girvan and O. Jefferson (Kingston: New World Group, 1971), p. 209.

16. See Government of the Cooperative Republic of Guyana, Second Development Plan 1972-76 (Georgetown: Ministry of Economic Development, 1973).

17. See Kempe Ronald Hope, W. David, and A. Armstrong, "Guyana's Second Development Plan 1972-76: A Macro-Economic Assessment," World Development 4, no. 2 (February 1976), pp. 131-41.

18. See Government of Guyana, Third Development Plan 1978-81 (Georgetown: Ministry of Economic Development, 1978).

19. Kempe Ronald Hope, "Strengthening Rural Cooperatives in Guyana," Journal of Rural Cooperation 6, no. 2 (1978), pp. 163-64.

20. For more on this see D. Seers, "Why Visiting Economists Fail," Journal of Political Economy 70, no. 4 (August 1962), pp. 325-38.

21. This idea of the "seven sins of development planners" was pioneered by a World Bank economist, Mahbub ul Haq. See the chapter of the same title in his book Poverty Curtain, pp. 12-26.

22. Kempe Ronald Hope, Development Policy in Guyana: Planning, Finance, and Administration (Boulder, Colo: Westview Press, 1979), p. 144.

13

Patterns of Investment and Expenditure
in the Caribbean

Investment and expenditure policy in the Caribbean has never really been consistent. As a result, it has generally been difficult to analyze, with some degree of certainty, the socioeconomic impact of the actualized patterns. However, investment and expenditures play an important role in the functioning of an economy, whether at a relatively low or high level, or at a relatively low or high degree of development. But, there is good reason to expect that this role will change in the course of economic development. This chapter examines the trends with respect to investment and expenditures in the Caribbean and their relative impact and changing role in the development process.

GROWTH AND STRUCTURE OF CARIBBEAN INVESTMENT AND EXPENDITURES

In Table 13.1, we see the gross domestic investment in the Caribbean for the period 1960–80. No consistent pattern emerges. In Barbados, gross fixed investment increased from 1960 through 1974, declined in 1975, and then increased again thereafter. In Guyana, there was a decline in 1970 and then again in 1977–78 and 1980. In Jamaica there were declines in 1976–77 and 1980. Trinidad and Tobago showed the same inconsistency with declines in 1970 and 1974.

Like the absolute gross domestic investment, investment ratios with respect to GDP showed erratic changes. Relative to the 1971–75 average, Jamaica was the only country that by 1980 was showing an increase. All of the other countries showed marginal decreases. This performance tends to indicate that gross domestic investment in the Caribbean has occurred whenever it has occurred rather than as a result of a conscious development effort and target setting.

Table 13.1. Gross Domestic Investment in the Caribbean by Country, 1960–80 (Millions of 1976 U.S. Dollars)

Year	Barbados[a]	Guyana	Jamaica	Trinidad & Tobago
1960	30.9	68.7	112.9	234.0
1965	29.4	59.8	122.9	236.5
1970	45.2	63.7	270.0	224.9
1973	50.6	75.5	358.1	351.3
1974	86.7	95.5	758.5	116.2
1975	76.9	131.1	759.4	177.4
1976	83.4	149.5	457.1	188.0
1977	91.3	93.3	439.3	252.1
1978[b]	115.8	90.8	450.1	359.5
1979[b]	118.2	101.4	458.3	367.8
1980	185.0	97.7	402.1	427.8

Sources: World Bank, World Tables 1976 (Baltimore: Johns Hopkins University Press, 1976); and Inter-American Development Bank, Economic and Social Progress in Latin America (Washington, D.C.: IDB, 1982), statistical appendix.

[a]Fixed investment only. Barbados does not publish figures for gross domestic investment.

[b]Millions of 1980 dollars.

Within the framework of domestic investment is the role of government expenditures. Total expenditures may be classified according to their economic characteristics and functions. In the economic classification, the nature of the transaction, whether it is for current or for capital purposes, is the principal criterion. The level and allocation of expenditures in the Caribbean reflects the sustained efforts of central governments to broaden the scope and diversity of public services, strengthen transfer payments to lower levels of government and public enterprises, and increase the proportion of fiscal resources allocated to capital formation and financial investment.

In 1980 total expenditures as a ratio of GDP surpassed the 1971–75 average in all four countries. The largest increase occurred in Guyana (21 percent), up from an annual average of 43.5 percent of GDP in 1971–75 to 64.5 percent in 1980, and in Trinidad and Tobago (up 15.2 percent). In Trinidad expenditures were up from 26.1 percent of GDP in 1971–75 to 41.3 percent in 1980, and in Jamaica from 29 percent in 1971–75 to 43.3 percent in 1980. The increase in Barbados was much smaller, from 29.5 percent of GDP in 1971–75 to 32.6 percent in 1980.

Upon examination, the increases in 1980 showed varying patterns. Guyana's increase was primarily in the form of current expenditures, since capital expenditures as a percentage of GDP increased by a smaller degree. In Jamaica, even though both current and capital expenditures increased as a percentage of GDP, current expenditures increased much more rapidly. The other two countries, Barbados and Trinidad and Tobago, were successful in directing more resources toward capital expenditures than to current expenditures. Current expenditures accounted for more than 50 percent of total expenditures in all of the countries except Trinidad and Tobago.

Fixed investment was the major component of capital expenditure in the Caribbean as seen in Table 13.2. The share of fixed investment was highest in Trinidad and Tobago, where it accounted for 46.7 percent of total expenditures in 1980. The rapid expansion of investment spending in Trinidad and Tobago stemmed from the government's commitment to diversify the economic structure and to ease the impact of inflationary pressures on low-income groups by providing social inputs such as health and education services. In Barbados, fixed investment improved in 1980 to 15.4 percent from the 1971–75 average of 10.9 percent. In Guyana there was an increase from 23.5 percent in 1971–75 to 29.3 percent in 1980, and in Jamaica there was a decrease from the 1971–75 average of 15.9 percent to 14.9 percent in 1980.

The magnitude of fixed investment in the Caribbean has a dual role in influencing the growth of output. First, with respect to generating demand and, secondly, with respect to creating capacity. On the one hand, expenditure on such things as buildings, plant, and equipment creates a demand for current output in the economy and the satisfaction of this demand generates a concomitant flow of income. Thus an increase or decrease in the rate of capital formation is directly reflected in the annual flow of goods and services.

**Table 13.2. Structure of Central Government
Capital Expenditure by Country, 1971–75 and 1980
(Percentage of Total Expenditure)**

Component	Barbados		Guyana		Jamaica		Trinidad & Tobago	
	1971–75	1980	1971–75	1980	1971–75	1980	1971–75	1980
Fixed Investment	10.9	15.4	23.5	29.3	15.9	14.9	33.5	46.7
Capital Transfers	8.0	7.1	5.0	9.9	13.5	7.4	1.2	0.3
Financial Investment & Net Lending	0.2	2.0	10.3	—	—	—	3.6	8.8
Total	19.1	24.5	38.8	39.2	29.4	22.3	38.3	55.8

Sources: Same as for Table 13.1.

On the other hand, capital formation creates a capacity to produce goods and services in the future. But those countries having the same proportion of fixed investment in relation to their output may not have the same rate of growth of output. The contribution of investment to the growth of output also depends on the pattern and composition of investment, the allocation of investment into various sectors of the economy, the technological forms assumed by the capital investment, the durability and degree of utilization of the capital assets and replacement requirements, because of wear and tear and obsolescence. Thus the growth of productive capacity is related both to the annual volume of capital formation and its productivity. As has been observed, "the problems of economic investment are not merely those of collecting quantities of capital, but of deciding the forms it should take and the specific uses to which it should be put."[1]

Capital transfers were used as a major instrument for the purpose of financing the acquisition of fixed and financial assets in Guyana while in Barbados, Jamaica, and Trinidad and Tobago there were decreases in 1980, compared with the annual average for 1971–75, as seen in Table 13.2.

Financial investment and net lending, the third category of capital expenditure, including loans, equity investment, and debt instruments issued by public and mixed enterprises, accounted for more than 8 percent of total expenditures in Trinidad and Tobago. This category of expenditure is used primarily in Trinidad and Tobago and its share has been steadily increasing as the number of development funds grew from 9 in 1974 to 47 in 1980.

The pressure for increasing public expenditures in the Caribbean is obviously continuous — to meet the needs of population growth, urbanization, and urban employment, and to enable the governments to expand their economic and social infrastructure.[2] Increased recurrent expenditures may mean reduced capital expenditures and the slowing down of capital formation. Increased public capital expenditures may mean reduced current expenditures. Yet increasing current expenditures may be necessary to support an expansion of public capital investment.[3]

In any case, however, increased expenditures are dependent on increasing revenues, and the boundary conditions to expenditures are set by the revenue capacity of the region, the rate of general development, and the possibility of filling the gap in capital and recurrent requirements through external financing.[4]

Such constraints tend to reduce the efficiency of public spending. However, in Guyana, for example, this inefficiency, instead of dampening the enthusiasm of the government sector for acquiring a larger and larger proportion of the nation's resources, paradoxically contributed to increased public expenditure, partly because a more than optimum amount had to be spent to achieve any given objective and partly because the resultant rate of growth of national income and employment, being slower than expected, increased frustration and encouraged further government intervention.[5]

In Barbados, other constraints, such as market prospects and organizational capacity, have limited investmment.[6] The country, however, has not suffered from an investment constraint for any length of time during the period 1960–80. The incremental capital/output ratio has varied considerably, ranging from between 14 in 1955 and 19 in 1972.[7]

Now let us move on to private direct investment. Net private direct investment has changed unevenly in the Caribbean, as seen in Table 13.3, though there was a recovery in Barbados in 1979 and Trinidad and Tobago in 1980.

The bulk of private investment in the Caribbean is of foreign origin. The Caribbean's desire to industrialize during the pre-independence era made private investment attractive to transnational corporations (TNCs). The Caribbean host countries wanted to acquire technological and management skills, increase their rate of economic growth, and reduce their rates of unemployment; the TNCs, on the other hand, wanted to acquire the vast new markets that had become available to them. But, after independence, government as well as popular attitudes toward foreign investment began to change and the growing nationalism fueled opposition to foreign investors, thus resulting in voluntary as well as forced reduction in private foreign investment in the region.

However, the attractiveness of TNC investment in the Caribbean is that it is a convenient way to help fill the gap between the available finance

Table 13.3. Net Private Direct Investment in the Caribbean, 1971–80 (Millions of U.S. Dollars)

Year	Barbados	Guyana	Jamaica	Trinidad & Tobago
1971	14.7	− 55.6	175.5	103.0
1972	17.4	2.5	97.8	86.6
1973	4.8	8.2	75.1	65.6
1974	10.0	1.3	23.3	120.1
1975	22.2	0.8	− 1.8	202.9
1976	6.2	− 26.1	− 0.6	107.1
1977	4.7	− 0.8	− 7.0	140.1
1978	9.1	—	− 26.7	140.1
1979	14.9	0.6	− 26.4	130.1
1980	0.9	0.5	− 11.1	216.5

Source: Inter-American Development Bank, *Economic and Social Progress in Latin America* (Washington, D.C.: IDB, several years), statistical appendixes.

for development and the rate of investment deemed necessary to achieve national economic goals. Investment by transnational corporations contributes more than just financial resources. The TNCs also provide managerial, administrative, engineering, and other technical skills that are in short supply in the Caribbean. The petroleum-exporting and the bauxite-mining industries could not have been developed in Trinidad and Tobago and Guyana, for example, without assistance from TNCs.

In Jamaica, a change in political orientation, which led to a decline in investment by TNCs, occurred in 1976 when Prime Minister Michael Manley committed his government to a path of democratic socialism involving public ownership of utilities and worker participation in industry. As a result of this policy, U.S. investment in Jamaica in 1976 was $50 million less than it was in 1972.[8]

With respect to Guyana, a change in political orientation occurred in 1970 when the government of the late President Forbes Burnham declared Guyana a Cooperative Socialist Republic and the country proceeded to engage itself in the process of nationalization of the major industries in the economy. Through this process President Burnham had hoped to use the cooperative movement as the main instrument for the promotion of Guyana's economic growth by supposedly allowing the Guyanese populace to participate fully in the development process. As a result of this, in 1981 U.S. direct investment in Guyana was one-quarter of what it was in 1970 as shown in Table 13.4.

U.S. direct investment in Barbados, though marginal, has been increasing in recent years while in Trinidad and Tobago it increased from US$198 million in 1970 to US$932 million in 1981. About 76 percent of the foreign direct investment in Trinidad and Tobago is from the U. S. and about 90 percent of that investment is in the petroleum industry, while in Jamaica the majority of the U.S. direct investment is in the mining sector.

Not as large as investment originating from the United States, investment originating from the United Kingdom has also declined in the Caribbean. Most of the U.K. TNCs' investment flow is in the manufacturing sector, primarily in Jamaica and Trinidad and Tobago. The same is true of TNC investment flow from Germany and Japan; Canadian direct investment is concentrated mainly in banking and mining.

Investment by transnational corporations in developing countries dates back to the nineteenth century. During the colonial and neocolonial period, it was concentrated in export-oriented mineral and agricultural production and in public utilities. But, as nationalist movements emerged, the corporations came to be regarded as exploiters. As such, attitudes in developing countries toward investment by TNCs have ranged from cautious to prohibitive and, of course, the Caribbean has been no exception to such a range of attitudes.

Table 13.4. U.S. Direct Investment in the Caribbean, 1970–81 (Millions of U.S. Dollars)

Year	Barbados	Guyana	Jamaica	Trinidad & Tobago
1970	9	40	507	198
1971	12	35	618	262
1972	18	36	624	280
1973	20	—	618	433
1974	20	20	609	549
1975	19	22	654	656
1976	20	21	577	713
1977	26	3	378	971
1981	41	10	385	932

Sources: U.S. Department of Commerce, *Selected Data on U.S. Direct Investment Abroad 1966–76* (Washington, D.C.: U.S. Department of Commerce, 1977); and U.S. Department of Commerce, *U.S. Direct Investment Abroad, year-end, 1982* (Washington, D.C.: Department of Commerce).

But there are issues other than economic ones that must be noted. Investment by TNCs cannot be analyzed in purely economic terms; it is a political phenomenon as well. Developing countries fear investment by TNCs because it has neoimperialist connotations while some other countries welcome it for the same reasons.[9] In some sectors, investment by TNCs is seen as having both a cultural and political influence and, as such, the TNCs are usually barred from these sectors.

Any trained economist would agree that investment by TNCs has costs as well as benefits. There is a divergence between private and social benefits and the benefits accruing to various groups in a country. Basically, it is up to the governments of host and home countries to decide whether, and to what extent, they want to use or promote investment by TNCs as an instrument of development.

For host country governments, the real issues are how to provide an environment in which TNCs can contribute to national goals while minimizing the costs and maximizing the benefits. For home country governments, the central question is how to prevent adverse effects to the home economy as a result of economic activities abroad.[10]

But, irrespective of political ideology, unless countries develop and have attained some degree of self-sufficiency there will continue to exist a reliance on investment flows from the TNCs, no matter how marginal that reliance may be. Since none of the Caribbean countries has achieved economic independence, rationality would suggest that the climate for investment flows from abroad should be made as conducive as possible to encourage such flows, despite their magnitude, within the framework of the development thrust. This undoubtedly will also assist in improving the balance-of-payments and foreign exchange positions of these countries.

It seems overwhelmingly clear that investment by TNCs does make some meaningful contribution to the development process and there is considerable literature in support of that point of view.[11] The fact that the overseas investor is in a far more favorable position than the local investor in raising finance either abroad or in the host country, allows faster growth possibilities, which in turn reinforces the foreign sector and Gross Domestic Product. Thus, at the same time the foreign firm brings with it foreign resources and availability of imports and, where aid is also given, this advantage is intensified.[12]

However, we must also recognize the adverse external effects of direct investment by TNCs. Primarily, investment by TNCs can result in the development of a foreign enclave within the host countries with the probability of little or no economic contact with the local economy, along with the possibility that overly heavy dependence on such investment may pose a threat to a country's balance-of-payments position, which, in turn, may seriously constrain domestic economic policies with the resultant effect of a loss of control, in a number of ways, over the private sector of the economy.[13]

Given this possibility, Caribbean countries ought to try to obtain a package that includes both development assistance and foreign-investment flows in accordance with their individual development thrusts. This assumes development thrusts that give prominence to the private sector and which may better ensure some degree of flexibility in their growth strategy and reduce the possibility of a mass exploitation of local resources and the citizens.

Another interesting point that should be made here is the fact that it has long been evident that private foreign investors will conduct business, whether in the form of equity or management participation, without incentives from host or home governments. Provided that the political and economic environment is favorable to private business, the decision to participate directly in an enterprise in a developing country is usually almost independent of host and home countries' private-investment policies.[14] The motivation to enter or remain in developing countries is an integral part of a private foreign investor's strategy. It is the form of participation and its location that can be more readily influenced by host- and home-country policies.

Investment by TNCs has multiple effects on the economy of a host country in terms of production, employment, income, the balance of payments, and general welfare. Some of these effects confer benefits on the host country; some of them incur costs. Some effects occur almost immediately, and some may be long-term in nature. However, the fundamental effect of direct foreign investment is its contribution to the national income of the host country over time.

But, in looking at investment of TNCs a distinction must be made between income generated through investment by TNCs and income due to investment of TNCs. A distinction is necessary between these two expressions because it is questionable whether evidence presented on income generated through investment of TNCs, even if the data are correct, is acceptable as evidence of income due to investment of TNCs. The latter would only be appropriate if the productivity of factors of production employed in investment by TNCs would have had a zero productivity in the absence of investment by TNCs. In other words, it would require that all labor and capital used in the private foreign-investment sector be deducted from the value added and generated in the private foreign investment sector, in order to obtain the contribution made to GNP.

A simple, but unsuccessful, attempt to measure the contribution of investment by TNCs to national income was made by Herbert May.[15] In his report for the Council for Latin America, he came to the conclusion that in 1966 alone, U.S.-owned TNCs' investment generated an income of US$12,885 million or 13.7 percent of the GDP of the region. These findings have to be rejected, however, as May equates total sales volume with contribution to GDP.[16] As no detailed breakdown of production costs is presented in his report, it is not possible to come to a corrected estimate of income generated through investment by TNCs in Latin America and the Caribbean.

The ground is no firmer if we try to establish correlations between TNCs' investment rates and the rate of growth of the Caribbean economy. There are a number of reasons for this. First, there is the declining trend in foreign resource flows, coupled with increasing government expenditure. As such, increases in output were dependent primarily on the stimulus provided by government expenditure. In addition, the import bill of the Caribbean economies has been increasing rapidly despite attempts at import-substitution. These increases, naturally, have to be met by increases in government expenditure and foreign exchange outflows. This represents, therefore, an important leakage from the Caribbean economies and is not conducive to maximizing their rate of growth.

Also, recent data indicated that there are further revenue leakages from the Caribbean economies due to the nature of their tax incentives for foreign investors. In Jamaica, for example, data for 1977 revealed that the pretax rates of return on equity for a sample of incentive firms have been from 40 to about 75 percent.[17] Though in most developing countries the sacrifice of tax revenue has been justified as a small cost necessary to induce foreign corporations to invest in productive activities, it can be argued, however, that pretax annual rates of return of between 40 and 75 percent are far too high to warrant generous tax incentives, particularly with respect to the long duration of the exemption period. Moreover, the incentives were of limited value to TNCs based in the United States since neither their after tax nor cash flow positions on repatriated profits was altered because there are no tax-sparing provisions in the United States. The real effect was a loss to the Jamaican treasury and a gain for the treasury of the United States.

With respect to employment effects of investment by TNCs in the Caribbean, one study published in 1971 estimated that investment by TNCs in Jamaica between 1950 and 1967 created 168 new factories that produced jobs for 10,000 people, roughly 15 percent of the industrial labor force.[18] A large part of the employment was generated by enclave factories manufacturing exclusively for export, and between 1960 and 1967 these latter factories accounted for 65 percent of the jobs created by the "incentive" factories.[19]

The same study indicated that in Trinidad and Tobago investment by TNCs was responsible for the establishment of 149 factories by the end of 1967. These factories provided jobs for 8,000 people, which was roughly 16 percent of the employment in the manufacturing sector. In addition, a number of factories were assisted by the import duty concessions on their new plant, machinery, and raw materials without the benefit of exemptions from income tax. The total employment provided by these assisted establishments was about 6,000.[20]

Another study published in 1973 and done by the United Nations, indicated that between 1968 and 1970 TNCs investing through special fiscal concessions were responsible for the creation of 75 percent of the jobs in the manufacturing sector in Barbados and 34 and 20 percent, respectively, in Trinidad and Tobago and Jamaica. The main conclusion that can be drawn from these figures is that the employment created by transnational enterprises enjoying concessions in the manufacturing sector is extremely important for Barbados while it is less important for Jamaica and Trinidad and Tobago. A more recent study published in 1982 also confirmed this finding, despite the revelation that the share of employment generated by TNCs in Trinidad and Tobago increased to, and appears to have held more or less constant at, 44 percent throughout the 1970s if account is taken of state interventions in ownerships.[21]

Investment by TNCs may create, directly and indirectly, employment opportunities. However, the extent of the employment opportunities created will be determined by the nature of the investment, that is, whether the investment is more labor intensive than capital intensive, or vice versa. Moreover, general policies play an important role in determining the employment effects of investment by TNCs.

As far as the direct employment effects are concerned, technological requirements generally imply a very high capital intensity. Technological development has been input-saving over time and particularly labor-saving, rendering older processes technically inefficient. This is particularly true in the extractive industry, which is very important to all of the

Caribbean economies except Barbados. In Trinidad and Tobago, for example, despite the importance that the foreign extractive industry has had for the economy, its share of employment increased by only 8 percent during the past decade.

CONCLUSIONS

Patterns of investment and expenditure in the Caribbean have been erratic. What seems clear, however, is that the level of development has a direct relationship to the magnitude of government expenditures and that the rate of investment in new production activities determines the region's growth capacity.

It is also clear that private sector initiatives have in the past contributed greatly to economic growth and employment in the Caribbean, and can continue to do so in the future. With the appropriate public programs and incentives, private-sector development will not only improve the growth performance of the Caribbean countries, but will also help alleviate unemployment and improve social conditions.[22] For the Caribbean host governments, the real issue ought to be how to provide an environment to which TNCs can contribute to national goals while minimizing the costs and maximizing the benefits of private investment. Host countries can provide a better framework for private investment and avoid many of the negative aspects by following policies that allow prices of products and resources to reflect real scarcities more closely. Sound general economic policies help to build a good image for the host country and its economic development and create confidence. And, indeed, many case studies have shown that these factors are much more effective in attracting foreign investors than the most favorable tax incentives.[23]

One aspect of providing such an environment and framework is for those Caribbean governments that have acquired enterprises engaged in production or trade to consider divesting ownership, in selected cases, to increase yield and efficiency as well as provide a signal to investors of their interest in improving confidence in the private sector.

Without a viable private sector, Caribbean governments, for the most part, cannot stimulate or sustain economic growth. Conversely, without a reasonably efficient public sector capable of providing — at a manageable economic cost — the necessary infrastructure and an overall environment conducive to sound investment, the private sector is unlikely to make its full contribution to development. If governments are inefficient and ineffective, or if they pursue policies that significantly distort private sector decision making, both the private sector and the overall prospects for economic development suffer.[24]

It is partly within that context that the Reagan administration developed its Caribbean Basin Initiative (CBI) in early 1982. The CBI proposal consists of integrated, mutually reinforcing measures in the fields of trade, investment, and financial assistance. The centerpieces of the program are tax incentives for investment in the Caribbean along with the offer of one-way free trade. Moreover, the program's integrated nature assures, to some extent at least, that symptoms are not just treated but root causes are also addressed. The total proposed expenditure to the end of 1983 was US$664.4 million for economic assistance and US$106.2 million for military assistance. The program is expected to run for twelve years and as of February 1985 there were 285 new CBI-related private investment projects underway or about to get started with more than US$200 million committed to them. These projects are expected to create 36,000 new jobs in nontraditional areas in the Caribbean.

Despite such a bold initiative, however, some Caribbean leaders and a few academics have been critical of the CBI's thrust. The primary argument seems to be too little too late. Also, the program excludes such countries as Nicaragua, which is seen as lacking a democratic government while Jamaica, with its current pro-U.S. government, is targeted for a large share of the assistance.

However, given the region's deeply rooted structural problems which have resulted in serious inflation, high unemployment, declining economic growth, enormous balance-of-payments deficits, a pressing debt-servicing problem — all of which threaten the political and social stability of the individual nations — the CBI needs to be given a chance to evolve to its fullest capability. No one can really argue successfully that the region would be better off without such types of initiatives.

NOTES

1. Peter T. Bauer and Basil S. Yamey, The Economics of Underdeveloped Countries (Chicago: University of Chicago Press, 1957), p. 130.

2. Farley, Economics of Latin America, p. 235.

3. Ibid.

4. Ibid.

5. Maurice Odle, The Evolution of Public Expenditure: The Case of a Structurally Dependent Economy: Guyana (Kingston, Jamaica: Institute of Social and Economic Research, University of the West Indies, 1976), p. 221; Kempe Ronald Hope, "Patterns of Government Expenditures in Guyana, 1956–72," Journal of Caribbean Studies 1 (Spring–Autumn 1980), pp. 162–72.

6. DeLisle Worrell, "An Economic Survey of Barbados, 1946–1980" in Economy of Barbados, pp. 16–17.

7. Ibid.

8. R. Palmer, Caribbean Dependence on the United States Economy (New York: Praeger, 1979), p. 14.

9. K. Billerbeck and Y. Yasugi, *Private Direct Foreign Investment in Developing Countries* (Washington, D.C.: World Bank staff working paper no. 348, July 1979), p. 2.

10. Grant Reuber et al., *Private Foreign Investment in Development* (London: Oxford University Press, 1973), pp. 15–46.

11. See, for example, Gustav Papanek, "Aid, Foreign Private Investment, Savings and Growth in Less Developed Countries," *Journal of Political Economy* 81 (January–February 1973), pp. 120–30; and other studies cited therein.

12. P. Ady, "Private Overseas Investment and the Developing Countries" in *Private Foreign Investment and the Developing World*, ed. P. Ady (New York: Praeger, 1971), p. 30.

13. See Raymond Vernon, "Conflict and Resolution Between Foreign Direct Investors and Less Developed Countries," *Public Policy* 17 (1968).

14. Yair Aharoni, *The Foreign Investment Decision Process* (Cambridge, Mass.: Graduate School of Business Administration, Harvard University, 1966), pp. 235–42.

15. See Herbert K. May, *The Contributions of United States Private Investment to Latin America's Growth*. A report for the Council for Latin America, January 1970.

16. Ibid., pp. 3–4.

17. Ayub, *Made in Jamaica*, p. 194.

18. Frank Rampersaud, "Overseas Investment and Fiscal Policy in Puerto Rico, Jamaica and Trinidad and Tobago," in *Private Foreign Investment and the Developing World*, ed. Peter Ady (New York: Praeger, 1971), pp. 167–89.

19. Ibid.

20. Ibid.

21. See United Nations Division of Public Finance and Financial Institutions, "The Role of Fiscal Incentives for Employment Promotion in the Manufacturing Industries in Central America and Selected Caribbean Countries," in *Fiscal Incentives for Employment Promotion in Developing Countries*, eds. ILO (Geneva: ILO, 1973), pp. 183–211; and Terisa Turner, *Multinational Enterprises and Employment in the Caribbean with Special Reference to Trinidad and Tobago* (Geneva: ILO, working paper no. 20, 1982), pp. 3-1–5-5.

22. Task Force on Private Sector Activities, *Measures to Promote the Role of the Private Sector in Caribbean Development: A Report to the Caribbean Group for Cooperation in Economic Development* (Washington, D.C.: International Finance Corporation, June 1980), p. 7.

23. See, for example, I. Frank, *Foreign Enterprise in Developing Countries* (Baltimore: Johns Hopkins University Press, 1980), pp. 35–36.

24. Barend A. de Vries, "Public Policy and the Private Sector," *Finance and Development* 18 (September 1981), pp. 11–12.

PART VI

DEVELOPMENT FINANCE AND RESOURCE MOBILIZATION

14

The Growth and Trends of Tax Revenues in the Caribbean

In recent times a number of articles have appeared in various international journals pertaining to the role of external borrowing and its changing composition and importance to the developing countries. This chapter, however, demonstrates that despite the growing significance of external borrowing by the Caribbean countries, the role of tax revenues is still of major importance in the development process as well as an important fiscal tool. This is so primarily because the nature and rate of taxation are internally controlled and, as such, not subject to developments, in the international money markets, which are difficult to foresee.

Taxation remains the major fiscal tool on the revenue side. It is that fact that rationally dictates that borrowing should only occur when government expenditures exceed revenues and tax revenues cannot be beneficially increased.

INDIRECT TAXES

First we look at the indirect taxes in the Caribbean, which consistently constituted the major component of total tax revenues, as seen in Table 14.1, in Jamaica and in Barbados after 1978. In Jamaica, the indirect taxes steadily increased until 1979 before declining in 1980. In contrast, in Guyana, direct taxes have been increasing along with the uneven increases in indirect taxes. In Trinidad and Tobago the indirect taxes are not the major component of total tax revenues. During the period 1960–75, indirect taxes in Guyana and Jamaica increased significantly. The increases were more than 600 percent in Guyana and 700 percent in Jamaica during that period. After 1975, indirect taxes in both countries exhibited uneven changes.

The indirect taxes are composed primarily of production and sales taxes and international trade taxes, as shown in Table 14.2. In all of the

TABLE 14.1. Central Government Tax Revenues, 1960–80 (Millions of U.S. Dollars)

Country/Component	1960	1965	1970	1975	1978	1979	1980
Barbados							
Direct Taxes	3.8	7.2	13.8	39.2	48.4	77.1	83.2
Indirect Taxes	9.3	11.8	16.7	28.7	41.6	78.8	90.7
Total	13.1	19.0	30.5	67.9	90.0	155.9	173.9
Guyana							
Direct Taxes	11.6	12.9	26.3	44.6	59.4	77.3	80.3
Indirect Taxes	18.9	24.5	33.3	139.7	56.2	73.0	77.3
Total	30.5	37.4	59.6	184.3	115.6	150.3	157.6
Jamaica							
Direct Taxes	30.9	58.9	67.6	235.1	187.6	233.4	233.4
Indirect Taxes	58.2	113.3	82.4	439.0	469.5	549.9	454.7
Total	89.1	172.2	150.0	674.1	657.1	783.3	688.1
Trinidad & Tobago							
Direct Taxes	34.5	45.1	144.3	324.4	425.9	650.9	859.9
Indirect Taxes	32.9	51.1	130.3	103.5	138.3	221.9	231.9
Total	67.4	96.2	274.6	427.9	564.2	872.8	1091.8

Sources: Inter-American Development Bank, *Economic and Social Progress in Latin America* (Washington, D.C.: IDB, several years); and World Bank, *World Tables 1980* (Baltimore: Johns Hopkins University Press, 1980).

countries the changes in each component of the indirect taxes have been inconsistent. In Trinidad and Tobago, after 1973, trade taxes declined in importance and production and sales taxes became the major source of indirect tax revenues until 1978. The increase in production and sales taxes in Trinidad and Tobago has been due to the government's immediate response to the boom in world petroleum prices by overhauling the tax system to tap windfall profits of the petroleum companies. The government enacted a refinery tax on each barrel of oil and instituted a production levy designed to fund a domestic subsidy on petroleum products.

In Jamaica, except during 1976 and 1978, the trade taxes have consistently dominated the indirect taxes. A major part of Jamaica's indirect taxes is derived from the bauxite industry, which provides approximately 23 percent of central government revenues. In 1974, the Jamaican government launched an ambitious plan to (1) increase its share in the profits of the bauxite industry, and (2) extend its control over bauxite and alumina opeations. One of the results of that plan was the enactment of a bauxite levy, which obliged the bauxite and alumina companies to pay a levy for all bauxite

TABLE 14.2. Composition of Indirect Tax Revenues, 1970–80 (Millions of U.S. Dollars)

Country/Component	1970	1974	1975	1976	1978	1979	1980
Barbados							
Production & Sales Taxes	6.8	10.5	13.5	19.3	20.8	36.5	38.8
Trade Taxes	9.4	18.3	14.6	15.8	19.8	40.3	50.0
Other	0.5	0.5	0.6	7.9	1.0	2.0	1.9
Total	16.7	29.3	28.7	43.0	41.6	78.8	90.7
Guyana							
Production & Sales Taxes	9.1	24.9	25.1	32.2	33.9	46.5	51.7
Trade Taxes	21.9	57.2	110.5	55.9	16.8	21.3	19.4
Other	2.3	4.1	4.1	5.4	5.5	5.2	6.2
Total	33.3	86.2	139.7	93.5	56.2	73.0	77.3
Jamaica							
Production & Sales Taxes	36.1	154.1	170.7	192.8	272.2	225.2	205.3
Trade Taxes	34.1	240.9	250.7	163.6	197.3	278.6	226.2
Other	12.2	21.1	17.6	14.7	0	46.1	23.2
Total	82.4	416.1	439.0	371.1	469.5	549.9	454.7
Trinidad & Tobago							
Production & Sales Taxes	18.0	75.8	70.5	80.2	77.6	74.9	81.1
Trade Taxes	88.1	25.3	27.9	37.7	52.9	135.9	139.3
Other	24.2	4.8	5.1	6.0	7.8	11.1	11.5
Total	130.3	105.9	103.5	123.9	138.3	221.9	231.9

Sources: Same as for Table 14.1

mined in Jamaica. However, since 1976, receipts from the bauxite levy have been declining considerably, owing to large declines in production.

In Guyana, except for 1977–80, the trade taxes were the major component of indirect taxes. In 1974 and 1975, there was an increase in the consumption tax revenue and windfall amounts were also collected in those same two years after the imposition of a sugar export levy in 1974. After 1976, however, the output of Guyana's three major industries—bauxite, sugar, and rice—declined considerably as a result of poor weather and labor disputes. This resulted in a decline in indirect tax revenues and in overall government revenues.

Except for 1976 and 1978, Barbados's trade taxes were the major component of indirect taxes. During 1977 and 1978 the Barbadian government took a number of fiscal measures in recognition of the growing precariousness of public-sector finances. This resulted in increases in the consumption-tax rates on luxury goods and the enactment of an employment levy, which considerably boosted government revenues.

The indirect taxes in developing countries tend to work positively, for the most part, by encouraging savings and conserving foreign exchange for the necessary import of capital goods. Such taxes also help to prevent prices from rising too rapidly when ongoing investment is increasing personal incomes faster than the output of finished goods and services is rising. These taxes are popular not only because of their administrative simplicity, but also because they can satisfy the principles of progressivity and built-in stability, as well as equity. One additional property of indirect taxes of particular interest to developing countries is their ability to allocate resources to desired areas of development.

Equity is served by exempting necessities and the produce of peasant farmers from taxation while graduated taxes imposed on nonessentials and luxuries, especially if established through scientific studies of family budgets, allow indirect taxes to satisfy the principle of ability to pay and the built-in flexibility property. By raising the cost of consumption relative to saving, indirect taxes tend to encourage the latter at the expense of the former. In a system of indirect taxes, saving is stimulated as it virtually escapes taxation and resources are released from consumption to capital formation, of which the contribution to economic development cannot be overemphasized.

Indirect taxes serve the purpose of industrialization by diverting resources to desirable activities. On the one hand, import duties being graduated according to the degree of luxury of imported commodities provide incentives for domestic production. The particular stimulation given to semi-luxury or luxury goods should be dealt with carefully and their local production discouraged at times by heavy sales or excise taxes or even by outright prohibition because resources should be used for the production of more urgently needed commodities.

Indirect taxes imposed on locally produced goods are, on the other hand, designed to divert resources from the production of luxuries to semi-luxuries and necessities, by affecting the rate of return. This goal is not always easy to achieve and its attainment depends, in the final analysis, on the diversionary effect of taxes on particular commodities with different elasticities of supply and demand. If, however, indirect taxes fail to change the allocation of resources and the pattern of investment, other measures affecting relative prices and relative profitability must be employed.

The structure of indirect taxes should be such as not to stifle altogether the production of semi-luxury goods, defined as those widely consumed by people, above the subsistence level, but kept at low levels as a stimulant for increased participation in the development process. The favorable tax treatment of necessities should not be taken to mean that the majority of resources released through taxation are used to expand the production of necessities. It is important that the production of necessities does increase at least at the same rate as the population growth, but due to the prevailing poverty in the Caribbean, it is easy for income increases to be spent exclusively on consumption. As such, to protect the long-term development interests of the Caribbean countries, part of the increased incomes must be diverted to investment through mass commodity taxation. Indirect taxes have an important role to play in this respect by transferring resources from consumers to the public sector, which in turn uses these resources for investment. Mass commodity taxation is therefore fully justified as it serves to raise the incremental saving ratio.

Taxes are commonly classified according to the kind of action that creates the liability or the nature of the base on which the tax is levied. Taxes on goods and services may include all taxes and duties levied on production, sale, transfer, leasing, and delivery of goods and rendering of services, or in respect of taxes on the use or ownership of goods or permission to use goods or perform activities.[1]

Historically, excise taxation has been associated with domestically produced commodities. Any countervailing duty on goods coming from abroad is incorporated in the import duty, and sales taxes are levied as general taxes on the sale of goods and services. The scope of coverage emerges as the most useful distinction between excises and sales taxes. Under an excise system, taxable commodities are individually enumerated in the law; while under a sales tax the tax base is typically defined as including all commodities for sale other than those specifically exempted. In Jamaica and Trinidad and Tobago there are no sales taxes while Barbados has a sales tax at the retail level and Guyana has a manufacturers sales tax. In Barbados, Jamaica, and Trinidad and Tobago the excise tax coverage is extended, which means the tax spans almost the whole range of production activities in those countries. In Guyana, the excise tax coverage is limited to specified, domestically produced goods and similar goods imported from CARICOM.

While indirect taxes are inadequate, by usual standards, as sole measures of tax capacity, the traditional case for indirect taxes in the Caribbean has been made on the basis of their potential revenue yield and their administrative simplicity when compared with the income tax. It would seem though that the prevailing indirect tax structure is satisfactory from the point of view of the criterion of income elasticity. In order to conform to the criterion of economic stabilization, indirect taxes should be levied on goods with a high income elasticity of demand. The significance of this criterion lies in the fact that such indirect taxes would be ideally suited for maximum volume of resouce mobilization.

The rate of change of indirect taxes as a percentage of total current revenue and Gross Domestic Product during 1960–80, for all of the countries, was uneven and inconsistent. However, a better gauge of the relevant significance of indirect taxes in the Caribbean can be obtained from examining indirect tax revenues as a ratio of total tax revenue as exhibited in Table 14.3. In Barbados between 1974–78, indirect taxes declined to less than 50 percent. A similar situation prevailed in Trinidad and Tobago and Guyana after 1972 and 1976–79 respectively while, in Jamaica, indirect taxes have never been less than 50 percent during 1960–80, indicating the growing and significant importance attached to indirect taxes as a source of development finance in Jamaica. Moreover, it has been claimed that Jamaican indirect taxes are essentially proportional to both income or expenditure, except in the highest income bracket.[2] In Guyana, indirect taxes were found to have an income elasticity coefficient of 2.1; in Jamaica the income elasticity was 1.9; and in both Barbados and Trinidad and Tobago it was 0.9.[3] The average income elasticity of indirect taxes for the four countries as a whole is 1.5.

The coefficient of income elasticity of tax revenue indicates by how many percentage points a specific revenue source increases with a one percentage point increase in income, as well as it expresses the ratio between the marginal tax rate and the tax ratio of the earlier period. When the elasticity coefficient is greater than one, taxes are considered to be elastic and regarded as inelastic if the coefficient is less than one. In terms of the individual indirect taxes, the elasticity coefficients are shown in Table 14.4.

Table 14.3. Percentage of Total Tax Revenue from Indirect Taxes, 1960–80

Year	Barbados	Guyana	Jamaica	Trinidad & Tobago
1960	70.9	62.0	65.3	48.8
1965	62.1	65.5	65.8	53.1
1970	54.8	55.9	54.9	47.5
1971	49.2	59.1	52.9	49.1
1972	50.5	50.0	51.9	50.1
1973	60.6	52.9	50.9	46.9
1974	47.5	69.9	62.5	26.9
1975	42.3	75.8	65.1	24.2
1976	48.2	64.3	61.6	25.9
1977	44.8	45.8	64.0	26.0
1978	46.2	48.7	71.5	24.5
1979	50.5	48.6	70.2	25.4
1980	52.2	52.5	66.1	21.2

Sources: Same as for Tables 14.1.

Table 14.4.   Income Elasticities of Indirect Tax Revenues, 1970–79

Country	Production & Sales Taxes	Trade Taxes	Total Indirect Taxes[a]
Barbados	1.5	1.1	0.9
Guyana	1.1	1.1	2.1
Jamaica	2.9	4.2	1.9
Trinidad & Tobago	0.7	0.1	0.9

[a]1960–76.

As one might except, there is considerable variation in the value of the coefficient for the indirect taxes in the four countries. However, both Guyana and Jamaica have elastic indirect taxes while only the trade taxes and production and sales taxes indicate some degree of elasticity in Barbados. With the exception of Jamaica, all of the countries seemed to have relied relatively more on their production and sales taxes than on the international trade taxes, in terms of tax effort, as suggested by the data. These data, therefore, lend some support to the general impression that with the growth and diversification of their economies the developing countries have been turning more effort toward the exploitation of internal taxes with diminishing relative reliance on international trade taxes.

Indirect taxes in the Caribbean have been instrumental in bringing about an allocation of resources to some priority uses. Excise taxes have resulted in the reduction of the production of goods not regarded as essential for development and thus, resources have been channeled into the production of high-priority goods under the assumption that demand is not perfectly inelastic. In the context of the growth of industrial production, which in many cases means the production of domestic goods as substitutes for foreign imports, excise taxation not only makes up the loss in revenues caused by a fall in the proceeds from import taxes, but also becomes a very productive and expansive source of development finance.

One of the greatest weaknesses of indirect taxes in developing countries, and the Caribbean is no exception, is their inability to reach high concentrations of income and wealth as effectively as direct taxes. To that extent, indirect taxes can be regarded as regressive. Under the ability-to-pay principle, taxes should bear some relationship to people's capacity to pay them. That is, the amount of taxes should be the same for people in the same economic position (horizontal equity), but different for people in different economic positions (vertical equity). Historically, however, indirect taxes, by their very nature, have never been able to satisfy these two criteria completely both in developed and developing countries.

DIRECT TAXES

As for the direct taxes in the Caribbean, Table 14.5 indicates that they have been growing as a source of revenue. In all of the four countries, total direct taxes have shown an uneven growth during the period 1970–80. In terms of the relative magnitude of the growth with respect to current revenues, increses in direct taxes as a percentage of current revenues were most pronounced in both Guyana and Trinidad and Tobago. In Guyana, direct taxes were up from an annual average of 32.7 percent of current revenues in 1972–76 to 43.1 percent in 1980, and in Trinidad and Tobago, from 59.7 percent to 75.3 percent.

Regarding the composition of direct taxes, Table 14.6 shows that income taxes (personal and corporate) constitute by far the most important form of direct-tax revenue. However, only in Trinidad and Tobago did income taxes average more than 50 percent of current revenues while only Barbados had property taxes of more than 4 percent. Income taxes in Trinidad and Tobago reflect a wide range of modifications in oil taxation designed to enable the government to make more flexible use of fiscal measures to control the depletion of a finite, nonrenewable resource.

The personal income tax is a compulsory payment to government that is imposed by legislation. Income taxes really belong to a fairly

TABLE 14.5. Composition of Direct Tax Revenues, 1970–80 (Millions of U.S. Dollars)

Country/Component	1970	1974	1975	1976	1978	1979	1980
Barbados							
Income Taxes	13.0	27.0	35.0	41.9	43.6	68.4	74.6
Property Taxes	0.8	5.4	4.2	4.4	4.8	8.7	8.6
TOTAL	13.8	32.4	39.2	46.3	48.4	77.1	83.2
Guyana							
Income Taxes	24.1	35.6	43.4	49.3	57.2	74.9	78.7
Property Taxes	2.2	1.6	1.2	2.5	2.2	2.4	1.6
TOTAL	26.3	37.2	44.6	51.8	59.4	77.3	80.3
Jamaica							
Income Taxes	66.5	234.0	210.3	209.3	184.4	213.7	216.9
Property Taxes	1.1	15.4	24.8	21.6	19.2	19.7	16.5
TOTAL	67.6	249.4	235.1	230.9	187.6	233.4	233.4
Trinidad & Tobago							
Income Taxes	124.1	277.4	315.3	344.9	411.4	631.5	841.7
Property Taxes	20.2	10.0	9.1	10.0	14.5	19.4	18.2
TOTAL	144.3	287.4	324.4	354.9	425.9	650.9	859.9

Sources: Same as for Table 14.1.

Table 14.6. Direct Taxes as a Ratio of Current Revenues, 1972–76 and 1980 (Percentages)

Country	Income Taxes 1972–76	1980	Property Taxes 1972–76	1980	Total Direct Taxes 1972–76	1980
Barbados	39.8	39.2	5.7	4.5	45.5	43.7
Guyana	31.2	42.2	1.5	0.9	32.7	43.1
Jamaica	36.4	30.1	2.5	2.3	38.9	32.4
Trinidad & Tobago	55.8	73.7	3.9	1.6	59.7	75.3

Sources: Same as for Table 14.1.

advanced stage of economic development; yet they are found in operation in a large number of developing nations. The reason is quite simply that everyone is expected to contribute toward the expenditures that lead to development, this contribution being derived primarily from income.

Taxation of net income in the Caribbean is complicated by many problems relating to permissible business expenses, including treatment of depreciation, exemptions and credits, and capital gains or casual profits. Hence, the measurement of net income for tax purposes is difficult and, as such, requires a high standard of administration for equitable results. However, personal income taxes in the Caribbean have been reasonably effective in reaching wage and salary income, where concealment is difficult.

As a percentage of total tax revenue, direct taxes in Barbados increased during 1974–78 to more than 50 percent. A similar situation prevailed in Trinidad and Tobago after 1972 and in Guyana after 1976. In Jamaica, direct taxes have always been less than 50 percent of total tax revenues during 1960–80.

Direct taxes, or more specifically, income taxes, are a very convenient device for introducing the principle of equity in tax structure. Due to their capacity to introduce an element of built-in flexibility in the tax structure, they are regarded, even in developed countries, as a very important countercyclical device for achieving economic stabilization. Thus, in the analysis of taxation in developing countries, the traditional objectives of progressivity and equity in taxation have pointed strongly to, and have resulted in, more aggressive use of net income and wealth taxation.

Though a highly progressive income tax with high marginal rates on upper income ranges is a very desirable fiscal instrument, both on grounds of resource mobilization for the public sector and redistributive considerations, which are very important in developing countries, it tends to conflict with the criteria of economic efficiency and progress in a context where the growth of savings and investment occupies an important place in the

Table 14.7. Percentage of Total Tax Revenue from Direct Taxes, 1960–80

Year	Barbados	Guyana	Jamaica	Trinidad &Tobago
1960	29.1	38.0	34.7	51.2
1965	37.9	34.5	34.2	46.9
1970	45.2	44.1	45.1	52.5
1971	50.8	40.9	47.1	50.9
1972	49.5	50.0	48.1	49.9
1973	39.4	47.1	49.1	53.1
1974	52.5	30.1	37.5	73.1
1975	57.7	24.2	34.9	75.8
1976	51.8	35.7	38.4	74.1
1977	55.2	54.2	36.0	74.0
1978	53.8	51.3	28.5	75.5
1979	49.5	51.4	29.8	74.6
1980	47.8	90.4	33.9	78.8

Sources: Same as for Table 14.1.

process of economic development,[4] as is the case in the Caribbean. Moreover, except in Trinidad and Tobago, income taxes are relatively elastic, as seen in Table 14.8.

For the period 1970–79, there is considerable variation in the elasticity coefficients for direct taxes in the Caribbean. In both Barbados and Jamaica, property taxes have a higher than average income elasticity coefficient. Since 1973 Jamaica has been unevenly increasing its property tax yield, due to increasing property tax rates. However, overall, it may be said that all of the countries have relied relatively more on income taxes. In 1973, the Jamaican government proposed income-tax relief for pensioners, payments of mortgage interest, health insurance and medical expenses, and premiums for equity-linked life insurance. But since the advantages of these reliefs are available only to Jamaicans paying income tax, and because the benefit of the reliefs rises with the taxpayer's marginal tax rate, these tax reductions reduce the burdens on upper-income households, and therefore weaken the progressivity of the income tax and of the overall Jamaican tax system.[5]

Since 1974 the structure of the tax system has not undergone any major modification in Trinidad and Tobago. Largely because of the unique position of the country's petroleum sector and measures designed to tap the increased petroleum profits, income taxes now account for more than two-thirds of total current revenues. In Barbados, the domestic-revenue effort has been relatively stable since 1970, except for the strongly recessionary years of 1974–75. The country's income tax effort has shown some improvement, due to increases in corporation tax rates and higher wages and salaries.

Table 14.8. Income Elasticities of Direct Tax Revenues, 1970–79

Country	Income Taxes	Property Taxes	Total Direct Taxes
Barbados	1.6	3.4	1.6
Guyana	2.0	0.1	1.9
Jamaica	1.2	9.4	1.4
Trinidad & Tobago	0.9	-0.1	1.0

The increasing importance of the taxation of income and company profits in the Caribbean underline the need, therefore, for encouraging the growth of individual and business savings, and the ploughing back of retained profits of business into the expansion of investment. The tax policy should therefore be directed to further mobilization of resources for development and allocating them according to development planning priorities.

AN ASSESSMENT

Tax revenues represent the major proportion of all revenues collected in the Caribbean by the central government. Current tax revenues averaged about 87 percent of total current revenue in Barbados, about 84 percent in Guyana, about 93 percent in Jamaica, and about 90 percent in Trinidad and Tobago during 1970–80. Taxes, therefore, constitute an important part of the public finances of the Caribbean economy and as such a very important fiscal tool. The significance of tax revenue in the Caribbean can also be determined by examining the ratio of tax revenues to GDP. Tax revenues averaged 22.2 percent of GDP in Barbados, 25.9 percent in Guyana, 21.2 percent in Jamaica, and 26 percent in Trinidad and Tobago during 1970–80. The yield from taxation seems to indicate the response that might be expected in a period of growing investment and national income as the countries attempt to move forward on their developmental paths. The tax ratios in the Caribbean are substantially higher than the average ratios in developing nations. The average ratios in developing nations, according to the most recent study, is 16.1 percent.[6]

As a fiscal tool, taxation has to aim at directing productive resources to uses which are necessary for development but which the private sector is unwilling to provide for, as is the case in the Caribbean. Such a direction of resources may be needed at certain times in developed countries also and may be engineered through a system of checks and incentives operating on decision-making units in the private sector. In the developing nations, however, this may require, in addition, direct participation by government in production and investment activities. The major point being made here is quite simply that if fiscal policy is to make net contribution to growth, its operations have to be supplemental to whatever can normally be expected to be achieved by the existing constellation of forces in the economy.

The object of both fiscal and development policy, therefore, is not to balance the budget of the public sector, but to balance the economy as a whole. In this respect, budgetary rules are different for governments than for individuals. It is important that governments should feel free to make appropriate use of budget surpluses or deficits, in conjunction with monetary and other policies, to counteract excess or deficiencies of demand in the rest of the economy.[7]

In determining the size of the budget, the tradition in the theory of public finance takes its cue from welfare economics: It is rewarding to transfer money from the private sector through taxation—and to give up individual decision power in the process—only to the extent that the public authority is presumed to spend the money better (i.e., to the extent that the public services provide better value than would have been derived from spending the money on individual goods and services).[8]

Though some advances in economic thought have conquered sufficient ground for these principles to have been accepted among most policy-makers, one of the obstacles to their effective implementation has been the persistence of widespread public suspicion of unbalanced budgets. It is true that, as spending is generally popular and taxation is not, the temptation to political leaders to run budget deficits, not justified by the overall state of the economy, can be great. This can bring about all those consequences of excess demand and inflation, frequently combined with misallocation of resources, which prudent governments would seek to avoid. But no simple, predetermined rules for the balancing of budgets guarantee responsible government. Protection against irresponsible fiscal policy must rest on informed leadership, coupled with the development of wide public understanding of the questions at issue.[9] Methods of ensuring that the leadership is adequately informed and public understanding sufficiently developed are, accordingly, subjects to be emphasized.

In light of the currently accepted social goal of an equitable distribution of the national product and on the basis of the above discussion of fiscal policy, the main objectives that should govern tax and budgetary policy in developing countries, such as those in the Caribbean, may be stated as follows: (1) a further increase in the rate of investment by further control over actual and potential consumption, (2) a further encouragement of the flow of investment into channels judged to be most desirable from the point of view of maximum benefit to society, and (3) a regulation of the flow of purchasing power in accordance with the overall pattern laid down in the development plans.

All of these objectives have been advocated and imposed by the International Monetary Fund on most of the Caribbean economies in recent years. These objectives are related to the ultimate goals of rapid increase in national income and of improvement in its distribution. The problem is to design and maintain a tax structure that will be conducive to the accomplishment of these objectives.

Given the level of revenue now derived from taxation, then the tax system in the Caribbean need only to be directed increasingly toward meeting the long-term needs of development. This, therefore, implies a tax system with more administrative flexibility, one where incidence can be rationalized, and one which can be used as a means of controlling inflation—a major problem in the Caribbean. One of the major objectives of taxation in the Caribbean should be that of the mobilization of internal resources to meet development financing requirements. The amount raised by a government is not necessarily linked to the amount it spends in providing services. Public funds come from other sources than taxation, but the power to tax is uniquely a power of government and its exercise is a matter of crucial importance to the economic and social life of a nation.

CONCLUSIONS

It seems that the determing factors of tax structure for the Caribbean are primarily economic. The character of and change in the economic bases to be taxed are more important than the style of taxation. Taxation policies should be viewed in terms of their ability to pay the government's needs for capital to finance economic development within the framework of the limits to the sources of the taxes. Excessive taxation may restrict economic incentives and productive efforts and may cause business activity and national income to decline. However, no definite answer can be given to the question of what is the optimum taxation level that could be carried by the Caribbean economies, or any economy for that matter. It seems, however, that given the elastic nature of the total direct taxes in all of the countries, they are prime candidates for increased tax rates. But, of course, these increased tax rates must be considered within the context of increased revenue, encouragement to noninflationary impact, and administrative feasibility.

NOTES

1. S. Cnossen, *Excise Systems: A Global Study of the Selective Taxation of Goods and Services* (Baltimore: Johns Hopkins University Press, 1977), p. 7.

2. Charles E. McLure, Jr., *The Incidence of Jamaican Taxes 1971–1972* (Kingston, Jamaica: Institute of Social and Economic Research, University of the West Indies, working paper no. 16, 1977), pp. 74–75.

3. Estimates of elasticities have been derived by fitting a long-linear function to the data with Gross Domestic Product as the independent variable.

4. Hope, *Development Policy*, p. 164.

5. McClure, *Incidence*, p. 40.

6. See Alan Tait et al., "International Comparisons of Taxation for Selected Developing Countries, 1972–76", *IMF Staff Papers* 26 (March 1979), pp. 129–30.

7. Walter Heller et al., *Fiscal Policy for a Balanced Economy* (Paris: OECD, 1968), p. 15.

8. Dirk J. Wolfson, *Public Finance and Development Strategy* (Baltimore: Johns Hopkins University Press, 1979), p. 33.

9. Heller et al., *Fiscal Policy*, p. 16.

15

The Role of Savings in Financing Development in the Caribbean

This chapter investigates the nature and structure of savings in the Caribbean with an analysis of the implications of the existing savings structure for the development finance process. The underlying premise herein is that one of the primary objectives of fiscal policy in the countries of the region is to raise the ratio of savings to national income so that the rate of net investment could be stepped up without the danger of inflation.

SAVINGS AS A SOURCE OF DEVELOPMENT FINANCE IN THE CARIBBEAN

Table 15.1 exhibits the gross national savings of the Caribbean for the period 1960–80. Gross national savings, on an absolute basis, changed unevenly in all of the countries. In Barbados, savings were negative in 1970 and 1972 and increased during the period 1974–80. In Guyana, gross national savings declined over the previous year's amount during the years 1971–73 and 1978–80. For Jamaica, national savings increased during 1970–73 and then declined precipitously thereon before increasing again in 1979. In Trinidad and Tobago, gross national savings have been most erratic. The country's national savings declined in 1971, increased in 1972, declined consistently during 1973–75, and then increased again during 1978–79.

The ratio of gross national savings to Gross Domestic Product is an indicator of internal resource mobilization. Looking at the savings ratio for the four countries, as seen in Table 15.2, it can be gleaned that in 1979, with the exception of Trinidad and Tobago, the coefficient declined in all of the countries. In Barbados and Guyana the registered decreases exceeded 5 percent over the 1978 ratio. During the period 1975–79, the

Table 15.1. Gross National Savings in the Caribbean, 1960–80 (Millions of U.S. Dollars)

Year	Barbados	Guyana	Jamaica	Trinidad & Tobago
1960[b]	12.5	32.2	279.5	43.9
1970[a]	-0.6	60.5	189.3	369.5
1971[a]	4.5	48.5	394.1	350.2
1972[a]	-2.9	43.8	478.5	379.3
1973[b]	29.8	25.6	649.3	185.5
1974[b]	17.4	98.3	465.2	102.3
1975[b]	25.6	141.2	423.8	95.4
1978[c]	157.0	51.9	57.7	161.2
1979[c]	157.0	38.2	129.8	166.0
1980[c]	173.0	28.1	16.8	n.a.

Sources: Inter-American Development Bank, Economic and Social Progress in Latin America (Washington, D.C.: IDB, several years); and United Nations, Yearbook of National Accounts Statistics (New York: United Nations, several years).
[a]Millions of 1973 dollars.
[b]Millions of 1976 dollars.
[c]Millions of 1980 dollars.

Table 15.2. Gross National Savings in the Caribbean, 1960–79 (Percentage of Gross Domestic Product)

Country	1960–64[a]	1965–69[a]	1970–74[a]	1975	1978	1979
Barbados	4.0	5.2	2.6	9.3	11.1	5.4
Guyana	15.9	14.3	15.3	30.3	15.2	9.1
Jamaica	23.0	24.1	21.3	14.9	14.9	12.8
Trinidad & Tobago	17.7	15.6	20.1	25.2	n.a.	40.1

Sources: Same as for Table 15.1.
[a]Average.

savings ratio was higher than 25 percent in Trinidad and Tobago only. This can be explained as being due to the country's general improvement in its internal resource mobilization effort and the increased revenues resulting from its oil exports.

A long-term analysis of the changes in the savings ratios during 1960–74, based on a comparison of the five-year averages for 1960–64, 1965–69, and 1970–74, showed that there was no sustained increase in the savings ratios of the four countries during the entire 15-year period. Barbados, Guyana, and Jamaica achieved savings ratios in the last five-year period that were below those of the initial period.

Increases in gross national savings in the Caribbean, given the declining private-sector activity in most of the countries, necessarily implies increases in revenues or decreases in public expenditure. However, attempts should be continued to maximize private sector savings through encouragement of savings from households. This can be done through two mechanisms primarily.

First, assurance should be given by the governments against loss of savings due to inflation. Or better still, a major effort should be made by the authorities to curb inflation. A most important deterrent to household saving is inflation. Most households, particularly savers of small amounts, have no satisfactory means of protecting their savings from depreciation due to inflation. When prices have risen steadily, the will to accumulate savings is undermined and eventually destroyed. Once assurance is given against loss from inflation, the will to save can be quickly restored.

The second mechanism relates to the use of interest rates. There is a tendency to underestimate the beneficial effects of a high rate of interest in the developing countries. The savings rates of interest need to be raised. A higher rate of interest will induce the public to increase its savings further and to hold more of its savings in the form of deposits and bonds, rather than in hoards of foreign exchange, which is already very scarce in the Caribbean. In Guyana, for example, higher interest rates in 1979 resulted in increased savings deposits. Furthermore, higher rates of interest will tend to encourage a more economical use of capital and thus diminish the deficiency of resources for development. This argument can be further supported through recent studies which have shown that the major part of household savings are in the form of claims on financial institutions. Households clearly prefer to hold their savings in the form of claims on financial institutions rather than in the form of direct claims on the government and corporate sectors. Hence, any further incentives provided by these financial institutions, in the form of higher interest rates, will tend to increase the volume of household savings. It is reasonable to pay a high rate of interest to attract savings, for savings have high value in the developing countries.

However, it must be pointed out that, at least in Guyana and Jamaica with their shrinking private sector, increases in gross national savings would have to come primarily from the public sector. However, the performance of government savings in both economies has been less than impressive, as shown in Table 15.3. Except in Trinidad and Tobago, all of the countries had deficits in their current accounts as a percentage of Gross Domestic Product during the 1970s. As an average, during the 1972–76 period, Jamaica had the lowest ratio of government current savings as a percentage of Gross Domestic Product. In contrast, in Trinidad and Tobago, government current savings as a percentage of Gross Domestic Product has been steadily increasing since 1972 due to the buoyancy of petroleum revenues.

**Table 15.3. Central Government Current Savings, 1970–80
(Percentage of Gross Domestic Product)**

Year	Barbados	Guyana	Jamaica	Trinidad & Tobago
1970	1.9	3.0	0.9	3.6
1971	1.1	− 0.4	2.0	1.3
1972	3.3	2.7	—	0.5
1973	0.8	− 3.5	0.2	2.1
1974	− 2.5	7.4	2.6	16.1
1975	− 0.1	14.0	1.6	17.3
1976	− 0.2	− 5.7	− 4.0	17.4
1977	0.6	− 5.4	− 6.0	19.6
1978	4.0	− 9.4	− 2.4	16.0
1979	3.1	− 5.6	− 4.0	16.0
1980	3.3	− 7.8	− 5.0	23.3

Sources: Same as for Table 15.1.

Central government savings in the Caribbean have been extremely volatile, except in the case of Trinidad and Tobago. The savings of Caribbean central governments have an important role to play in the accumulation of both total public sector savings and gross domestic savings. This is so because of the increasing scarcity of funds from the international financial institutions. This increased savings performance will require careful budgetary management by the various central governments as well as a reduction in the dependence of the public corporations on the central governments for both current and capital transfers. The reduction of the dependence of the public corporations on the central government would require that measures be taken to improve the net earnings of the public enterprises. This would require, among other things, that these enterprises be managed efficiently and be allowed to charge prices that would enable them to earn profits which could then be invested in accordance with government policies. In effect, it means prudent fiscal policy.

Fiscal policy is now widely recognized to be a potent instrument for achieving important economic and social objectives in developing countries. One of the primary objectives of fiscal policy in these countries is to raise the ratio of savings to national income so that the rate of net investment could be stepped up without the danger of inflation. As the role of the public sector expands, public savings undoubtedly assume further importance and it becomes necessary to reorient fiscal policy to generate sizable surpluses in the public sector.

Inasmuch as the main sources of public sector savings are taxes and surpluses of public enterprises, it may be taken to represent collective compulsory savings by the community, as distinguished from voluntary savings by households and private corporations. Public savings have a dual role to play. On the one hand, they constitute a convenient source of finance for public investment; on the other hand, they may serve to raise the rate of savings in the economy.

Table 15.4 shows the contribution of national savings to the financing of gross domestic investment in the Caribbean. This is obtained by dividing the savings coefficients by investment as a percentage of Gross Domestic Product. The resultant ratio, by implication, also provides an indication of the share of net external resources in the financing of gross investment.

The ratio of national savings to gross domestic investment in the Caribbean showed considerable annual fluctuations during 1973–79. National savings did not exceed gross investment during any of the years of the period in any country. Nevertheless, Trinidad and Tobago achieved a savings surplus in individual years during 1974–79. Barbados, Guyana, and Jamaica were, to one extent or another, dependent on foreign capital for financing investment in recent years.

The longer-term trends in the relationship between savings and investment during 1960–74, based on a comparison of averages for the five-year periods of 1960–64, 1965–69, and 1970–74 show Jamaica with a sustained decrease in the averages, Trinidad and Tobago with sustained increases, and Barbados and Guyana with uneven changes. Furthermore, Trinidad and Tobago showed the strongest growth in domestic financing in the region during the past decade, primarily because of increasing oil revenues during that period.

Table 15.4.   Relationship between Savings and Investment, 1960–79 (National Savings as a Percentage of Domestic Investment)

Year	Barbados	Guyana	Jamaica	Trinidad & Tobago
1960–64[a]	19.0	84.2	85.5	67.5
1965–69[a]	23.1	62.8	77.1	75.2
1970–74[a]	11.1	67.9	70.1	88.2
1973	0.8	20.8	64.9	57.6
1974	20.1	87.6	68.0	122.1
1975	45.2	91.6	60.3	124.7
1976	7.5	16.9	41.9	106.6
1977	30.8	16.9	70.5	n.a.
1978	46.6	78.4	99.6	n.a.
1979	22.9	38.7	81.4	148.4

Sources: Same as for Table 15.1.
[a]Average.

CONCLUSIONS AND POLICY ISSUES

An increasing volume of savings needs to be mobilized in the Caribbean. However, this can only be done when the rate of voluntary savings is progressively increasing. This means, therefore, an encouragement of voluntary savings. One aspect of that encouragement is to tap the enormous reservoir of rural savings that is seemingly hoarded in the Caribbean because of lack of access to financial institutions. The generation of savings is, admittedly, a function of income and wealth, but the existence of financial intermediaries may contribute to raising the savings ratio by providing a convenient form of savings.[1]

Voluntary savings by households accumulate as either residual (discretionary savings) such as bank deposits and government and corporate securities or as long-term contractual savings, such as insurance policies, pension funds, or payments on mortgage loans. Households as "surplus" units are potentially capable of providing the national economy with financial resources directly as well as indirectly. As such, one of the major tasks confronting the developing countries and their governments is to encourage and facilitate the economy's monetization for the benefit of productive savings accumulation. Understandably, the purpose of these efforts is to discourage unproductive hoarding of physical goods, such as real estate, livestock, and precious metals, which have traditionally made up the bulk of savings in rural areas.[2]

The generation of savings is admittedly a function of income and wealth. But in the Caribbean, where private savings are clearly not sufficient to match the needs of development, public savings also automatically assume importance and it becomes necessary to reorient fiscal policy to generate sizable surpluses in the public sector.

The savings of the public sector in the Caribbean have a dual role to play. On the one hand, they constitute a convenient source of finance for public investment and, on the other hand, they may serve to raise the rate of savings in the economy. If public savings represent a genuine addition to private savings, they enable the countries to step up capital formation beyond the limits set by autonomous and induced savings performed by the private sector. It is essential to bear in mind, however, that the rate of savings in the economy is raised through public savings only if private savings are not correspondingly reduced thereby, and public revenue and public savings are increased at the expense of private consumption.

The role of savings is rather basic to any development finance process. Savings magnitude determines the extent of foreign financing required. As such, increasing the rate of domestic savings is considered to be of first importance in most discussions of economic development. However, much of the savings in the Caribbean is not being channeled in the right direction. Instead, it is being put into socially unproductive uses rather than being invested to yield a future income stream. As such, some emphasis must be placed on mobilizing domestic savings, which connotes both an increase in the domestic savings rate and the channeling of existing and new savings into uses that will increase the rate of economic growth.[3]

Mobilizing domestic savings in the Caribbean necessarily entails an attempt to tap rural savings. A large volume of savings originates in the rural sector, but these savings cannot be mobilized through taxation because a portion of the income in the rural sector does not flow through monetary channels. Most of the financial institutions in the Caribbean are concentrated in the urban areas and urban savings are mobilized through these institutions. Therefore, further large-scale mobilization of savings for development finance through public borrowing is dependent, to a large measure, on the development and extension of financial institutions into the rural areas.

Organized rural money markets may influence households' savings behavior in several ways.[4] On the one hand, they may augment the households' liquidity pool through credit. The additional liquidity allows rural households to maintain consumption which would otherwise be disturbed by uneven income flows. Credit further allows households to make major purchases of consumer durables and large productive capital goods. On the other hand, organized rural money markets may provide households with additional savings investment activities by offering various types of financial savings instruments. If these instruments provide positive real returns to the households, they may induce the households to convert some of their excess liquidity into financial savings. This may increase the average rate of return realized by the households on their savings portfolio and induce the households to divert more of their income to savings instrument activities by offering various types of financial savings instruments. If these instruments provide positive real returns to the households they may induce the households to convert some of their excess liquidity into financial savings. This may increase the average rate of return realized by the households on their savings portfolio and induce the households to divert more of their income to savings-investment activities.

NOTES

1. R.J. Bhatia and D.R. Khatkhate, "Financial Intermediation, Savings Mobilization, and Entrepreneurial Development: The African Experience," *IMF Staff Papers* 22 (March 1975), pp. 132–58.

2. K. Holbik, "Development Finance and Financial Intermediation in Developing Countries," *Journal of Economic Development* 4 (July 1979), pp. 189–217.

3. Kempe Ronald Hope, "The Role of Domestic Savings in the Financing of Economic Development in Developing Countries," *Economic Affairs* 25 (November 1980), pp. 259–60.

4. Dale W. Adams, "Mobilizing Household Savings Through Rural Financial Markets," *Economic Development and Cultural Change* 26 (April 1978), pp. 547–60.

16

The Use of External Borrowing in Financing Development in the Caribbean

This chapter examines the growth, structure, and use of external borrowing as a means of financing economic development in the Caribbean region during the past two decades.

In the present international economic context, the transfer of financial resources from the developed nations to the developing nations is a factor whose potential effects are of major importance for re-establishing the general trends of economic progress. To the traditional role of those financial resources as a complement both to domestic savings and to the current foreign-exchange inflows required for increasing investment and the rate of economic growth and social progress of the developing countries has been added in the last five years the task of contributing to the world monetary equilibrium and the adjustment to unprecedented external deficits caused by the recession of the industrial economies and the rise in fuel prices.

Toward the end of the 1940s capital flows to the developing nations were marginal. Some Third World countries had accumulated large international reserves after World War II as a result of relatively high prices for their exports.[1] But the situation changed rapidly as the flows between the developing and developed nations were reversed and official transfers became important.[2]

The experience of the 1960s and the early 1970s brings out the generally positive results of the contribution of international financial cooperation to the acceleration of the economic growth of the developing countries. That occurred during a period when international trade increased significantly and the economies of the developing countries became largely integrated into the world economy. As such, the international financial system succeeded during that period in placing a substantial part of its available resources in developing countries, which permitted them to cover extraordinary balance-of-payments deficits and to pursue adjustments that have depressed production and employment to only a minor extent. Because of the close correlation between monetary and trade flows, the maintenance of the import levels of the developing countries, in order to satisfy global demand, made it possible to lessen the intensity of the economic recession in the industrial countries and thus to avoid consequences that would probably have been worse.

As a result of the experience of recent years and a better understanding of the linkage of the economies of the developing countries with those of the industrial countries, policies of international financial cooperation may be expected to change in the near future. The new policies may endeavor to take advantage of the opportunities for mutual benefit offered by economic relations between the developing and the industrial countries. Given the trends of past relations, a possible increase in external financing to developing countries for investment purposes may be expected to return to the industrial countries in the form of larger import payments. In turn, the composition of those imports would continue to be dominated by the products of those manufacturing branches in the industrial countries that are presently having high indexes of idle capacity. Therefore, in these circumstances, the real economic cost of a larger transfer of resources to the developing countries would be substantially less than its nominal value, and its benefits for the two parties concerned would be significant.[3]

EXTERNAL DEBT OF CARIBBEAN COUNTRIES: GROWTH, STRUCTURE, AND IMPACT

Table 16.1 indicates the outstanding external public debt of the Caribbean for the period 1960–80. As can be seen, the external public debt has been increasing in all of the countries. This increase in recent years was mainly attributable to the large increases in the prices of oil, worldwide inflation, and the severe recession in the industrial countries. In the face of the reduced demand for their products, and their falling commodity prices and export revenues, many of the Caribbean countries had to borrow heavily from abroad in order to finance the large expansion of their current-account deficits and their investment program requirements. The bulk of the Caribbean countries' foreign borrowings, which supplemented their domestic savings and helped finance their import requirements, traditionally took the form of official bilateral and multilateral assistance. But beginning in the early 1970s, as the official flow of external funds grew at a slow pace, the current-account deficits swelled to unprecedented levels, which forced many countries to resort to the private capital markets, particularly commercial banks. This shift in the source of financing enabled the countries to finance their development programs during the recessionary period and to adjust to the impact of the higher oil prices.

The cost of foreign capital and the net transfer of resources from abroad depend to a great extent on the volume of external debt as well as its structure by type of creditor and its evolution over time. This is so, due to the diversity of interest rates and maturities existing in the various sources of international financing. The current of development in the Caribbean countries requires a net transfer of resources from abroad to cover the gap between savings and investment as well as the balance-of-payments deficit. This means that new indebtedness should exceed the outflow of foreign exchange to service the external debt and that the balance of total debt should continue to grow so long as requirements of economic efficiency and flexibility are met.

From the standpoint of economic theory, at a more advanced stage of economic development, the increase of external debt will stop as the growth of domestic savings enables the countries to finance, internally, the investment requirements to maintain the expansion of their productive capacity and the payments of interest and principal on their outstanding external debt.

As shown in Table 16.2, the composition of the Caribbean's external public debt changed drastically during the last decade, with an increasing use of commercial banks' credits and a lower proportion of debt

Table 16.1.   External Public Debt of the Caribbean Outstanding,[a] 1960–80 (Millions of U.S. Dollars)

Year	Barbados	Guyana	Jamaica	Trinidad & Tobago
1960	n.a.	50	n.a.	21
1966	13	69	143	76
1970	14	123	192	122
1973	38	254	501	190
1975	51	381	864	217
1976	60	458	1132	157
1977	79	480	1249	292
1978	103	651	1439	527
1979	122	719	1562	609
1980	154	743	1697	723

Sources: World Bank, World Debt Tables, 2 vol. (Washington, D.C.: World Bank, 1976); Organization for Economic Cooperation and Development, Total External Liabilities of Developing Countries (Paris: OECD, 1975); Inter-American Development Bank, Latin America's External Indebtedness: Current Situation and Prospects (Washington, D.C.: IDB, May 1977); and Inter-American Development Bank, Economic and Social Progress in Latin America (Washington, D.C.: IDB, 1982).
[a]Includes the undisbursed portion.

Table 16.2. Composition of Caribbean External Public Debt by Creditor, 1960–80 (Percentages)

Country/Creditor	1960	1970	1975	1980
Barbados				
Official Multilateral	n.a.	—	4.6	69.7
Official Bilateral	n.a.	21.4	34.1	18.7
Suppliers	n.a.	—	2.3	0.6
Private Banks	n.a.	—	52.3	11.0
Other Credits[a]	—	78.6	6.7	—
Guyana				
Official Multilateral	n.a.	10.6	14.6	29.0
Official Bilateral	n.a.	77.2	53.3	39.9
Suppliers	n.a.	—	2.7	3.1
Private Banks	n.a.	5.7	14.1	17.2
Other Credits[a]	n.a.	6.5	16.1	10.8
Jamaica				
Official Multilateral	n.a.	27.5	19.3	26.3
Official Bilateral	n.a.	27.5	20.4	41.7
Suppliers	n.a.	—	2.7	2.3
Private Banks	n.a.	10.2	50.9	24.6
Other Credits[a]	n.a.	34.8	6.7	5.1
Trinidad & Tobago				
Official Multilateral	—	42.4	42.7	12.2
Official Bilateral	—	25.3	21.6	21.7
Suppliers	14.3	4.0	3.3	—
Private Banks	38.1	15.2	29.1	60.2
Other Credits[a]	47.6	13.1	3.3	5.9

Sources: Same as for Table 16.1.
[a]Includes nationalization, bond issues, and credits from private financial institutions other than commercial banks.

contracted with foreign governments. This was due in general to a decline in the growth of financing from official sources in comparison with the expanding requirements for external financing by the Caribbean countries, a situation that led the countries to resort to private banks at a time when these institutions had ample liquidity. Except in Barbados and Jamaica, credits with foreign commercial banks rose progressively in all of the countries while, except in Trinidad and Tobago and Jamaica, obligations with foreign governments have been decreasing in terms of proportion. Suppliers' credits during the past decade have been a relatively stable component of the external public debt of the four countries.

The rapid growth in borrowing through financial markets by the Caribbean countries has affected the timing of their future debt service obligations. This may be seen in the changes of the maturity structure of external debt, as revealed by time profile ratios, which show future debt service payments as a percentage of debt outstanding at some base date. Interest rates and maturities constitute one of the main determining factors in the servicing of external debt. The accelerated growth in the past decade of interest and principal payments abroad may be explained by the expansion and change in the structure of the external public debt, together with a trend toward a progressive hardening of conditions in the loans contracted by the Caribbean countries.

Compared with borrowing from official sources, borrowing from private sources requires repayment in a shorter period of time and also at a higher rate of interest. Therefore, as the maturity of the countries' debt decreases and the average interest rate rises, the time profile ratio will increase accordingly. As such, the effect on the debt structure of the relative growth in private-source borrowing has been to bring about a net increase in the time profile ratios for the Caribbean countries.

The growing dependence on financial markets by the Caribbean countries puts more stress on their debt-management capabilities. One reason for this is, of course, that loans from private financial institutions now have, in large part, variable interest rates. Except in Trinidad and Tobago, the increment in the implicit average rate of interest of the outstanding external public debt reflects the higher cost of money in the industrial countries as well as in the international capital markets as a result of inflation, the adoption of restrictive monetary policies to deal with inflation, and risk and uncertainty factors prevalent in recent years.

Basically, interest rates charged by private lenders are higher than those applied to credits extended by government agencies or multilateral financing institutions. Although the practice of variable interest rates introduces greater uncertainties, it can have potential advantages to borrowers as well. The reference rate may rise as it did during 1973–74 but when it declines, as it did during 1974–76, the reduction in the cost of money is passed along to the borrower. This would not have been the case if the borrowing had been at a fixed rate. The funds which have been lent to the Caribbean countries in recent years have come, to a large extent, from institutions receiving Eurocurrency deposits. The lending rate has been on the rate paid on these deposits plus a margin. The margin is determined by the creditworthiness of the debtor and the external debt capacity of the country. The most common base rate for international lending by private financial institutions is the six-month London Inter-Bank Offered Rate (LIBOR). The debt servicing costs of the borrower therefore vary, parallel to the movements of the six-month swings of the Eurodollar rate, which is subject to substantial fluctuations.

The attractiveness of Eurocurrency lending for the developing countries lies primarily in the fact that the loans are untied and can be obtained with a minimum of red tape. But, in view of their relatively high cost, Eurocurrency flows will add importantly to the debt service burden of the borrowers. Moreover, it appears that these credits are extended at least by some of the lending banks primarily on insurance principles (spreading of risks) and only secondarily on a creditworthiness analysis of the borrower.

The foreign debt of a developing economy plays a complex role in its economic affairs. At the same time, the growth of external debt requires adequate growth in the amount of foreign exchange earnings which must be devoted to debt service. Debt servicing capacity of a developing economy may conveniently be discussed in terms of benefits and cost of foreign capital in the process of economic growth. Foreign capital supplements national resources and thus helps raise the rate of capital formation. By making possible a higher rate of investment than would otherwise be feasible, foreign capital raises the rate of income growth.

The debt-service ratio is the most frequently used measure in determining a country's creditworthiness. This ratio is the interest and amortization on external public debt expressed as a percentage of the value of exports of goods and services. The higher the ratio the greater is considered to be the pressure of debt service on the debtor's economy. Table 16.4 shows the debt service ratios for the period 1965–80. As can be gleaned, except in Trinidad and Tobago, the debt service ratio has increased unevenly in all of the countries from 1965 to 1980. In 1980, Guyana had the highest ratio while Barbados had the lowest. The size of the debt service ratio from year to year will vary widely from country to country and

Table 16.3. Interest Payments on the External Public Debt, 1966–80 (Millions of U.S. Dollars)

Year	Barbados	Guyana	Jamaica	Trinidad & Tobago
1966	1	4	5	4
1970	1	3	8	6
1971	1	3	10	5
1972	1	6	12	6
1973	1	6	18	8
1974	3	8	33	15
1975	2	10	49	12
1976	2	18	53	10
1977	2	16	59	7
1978	3	17	71	22
1980	6	26	111	45

Sources: Same as for Table 16.1.

Table 16.4. Debt Service Payments as a Ratio of Exports of Goods and Services, 1965–80 (Percentages)

Year	Barbados	Guyana	Jamaica	Trinidad & Tobago
1965	1.6	4.2	2.0	2.0
1966	1.4	5.6	1.8	1.9
1967	1.4	5.0	2.3	2.0
1968	1.3	6.1	3.1	1.4
1969	1.2	3.5	2.8	2.2
1970	1.0	3.4	2.7	2.5
1971	0.9	3.0	3.5	3.7
1972	5.5	5.5	4.7	1.5
1973	2.7	5.7	6.0	1.8
1974	2.1	5.1	6.1	2.2
1975	1.8	4.8	7.2	1.2
1976	1.9	10.4	11.6	2.9
1977	3.4	18.8	15.0	0.5
1978	2.0	16.1	17.0	2.0
1980	2.5	16.9	13.1	2.4

Sources: Same as for Table 16.1.

depends on, among other national and external factors, the management of financial and economic policies, the general economic performance, and the size of capital flows and export earnings.

The debt service ratio is usually calculated for a single year. The popularity of this ratio lies essentially in its simplicity and easy calculation. Its main value is that it shows the short-run rigidity in the debtor's balance of payments and the pressure to which debtor countries would be exposed if their export earnings declined or their imports increased. It also indicates how much debt a country has actually been able to service in the past.

But despite those advantages, the ratio has been recognized as an incomplete indicator of a country's debt position and, as such, international comparisons of these ratios have only limited meaning. Part of the deficiency of the debt service ratio is based on the fact that there seems to be no critical level beyond which default may be expected. In some developing countries difficulties have been met with relatively low debt service ratios while others avoided difficulties with high ratios. Moreover, the ratio may be particularly misleading for poor countries with a large export sector. In such countries, external debt liabilities may appear small in relation to export earnings but their more serious effect is on internal demand management, in particular, savings and the fiscal system.[4]

In attempting to determine a country's ability to service its debt, a number of factors must be considered. Among the factors are the stability and diversity of the composition of the country's exports, the prospects for growth of production and exports, the extent to which imports can be reduced without adversely affecting production, the size of foreign-exchange reserves and so on. Further, external public debt, though usually the largest debt, constitutes only a part of the total public debt of the developing countries and thus may considerably understate the extent of indebtedness in some cases.

Because of the above arguments it has been advocated that a new measure be used to indicate the debt service burden. The burden may be assessed in relation to the country's total resources, or GNP. This is regarded as a comprehensive indicator, relating the totality of a country's external liabilities to its total product. For the long run, this is the most important debt service indicator. However, in practical terms, as debt represents a contractual obligation of payments abroad, the levels of reserves and export earnings are more relevant in the short run.[5]

Table 16.5 shows the relationship between external public debt and GNP. The ratio of external public debt to GNP has consistently been highest in Guyana, primarily because of the greater openness of the Guyana economy. During 1960–80, the ratio never exceeded 30 percent in Barbados and Trinidad and Tobago, while in Jamaica the ratio exceeded 30 percent only after 1974. The annual variations in the ratio of external public debt to GNP in the Caribbean show no similarity to the variations in the debt service ratio. But, of course, this should not be surprising. The

Table 16.5. Ratio of External Public Debt to GNP, 1960–80 (Percentages)

Year	Barbados	Guyana	Jamaica	Trinidad & Tobago
1960	n.a.	17.9	n.a.	2.4
1966	9.6	24.6	11.5	9.2
1970	7.3	44.9	11.9	11.8
1971	8.6	63.1	15.2	10.9
1972	5.7	75.7	19.2	13.3
1973	10.1	62.9	17.2	13.8
1974	10.7	81.5	24.2	16.3
1975	13.8	81.5	30.4	14.8
1976	15.6	83.0	42.4	9.3
1977	19.7	93.0	49.2	18.6
1978	20.4	129.0	52.1	26.4
1980	23.6	135.1	54.0	14.1

Sources: Same as for Table 16.1.

debt service ratio, because of the contractual charge of debt service on exports, remains the relevant starting point in the analysis of creditworthiness but it cannot substitute for an in-depth knowledge of a country's situation, prospects, and total economic performance. Moreover, the evaluation of future debt service burdens must also take account of the interrelationships among economic, social, and political considerations, which may be subject to sudden and substantial change. In some instances, these changes may result from, or be amenable to influence by, a country's own choice of policies and its success in implementing them. But the pattern of future developments in a given country will also depend on factors outside its sphere of influence.

There is a consensus among economists, however, that, despite the nature of the measure used to determine a country's debt burden, the developing countries themselves bear the fundamental responsibility for their debt management. Most of the measures to avoid debt difficulties lie with them, rather than with the capital providers. Developing countries bear the responsibility to take all reasonable measures within their means to ensure that debt servicing difficulties are avoided. However, domestic policies designed to avoid debt servicing difficulties can only be fully successful in a suitable and favorable external environment. As such, it must be part of the development cooperation effort between richer and poorer countries that donors will do what they can to help poorer countries steer the difficult course between accelerating their development to the maximum extent and staying clear of a collapse in their external payments position. It means frank cooperation between debtor and creditor countries. The need for such cooperation becomes particularly important when the external payments position of any developing country is endangered by events beyond their control, such as a rapid deterioration of their terms of trade.

Avoiding debt service difficulties requires, among other things, policies with regard to the mobilization of domestic savings, which have an important bearing on investment programs and therefore on rates of growth of output. The avoidance of debt servicing difficulties under conditions that are consistent with an orderly development process in developing countries is, therefore, in the interest of both debtor and creditor countries. This means the use of policies that are in harmony. These policies may have many areas of overlap and a broad measure of understanding and complementarity should be promoted in order to achieve a fruitful rapprochement with regard to matters on which divergencies may exist.

Due to the importance of export earnings in determining total foreign-exchange availabilities in debtor countries, policies in creditor and debtor countries regarding trade have an important bearing on the capacity of the latter to service debt. In this connection, appropriate exchange rate and export promotion policies in debtor countries, including when necessary the prompt adjustment of exchange rates, will play an important role in fostering an expansion in export earnings. Most of the Caribbean countries seemed to have recognized this and during the last five years, particularly in Jamaica, there have been several changes in the exchange rates, some of which were imposed by the IMF.

The extent of foreign borrowing as a means of financing development in the Caribbean is shown in Table 16.6. As a percentage of Gross Domestic Product, net external borrowing has been relatively more stable in Jamaica during the past decade while in Guyana, Barbados, and Trinidad and Tobago there have been some fluctuations. The greatest fluctuations have occurred in Guyana. However, except in Trinidad and Barbados in 1980, net domestic borrowing as a percentage of Gross Domestic Product exceeded the similar ratios for net foreign borrowing.

It seems obvious though that if development is to proceed in the Caribbean there will be some need for capital inflows from the developed nations. If the terms on which this is provided are made more appropriate to the repayment capacity of the countries and if the regular and continuous flow of this capital can be better assured, the countries will be more able to ensure a more efficient management of their economies.

Table 16.6. Central Government Overall Surplus or Deficit Financed by Net Foreign Borrowing, 1970–80 (Percentages of GDP)

Country/Activity	1970	1971	1972–76	1980
Barbados				
Surplus or Deficit	– 1.0	– 2.5	– 4.2	– 5.5
Net Foreign Borrowing	– 1.0	n.a.	0.8	4.4
Guyana				
Surplus or Deficit	– 6.6	– 28.3	– 14.9	– 30.8
Net Foreign Borrowing	3.1	23.0	4.3	5.6
Jamaica				
Surplus or Deficit	– 5.1	– 4.3	– 10.3	– 18.1
Net Foreign Borrowing	2.5	2.1	2.7	4.6
Trinidad & Tobago				
Surplus or Deficit	– 3.3	– 6.4	1.9	6.5
Net Foreign Borrowing	– 0.2	2.6	1.3	1.1

Sources: Same as for Table 16.1.

CONCLUSIONS

The financing of the development effort in the Caribbean has displayed a tendency toward use of external financing primarily through borrowing from private banks in the international financial markets. However, the policy of deficit financing to expand economic activities and effect the infrastructural development to transform the economies has not been successful in terms of reducing unemployment and sustaining increases in national income. Moreover, despite the nationalism factor, the dynamics of international debt peonage are intimately tied to the dependent structures of Caribbean productive systems.

The recent increase in Caribbean external borrowing from private creditors has also contributed to the shortening of debt-maturity payments for the Latin American region. The portion of the external debt falling due in five years or less rose gradually from approximately 43 percent in 1973 to 50 percent in 1980. Payments maturing in more than 15 years dropped from 18 percent in 1970 to 5 percent in 1980.

However, the increase in private bank lending of Eurocurrency to the Caribbean countries must be subject to careful interpretation. This is so because the loans are new and therefore represent gross lending; with mounting repayments on earlier loans, the difference between gross and net figures will become increasingly important. Hence, the gross figures on Euro-loans do not necessarily reflect new indebtedness. These loans have tended to replace other forms of lending, especially export credits. The continued availability of Eurocurrency, however, depends on developments in the market which are difficult to foresee. On the one hand, some of the revenues of the oil-exporting countries are beginning to flow back into the Euromarket and provide available funds for lending but, on the other hand, the balance-of-payments problems of oil importers have led, and will lead, to large demands on the same funds. On balance, however, it seems likely that Euro-loans will continue to be available for lending to most established borrowers in the market for some time to come.

Foreign capital has played an important role in the economic development of many countries which are presently considered mature or developed economies. Most of the developing countries are still at a stage where their development depends, in part, on the flow of foreign funds in the form of grants, loans, and direct foreign investment. It is, therefore, not surprising that a substantial research effort, of both an empirical and theoretical nature, has been directed to the study of the relationship between economic development and foreign funds. However, whether it is a good idea to borrow or not obviously depends on whether the funds can be used to such an advantage as to warrant the cost of borrowing. If foreign loans are wasted, the obligation to service the debt will leave a country worse off than if it had never sought or accepted foreign loans at all.

At a conceptual level, it is possible for a country to have borrowed too much abroad, even if its debt service ratio is falling, if the return on the domestic investment were lower than the incremental interest rate on external debt. Debt service payments, like the amounts of outstanding debt, are generally affected by inflation and real growth of underlying variables.

For the Caribbean nations the primary issue with respect to their use of external borrowing to finance development is that of sound debt management. The key to sound debt management is to ensure consistency between a country's macroeconomic growth objectives, a current-account deficit, and the amount and terms of capital inflow that are available to assure servicing of old debt and provide the necessary net addition of foreign resources. This may mean acceptance of quantitative limitations on new external borrowing in certain maturity brackets and interest levels and the adjustment of related economic variables.[6]

In addition to pursuing effective economic and financial policies and adhering to debt-ceiling limitations, the Caribbean countries can strengthen their debt management by measures directly designed to assure control and surveillance of their total external debt. These measures include screening procedures to ascertain that foreign loans are contracted only for high-priority projects, prior authorization procedures for public loans, and central registration procedures for private loans.[7] This system for central debt recording enables a country to continually check its overall indebtedness and service obligations.

NOTES

1. Helen Hughes, "Debt and Development: The Role of Foreign Capital in Economic Growth," *World Development* 7 (February 1979), p. 99.
2. Ibid.
3. Inter-American Development Bank, *Economic and Social*, 1978, pp. 85–86.
4. Organization for Economic Cooperation and Development, *Debt Problems of Developing Countries* (Paris: OECD, 1974), p. 14.
5. Hughes, "Debt and Development," pp. 108–9.
6. Organization for Economic Cooperation and Development, *External Indebtedness of Developing Countries: Present Situation and Future Prospects* (Paris: OECD, 1979), pp. 20–21.
7. Marilyn J. Seiber, *International Borrowing by Developing Countries* (New York: Pergamon Press, 1982), p. 76; and Kempe Ronald Hope, "External Borrowing and the Debt Problem of the Developing Countries," *International Journal of Development Banking* 2 (January 1984), pp. 22–24.

17

Social Security Schemes and the Development Process in the Caribbean

In the past, social scientists have given little attention to the problem of social security and only in recent times some studies have begun to appear which integrate the economic significance of social security with the development process in the developing countries. These studies are beginning to recognize the fact that social security has undeniable effects on the economic and social development of nations.

But what is meant by social security? There are differing schools of thought concerning this concept. In this chapter we shall use a very wide definition which views social security as the result achieved by a comprehensive and successful series of measures for protecting the public (or a large sector of it) from the economic distress that, in the absence of such measures, would be caused by the stoppage of earnings during sickness, unemployment, or old age, and after death; for making available to that same public, medical care as needed; and for subsidizing families bringing up young children.[1] This definition is advantageous to the extent that it corresponds to internationally comparable statistics on social security published by the United Nations and the International Labor Office.

Social security, therefore, represents a guarantee by the whole community to all its members of the maintenance of their standard of living or at least of tolerable living conditions, by means of a redistribution of incomes based on national solidarity. It thus excludes the use of insurance techniques and particularist categories. It is essentially general, both as to the population covered and as to the elements of insecurity against which individuals and families are protected.[2] In the Caribbean, there are two distinct patterns of social security evolution. The larger, more-developed nations covered in this chapter have national insurance schemes while the microstates have opted for the provident-fund approach.

However, the efficacy of a social security system in the socioeconomic field depends on its scope, with regard to persons protected and risks covered, on the adequacy of benefits, on financial soundness, and the quality of the administration. This chapter examines the economic significance of social security programs vis-à-vis the development process in the Caribbean with primary emphasis on resource mobilization.

ECONOMIC IMPACT AND SIGNIFICANCE OF SOCIAL SECURITY PROGRAMS IN THE CARIBBEAN

The majority of the social security systems in the Caribbean nations were established either as separate government enterprises or as agencies operating out of a specific government ministry. Social security schemes in the Caribbean are institutions designed to provide comprehensive coverage to as many persons as the resources of the countries could possibly cater to while at the same time achieving the specific goals of mobilizing resources to increase the rate of economic development. An average of 68 percent of the labor force is covered by such plans in the Caribbean microstates while in the more-developed Caribbean nations the average is 70 percent with the largest coverage (82 percent) in Trinidad and Tobago.

Social security programs in the Caribbean, therefore, seem to emerge as government-operated and controlled, nonbank financial intermediaries. Financial intermediaries are economic units whose principal function is managing the financial assets of other economic units. Thus they bring savers and borrowers together by selling securities to savers for money and lending that money to borrowers. With respect to social-security plans, the securities sold are lifetime benefits of various sorts, as discussed before, and the borrowers here happen to be the Caribbean governments. Registration with social security programs is usually compulsory and so therefore are contributions. As such then, social security represents a form of compulsory savings and indeed it is, apart from commercial banks, the largest single institutional collector of funds in most Caribbean nations. Within the context of economic development, domestic savings are very important. The larger a developing country's level of savings, the lesser the degree to which the said developing country has to rely on external sources of finance for economic development. Any marked increase in the level of domestic savings in any developing economy requires deliberate government policies. Hence, the opening or widening of channels through which savings can flow (such as social security) is one means by which governments in the developing economies can encourage savings for use in financing economic development.

Domestic savings are used to finance all forms of capital formation. The essence of the growth process is that it is not possible without savings.

Expressed in a different manner, any failure to generate enough savings will inevitably slow down the growth process.

The relative importance of savings in the Caribbean, whether it be generated by social security or any other institution, has become more protracted in recent years in view of the fact that the sources of external finance for economic development in the Caribbean have become very limited. Increased mobilization of savings has therefore become more than necessary for the development thrust in the Caribbean. The use of social security as an institution for the mobilization of savings is essential in the Caribbean and attempts should be made to increase efficiency in these efforts.

Social security contributions are a form of compulsory or contractual savings as stated before. Compulsion is here regarded as necessary to increase the level of savings and to maximize the desirable flow of resources. The advocacy of compulsory savings presupposes that individual preferences are overridden, but the long-term advantages enable individuals to have a wider and more effective range of choice and an increased command over resources.

In the Caribbean, the relative size of the social security surplus with respect to gross national savings increased unevenly from an average of 2 percent in the early 1970s to a range of approximately 9 percent in Barbados to 22 percent in Guyana in the early 1980s.

Further economic significance of the social security surplus can be gauged by observing its relationship to gross domestic investment. Currently, it ranges from an average ratio of 11.4 percent in Barbados to 15.3 percent in Guyana. This performance is somewhat better in comparison with that of other developing countries whose national insurance and social security programs were at a similar stage of development.[3] Of course, this difference may be accounted for by the efficiency with which government and other employers' contributions are made in the Caribbean.

However, the foregoing revelation indicates that there is ample reason for advocating the further growth of social security plans. They specialize in creating financial instruments which meet the needs of employees in terms of safety and liquidity while at the same time fostering savings for development.

It seems desirable for the Caribbean nations to encourage and concentrate their efforts in bringing about those changes in their financial structure that will ensure, or at least make more likely, that a predominantly indirect and institutional—and largely contractual and compulsory—flow of personal savings contributes as much as possible to economic growth.[4]

However, there will no doubt be a tendency on the part of pressure groups to urge that these funds be expanded in increasing the benefits. But it has to be remembered that social security is responsible for providing over the whole of each insured person's life such benefits as he or she may become entitled to, and, after death, such benefits as may be payable to survivors. The surplus funds are capital accumulations to meet foreseeable commitments and their right use will be in the form of investments for the development of the countries rather than for increasing current benefits. The generation of surplus funds of this nature in a social security plan is accepted especially in developing countries as one of the means by which development can be expedited and further opportunities for employment increased.

The size of social security expenditures should not be taken as a measure of the value of the offered services. The expenditures include cash benefits and administrative costs. These components are valued at their cost to the institutions and not according to the value at market price to the beneficiaries.[5] In social security expenditures there is no market mechanism through which the supply of benefits is controlled by consumers' preferences.[6] As seen in Table 17.1, the major part of social security expenditures went toward payment of benefits. As a percentage of GDP, social security expenditures have ranged from 2.7 percent in Jamaica in 1965 to approximately 0.6 percent in Guyana at present.

Social security expenditures do not currently represent a large part of public expenditures in the Caribbean. Expenditures on social security, however, do have important economic effects on welfare and growth. Moreover, they constitute an important class of transfer expenditures and the relative magnitude of their importance among developing countries generally reflects the degree of economic development in those countries.

In the Caribbean, the low level of expenditures in relation to receipts may be a reflection of the infancy of the plans. However, one cannot help

Table 17.1. Social Security Expenditures in Barbados and Guyana, 1974–79 (Millions of U.S. Dollars)

Country/Component	1974	1975	1976	1977	1978	1979
Barbados						
Benefits	1.6	2.5	3.2	3.7	4.8	5.5
Administration	0.6	0.4	0.5	0.7	0.7	1.1
Total Expenditures	2.2	2.9	3.7	4.4	5.5	6.6
Guyana						
Benefits	1.1	1.2	1.4	1.8	2.8	3.3
Administration	0.9	1.1	1.2	1.4	1.6	1.9
Total Expenditures	2.0	2.3	2.6	3.2	4.4	5.2

Sources: Guyana National Insurance Board, *Annual Reports*; and Barbados National Insurance Board, *Annual Reports*.

but comment on the relative growing magnitude of the administration expenses in Guyana. Percentage-wise, administrative expenses in Guyana have been on a significant increase during 1971–76, from 42 percent in 1971 to 46 percent in 1976 of total expenses, and then declined to about 36 percent at present. The question then arises as to whether Guyana's social security plan, from an administrative point of view, is functioning efficiently. This question is a rather serious one, particularly when one observes the trend of administration expenses in other Caribbean countries. In Barbados, for example, administrative expenses currently represent approximately 17 percent of total expenditures.[7] If, as Henry Aaron points out, the expenditure level of social security automatically increases as these programs mature,[8] then it may be right to assume that, in the future, social security expenditures in the Caribbean will increase significantly and unless the expenses of administering the schemes are controlled, then we may also look forward to increases in administrative expenses in relation to total expenditures.

As mentioned before, the efficacy of any social security or national insurance plan in the economic and social fields depends on its scope, with regard to persons protected and risks covered, on the adequacy of its benefits, and on its financial soundness; but in actual practice it depends essentially on the quality of the administration. Hence, the human factor is fundamental since the training and qualification of staff is of decisive importance in efforts to attain the desired goals. In Jamaica, for example, social security is an institution that competes directly with other sectors, and consequently its efficacy depends also on the initiative and collaboration of the representative groups that are associated in the administration of the system.

Although social security is primarily humanitarian in purpose, its significant economic aspects have not been fully understood by the public. Social security can be described as a "built-in" economic stabilizer. These plans have frequently been supported not only for the benefits they bring to individuals and their families, but also because they increase the stability of the economy. Hence, there is no longer any serious disagreement among economists about the contribution of social security to economic stability and growth. Since a sound social security system constitutes a built-in stabilizer in the national economy, and as stability of purchasing power is one of the most powerful incentives to economic growth, it may be concluded that a sound social security system itself is a powerful incentive to economic growth.[9]

A distinction must be drawn, however, between the stabilizing effects of benefits which will remain fairly constant in total amount during boom and depression and those which are relatively small when trade is good and are much greater in recession periods.[10] Among the former are benefits for widows and orphans, sickness benefits, industrial-accident benefits, and old-age pensions. The constancy of these payments is in itself a stabilizing factor, but it is largely neutral to fluctuation in prosperity. Sickness benefits may increase somewhat in a period of recession and so may old-age pensions because of the earlier retirement of aged people who find increased difficulty in staying employed, but the changes would be small. The main benefit that falls in prosperity and rises in times of recession is that of unemployment insurance.

Social security systems are instruments for redistributing or transferring income among different sections of the community. These redistributive effects of social security do not take place in a vacuum but within the framework of conditions determining income distribution.[11] The distribution of income among the individuals and households of a nation is central to its economic welfare and, as such, an understanding of the interactions between the inequalities of income distribution and various aspects of economic and social modernization is therefore essential for the formulation of appropriate development policy. The causes of inequality of income have been dealt with elsewhere[12] and it would be beyond the scope of this chapter to summarize them here.

Given the current development thrust in most developing countries within the framework of creating an egalitarian society, then maybe one ought to examine social security as supplementary machinery for the redistribution of incomes. Social security systems in developing countries function in environments where there is much more scope for income redistribution than in developed nations, in view of the more unequal distribution of factor incomes. In developing countries, however, the social security systems operate on a much smaller scale, not only absolutely but also relatively, because the percentage of national income devoted to social security is much smaller than in developed nations. For this reason, one can expect social security to have a smaller redistribution effect in the Caribbean.

Ultimately, however, resources are transferred from the economically active to those in need. Hence, the poorest sections of society are within the redistributive impact of the various provisions of social security programs. The costs are largely borne by the main body of the population, who are also beneficiaries, since they are protected against risks. The transfers are among the beneficiaries as the risks are pooled among themselves.

It is obviously not enough just to know that social security transfers purchasing power to the needy insured individuals. What is required is some understanding of the deeper effects of the contribution of governments, which represent a reallocation of fiscal revenue and can be considered a horizontal redistribution of public sector income, in comparison with the vertical redistribution resulting from transfers among different income levels. This type of understanding is necessary if recognition is given to the fact that the economic effects of social security benefits and payments vary widely from one category to another.

Undoubtedly, the operations of social security programs are essentially transfers, that is, they amount to a redistribution of income. In all social security systems, large sums are involved in redistribution. These sums have in themselves an economic incidence, for beneficiaries do not use the amounts received in the same way as they would be used by those who contributed to the amounts.[13] Redistribution in Trinidad and Tobago, for example, operates in favor of the inactive population—the aged, invalid, and sick—so that the purchasing power of these groups is increased.

Social security represents a guarantee, by the whole community, to all its members of the maintenance of their standard of living or at least of tolerable living conditions, by means of a redistribution of incomes based on national solidarity. The scope of social security causes it to be considered as one of the rights of the individual and corresponds to the basic principle of redistribution.

The social security programs in the Caribbean cater to the whole society and they are instruments of change forming part of a conscious socio-economic policy. A policy, however, that is delimited only by the lack of integration of the schemes in the planning of the Caribbean economies. The purpose of the integration of economic and social security planning is to demonstrate that those programs relating to social security are in no respect contradictory to the economic and general development of a country.[14] Compared with economic planning, social security planning suffers from the disadvantage that it does not permit easy definition of measurable objectives to the same extent as do other items in social programs, such as education, health, or housing. On the other hand, it is possible to measure the mobilization of capital, as in the case of transfers between different sectors of the community.

As in any plan, the first task is to determine the purpose or objectives. Currently, the main lines of social security policy in the Caribbean have been fixed. It is, therefore, only necessary to ensure that the aims and objectives are in harmony not only with each other, but also with those of other economic and social programs. In fact, social security in the Caribbean must be considered as a part of general social policy. This is essential if it is to be properly integrated into national planning.

From a more general standpoint, planning of social security should be fully integrated in national development plans, which must fix the scope, rate of expansion, and limits of development of social security within the possibilities of the economy. It is only in this way that it will be possible to make a choice of priorities, ensure optimum use of resources, select the most effective technical methods and, most important of all, ensure that social security remains as an instrument for bringing equity and social justice and providing the majority of the people with the opportunity to belong to the community.

Social security programs are more and more acquiring the character of a public service that can be compared with all kinds of other public services in the developing countries. This is a much-espoused criticism by almost everyone who has had contact with social security. The underlying reason for this criticism lies in the administrative defects which have created an inefficient bureaucracy. These administrative problems aside for awhile, however, it must be pointed out that there is an important difference between social security and most other public services. The former entails individual expenditure, while the latter usually entails collective expenditure. Social security charges, to a certain extent, impose a restriction on individual expenditure, but on the other hand, it prevents a calamitous restriction of individual expenditure at the right moment, and ensures the continuation of purchasing power as much as possible.

As for the issue of administration, such as slowness of processing for the award of benefits, excessive number of forms, and multiplication of authorities for deciding entitlement to benefits, the primary reason is that these irregularities originated in the rules that established the administrative procedures rather than in defects of organization or methods. To a large extent, the formal organization of social security contains the causes of the pathology of the administration, which cannot be remedied without attacking the problem of administration as a whole, in some kind of internal decentralization of authority and duties. Ideally, the administration of social security should be a joint one, that is, by the parties who contribute to its financing—both employers and employees.

To sum it up, it may be said that the administrative problems of social security call for a new outlook unrelated to traditional practices and closely connected to the actual social conditions in the Caribbean and other developing countries.

CONCLUSIONS AND POLICY ISSUES

Social security programs have evolved in the developing countries. Policies governing their operation must be integrated with national economic policies in order that their maintenance and development can be promoted by the results of conscious and balanced effort.

Social security contributes, undoubtedly, to economic growth. But economic growth is only possible through the effort of workers as a whole. It cannot be expected that this effort will develop if the individuals concerned live in constant fear for tomorrow. Inhibition arising from fear for tomorrow can only be lifted by confidence and hope for the future through social security provisions. The behavior of the worker is directly influenced by the existence of an effective social security program which thus also favors economic growth and prosperity.

Within the framework of the growth process is the role of domestic savings. Social security can have three distinct effects on household savings ratios.[15] First, the income effect consists of the possible repercussion of changes in benefit or tax rates transmitted through the average level of disposable income and the degree of income inequality. Second, the wealth effect represents the direct savings response of households to expected future benefits. Third, the retirement effect indicates the positive indirect relationship between old-age benefits and the savings ratios.[16]

With respect to gross domestic savings, social security serves as an instrument of resource mobilization if the authorities invest the surplus in projects with an adequate social marginal rate of return, without inhibiting private savings and investment activity. Whether funds generated by such plans in the Caribbean have always been invested wisely is debatable, however.[17] Most of the investment has been in short-term financial instruments and government securities.

Resource mobilization is a fundamental aspect of the development process. For most social scientists it is of paramount importance in the development process and, as such, any institution that promotes that possibility must be given ample opportunity to continue to do so. Social security falls into that category and its overall value, both to individuals in society and nations as a whole, must be safeguarded and maintained.

Moreover, the redistributive impact of this resource mobilization is a major element of the process. Elements of redistribution are contained and caused both by benefits and contributions. Social security operations are essentially transfers. That is, they inevitably amount to a redistribution of incomes. Redistribution tends to operate in favor of those who are most needy, as it should. The universal scope of social security causes it to be considered as one of the rights of the individual corresponding to the basic principle of redistribution. In addition, social security has the potential to change the distribution of income indirectly.[18] To the extent that it alters the size of the capital stock, for example, it can change the rate of return on capital.

NOTES

1. This is the definition implicit in the Social Security (Minimum Standards) Convention, 1952, adopted by the International Labor Conference in that year. See ILO, *Social Security: A Workers' Education Manual* (Geneva: ILO, 1958), p. 11.

2. Pierre Laroque, "Social Security and Social Development," *Bulletin of the International Social Security Association* 19 (March–April 1966), p. 84.

3. For a comparison with other developing countries, see F. Reviglio, "Social Security: A Means of Savings Mobilization for Economic Development," *IMF Staff Papers* 14 (July 1967), pp. 324–62.

4. V.V. Bhatt, "Some Aspects of Financial Policies in Developing Countries", *Finance and Development* 11 (December 1974), p. 31.

5. F. Reviglio, "The Social Security Sector and Its Financing in Developing Countries," *IMF Staff Papers* 14 (November 1967), p. 506.

6. Ibid.

7. From M.A. Odle, *Pension Funds in Labour Surplus Economies: An Analysis of the Developmental Role of Pension Plans in the Caribbean* (Kingston: Institute of Social and Economic Research, University of the West Indies, 1974), p. 106; and Table 17.1.

8. H. Aaron, "Social Security: International Comparisons," in *Studies in the Economics of Income Maintenance*, ed. O. Eckstein (Washington, D.C.: Brookings Institution, 1967), p. 16.

9. G.M.J. Veldkamp, "Economic Aspects of Social Security," *International Social Security Review* 25 (1972), p. 72.

10. J.H. Richardson, *Economic and Financial Aspects of Social Security: An International Survey* (Toronto: University of Toronto Press, 1960), p. 215.

11. F. Paukert, "Social Security and Income Redistribution: Comparative Experience" in *The Role of Social Security in Economic Development*, ed. E.M. Kassalow (Washington, D.C.: U.S. Department of Health, Education, and Welfare; Social Security Administration, Research Report 27, 1968), p. 104.

12. For a refreshing and comprehensive coverage, see I. Adelman and C.T. Morris, *An Anatomy of Income Distribution in Developing Nations* (Washington, D.C.: U.S. Agency for International Development, 1971).

13. Laroque, "Social Security," p. 85.

14. For more on this, see G. Arroba, "Social Security Planning and National Planning in Developing Countries," *International Social Security Review* 25 (1972), pp. 215–41; also G. Arroba, "Social Security Schemes and the National Economy in the Developing Countries," *International Social Security Review* 22 (1969), pp. 28–60.

15. For more on these effects, see George Kopits and Padma Gotur, "The Influence of Social Security on Household Savings: A Cross-Country Investigation," *IMF Staff Papers* 27 (March 1980), pp. 161–90.

16. Kempe Ronald Hope, "Social Security Schemes and the Economic Development Process in Less Developed Countries," *Management and Labour Studies* 7 (December 1981), p. 124.

17. M. Jenkins, "Social Security Trends in the English-Speaking Caribbean," *International Labor Review* 120 (September–October 1981), pp. 637–38.

18. Henry J. Aaron, *Economic Effects of Social Security* (Washington, D.C.: Brookings Institution, 1982), pp. 80–81.

PART VII

DEVELOPMENT ADMINISTRATION AND INSTITUTIONAL MANAGEMENT

18

The Administration of Development in Emergent Nations: The Problems in the Caribbean

The administration of development in Commonwealth Caribbean countries is conducted primarily through politicians and the civil service operating within a ministerial system or government agency and characterized by its purposes, its loyalties, and its attitudes. The assumed purpose of development administration operating within this system of government is to stimulate and facilitate defined programs of social and economic progress. Put another way, development administration represents policies, programs, and projects to serve development purposes. It is the term used to denote the complex of agencies, management systems, and processes a government establishes to achieve its development goals.

This chapter discusses the experience at reconciling development administration with politicized governments under the ministerial system in the Commonwealth Caribbean nations.

THE STRUCTURE OF DEVELOPMENT ADMINISTRATION IN THE CARIBBEAN

The machinery of administration in the Caribbean was shaped primarily by the colonial government during the period of colonial rule and although, after achieving independence, there has been some attempt at reorganizing, changing, reforming, and improving the entire administrative structure to function effectively in the service of independent nations, administration in the Caribbean still remains a product of the colonial era, maintaining some of the features and attitudes of the former colonial establishments. During the colonial era the day-to-day administration was carried out through various departments and each of these was administered by a chief professional officer who was, in turn, responsible to a colonial secretary or governor as the case may be. The colonial secretaries or governors were responsible for overall administrative functions and they were in turn accountable to the imperial government.

With the achievement of internal self-government and political independence, decision making and executive authority in the Caribbean was transferred from the colonial governors and secretaries to local politicians serving as ministers. This new system gave indigenous elected officials the general direction and control of their respective governments and they were collectively responsible to their respective legislatures. With the creation of the ministerial system in the Caribbean, there was a shift of the locus of responsibility for policy formation from a chief professional officer to a minister of an elected government assisted by officials, the senior of whom are the minister's principal advisers.

Some Caribbean countries attempted to follow a model of public administration emphasizing the instrumental nature of administration and the idea of a politically neutral public service where the service is organized on a hierarchical basis and staffed by career civil servants with recruitment and advancement based on merit. However, they were unsuccessful in these attempts.

After independence in the Caribbean then, the bureaucratic colonial administration was transformed into a bureaucratic organization that emphasized the sovereignty of politics rather than the supremacy of administration.[1] Politics became the most important activity and the politician (minister) came to occupy a position of unquestionable supremacy in matters of decision making.[2] Bureaucratic power shifted from the technical development administrator as head of a department to the minister in office. As soon as the latter assumed power, he hastened to make this clear to the permanent officials.[3]

At the same time a political interest developed in personnel matters and this deteriorated into nepotism, pork-barrel appointments, and the denial of jobs to those who had not supported the governing party.[4] This situation is illustrated in Guyana where, to take one example, the late Dr. Walter Rodney, a brilliant historian, was denied a teaching position at the University of Guyana primarily because of his opposition to the government of President Burnham. The relationship between politicians and administrators in the Caribbean is aggravated by the highly personalized environment and the very sensitive political atmosphere in which political sympathies tend to be generally known and administrators become overexposed in the political arena.

Administrative structures served as patronage institutions, not agents of change. Moreover, the type of centralization that is characteristic of these Caribbean systems is not coordinated. The individual ministries and departments are centralized and this gives rise to undercoordination between departments and ministries in the conduct of national policy.[5]

What has therefore emerged in practice is the ascendancy of the political apparatus over the state bureaucracy. The ability of the political leader to utilize both the political apparatus and state to foster a growing personalization of political power and the use of the political apparatus for dispensation of patronage and for mobilization of the state as an instrument to legitimize these trends. Furthermore, there has been a tendency to extend this centralized control over the machinery of administration to incorporate other institutions in the society and use them as further instruments of control. In other words, while the formal acclaims to competitive democratic politics are being made, the practices of such politics are questionable. No better illustration can be found than in the changing relations between the political machinery and trade unions, that is, the subordination of the labor movement to politics with the resultant effect of the eventual absorption of the union apparatus into the political apparatus. Examples of this trend abound, whether in Jamaica, Barbados, Grenada, St. Kitts, or Antigua.[6]

The effect of these trends has been to create an elite in the Caribbean countries which is dependent for its position on its access to political power and acts to sustain the prevailing political order. This pattern of structuring administrative institutions fully reflects an elite bias and indicates that greater coordination at the systemic level would be resisted by the vested interests. Institution building on completely different premises would certainly reduce the number of access points open to the vested interests and, possibly, would also reduce their capacity to make personal extractions from the system through fair or corrupt means.[7] This style of administrative institution building therefore makes it very difficult to modify, effectively, the status quo or to innovate.[8]

The effect of this politicized and centralized control within the development administration has been to create a great deal of friction between government ministers and career officials. In the early years of self-government and independence, ministers, conscious of their newly acquired powers and determined to dispel any suggestion of inferiority, were anxious to assert their authority and to make it clear beyond doubt who the masters were.[9] Subsequently, ministers have exercised their authority to use the administration to preserve their political positions. Career civil servants are now in a position of great insecurity due to the enormous powers of the government ministers and, for reasons of survival within the civil service, career civil servants have to adopt a sycophantic attitude toward their ministers. At the same time these civil servants are usually better educated than their ministers and they have a professional competence and commitment to development administration, which leads them to distrust the decisions of their ministers and to be unhappy at the inadequate coordination, procrastination, and general ineptitude of government.

OVERCOMING ADMINISTRATIVE OBSTACLES TO DEVELOPMENT

One focus of reform designed to achieve more effective development-oriented administration places emphasis on the change in attitudes and practices of the politicians. Of major significance among factors affecting the administration of development in the Caribbean is that of the lack of total support on the part of the political leadership for improvement of the nation's administrative system. Administrative change inevitably involves a challenge to accepted modes of action and traditional values and prerogatives.[10] Projects for administrative reform, if they are other than routine and minor, must be backed fully by the chief executive of the nation and the cabinet. In speaking of the vital importance of leadership here, we are alluding to the critical place of authority in national development. If political leaders are to inspire a population and to direct the bureaucracy to higher levels of performance and development, their words and actions must carry an aura of legitimacy. Historically, political leaders in the Caribbean have been primarily concerned with maintaining their own existence as politicians and this has resulted in much confusion between the administrative and political function in the decision-making process and also in the creation of political elites—elites who among themselves alone cannot execute the services and achieve developmental goals.

Functional reform of development administration, as needed in the Caribbean, can only be brought about through a derived effort and the critical support of the political leadership. Constitutional changes and the pressures for development have brought about the need for new attitudes toward administrative reform, on the part of governments. Any continued lack of critical support by a government will inevitably continue to perpetuate and legitimize an inefficient and irresponsive bureaucracy, of which type the Caribbean cannot afford to have if the primary emphasis is on the promotion of growth, development, equity, and the meeting of basic needs for a once-colonized people.

However, the improvement of a nation's administrative and management capability is highly dependent on support from the political leadership. The role of the political leadership has been presented as the most crucial factor to be ascertained in the process of national development,[11] and hence in the improvement in the administration and management of development. Political leadership is the arbiter of, rather than one participant or factor among many in, the process of national development. In most emergent nations the lack of the political leadership's role in support of major administrative and management change can be traced to their own concern to maintain elite status and authority. The elite position is so crisply controlled that it is difficult for society to penetrate.

Lending support to administrative change and reform requires, therefore, commitment on the part of the political leadership. Commitment here involves an overriding desire to promote rationality, rise of productivity, social and economic equalization, and improved institutions and attitudes. When combined, these aspects of national development will hopefully produce the administrative and management machinery needed while at the same time generating future change. The promotion of these ideals points toward modernization and is directly opposed to the desire for the maintenance of the status quo. Not only should the political leadership be committed to these ideals in the interest of a just society and better development administration but it should also be resolute enough to recognize such actions as helpful in resolving any problems pertaining to any identity crises.

A second approach involves depoliticizing administration by placing a renewed emphasis on planning, particularly manpower planning. Manpower planning, with its emphasis on ensuring that there are sufficient human skills and resources in the economy, and the implied commitment to using these skills rather than, for instance, relying on jobs as a source of patronage, is an instrument for distancing staffing from politics. Urgency is given to the need for such planning due to the emigration from the Caribbean of high-level manpower. Such emigration has traditionally been to the United Kingdom. However, in the aftermath of the 1962 ban on West Indian migration to the United Kingdom and the liberalization of U.S. immigration policy in 1965, the volume of Caribbean migration to the United States increased sharply.[12] Migration to the United States as a percentage of the natural increase of the population during the period 1962–76 averaged from a low of 7.4 percent from Guyana to a high of 37.8 percent from Barbados. The majority of these individuals were from the category of professional, technical, and management (PTM) personnel. Annual migration from the PTM group represented roughly 10 percent of the incremental growth of manpower for that group in Jamaica, for example.[13] In Guyana, the same pattern prevailed but with a variance in the ethnic composition. Whereas in Jamaica the high-level manpower that emigrated was always predominantly Afro-Jamaicans, in Guyana the emigrants are no longer Afro-Guyanese but Indo-Guyanese instead. This change in the ethnic composition of Guyanese emigrants occurred in the 1970s, partly because of the sheer numbers of Indo-Guyanese in the labor force and partly for political reasons.[14] Emigration from Trinidad and Tobago, in recent years, has tended toward a balance between the two primary races: blacks and East Indians. The average rate of emigration among high-level manpower from Trinidad and Tobago is currently averaging 15 percent and has resulted in the lowering of national productivity and serious time lags in the execution of current operations.[15]

Development planning has been myopic in its lack of concern for the human factor and its preoccupation with economic factors. Planners appear to regard the development plans as self-implementing. But development entails more than economic factors and measures; it requires a far broader strategy and more comprehensive administrative initiatives than now prevail. Without any significant attempt on the part of the governments of the Caribbean to plan manpower within the framework of development plans, then the implementation of development plans will be anything but successful.

The importance of an integrated plan of manpower development on a long-term basis cannot be overstressed. The Caribbean countries need to review their manpower-planning policies with special reference to the need for stimulating the return flow and effectively utilizing the trained personnel currently available. Allowance should also be made for the individual need to find satisfactory and suitable reward. Yet in the context of attempts to overcome administrative difficulties the significance of manpower planning is not only that it helps in making available individuals with needed skills at the right time, but additionally it emphasizes the value to be placed on the skills, experience, and other qualities required for development administration, and on the need to make proper use of them.

In concert with the importance of integrated manpower planning is the role of training. By training, we mean the act or process of making a person fit to perform certain tasks. Training is necessary because no matter how well qualified a person may be at the time of recruitment, he or she still has certain inadequacies, and therefore much to learn before becoming a really effective development administrator.[16] Equally important is in-service training at the lower- and middle-management levels. Here, training must be conceived in very broad terms and result in an independent, development-oriented civil service with security to act effectively. Such training objectives can be easily attained in the Caribbean, given the fact that the institutions for managing training and training of development managers already exist in most of the countries. In Barbados, for example, there is the Institute of Management and Productivity; in Trinidad and Tobago there is the National Institute of Higher Education, Science, and Technology which has a mandate to coordinate management training and advise the cabinet; in Jamaica there is an Administrative Staff College and a Public Service Training Center; and in Guyana there is the almost-defunct Management Development and Training Center. These institutions need to be revitalized, energized, and restructured within the framework of rational policy in which the ends of more effective performance of development administrators can be realized in the Caribbean.

Additionally, there now exists the Caribbean Center for Development Administration (CARICAD), which has its headquarters in Barbados and has as a general objective "to render assistance to the countries of the English-speaking Caribbean thereby helping them to improve their administrative capability and accelerate their social and economic development."[17] CARICAD, as an institution, was created in 1979 and became fully operational in 1980. It is funded by the member Caribbean governments with some financial and technical assistance provided by international organizations and the Development Assistance countries. CARICAD is a timely institution for the promotion of administrative reform. Its role is even of greater importance to the Caribbean microstates which lack the necessary resources and expertise to attempt relevant administrative reform. To that end, CARICAD has embarked on a number of programs designed to train development administrators and provide relevant management-training material and basic equipment to allow for the use of a wide range of modern management-training techniques.[18]

A third approach to reform involves, similarly, containing the area of politicized administration by stressing the need for decentralization. Centralized control is an instrument of political dominance, whereas decentralization creates opportunities for administrators to exercise their professional competence in accordance with commitments to development. Decentralization is regarded here as the transfer or delegation of decision making and authority to plan and manage development related activities from politicians and higher-level officials to middle- and lower-level civil servants as well as the populace. In other words, decentralization is seen both as a political and administrative phenomenon. It is coordinated decentralization which would relieve the politicans and the higher bureaucracy from time-consuming local matters and tasks and thereby increase administrative speed and effectiveness at the various levels of government. Such was the intent and practice of the Maurice Bishop government in Grenada, an example of a typical microstate where smallness allowed for greater familiarity between the citizens and the politicians.

Through administrative decentralization it is possible to emphasize national standards to deal with problems which are national in scope, while at the same time to allow for adjustments to meet particular regional needs. The expertise of professionals is promoted through a vertical integration of the agencies and bureaus of the national government. It is generally agreed that administrative decentralization should have some place in all systems of modern government. By applying that concept to the structure of government administration in the Caribbean, the central government can be "decongested," so that its top administrators are freed from onerous and minor, detailed administration and unnecessary involvement in local affairs. As a result, the various national governments can devote more energy and time to national problems and at the same time facilitate and expedite action on the lower levels. Furthermore, greater civic participation in self-government and feeling for national unity are stimulated and this will bring about an increase in the people's understanding and support of social and economic development activities and, as a result, gain the benefit of their own contributions to these activities, and of personal and group adjustments to needed changes.[19]

A recurring problem with decentralization is that rather than serving to insulate administration from politics, it can serve the purpose of increasing the scope for patronage appointments and in the process produce a multiplicity of organs, duplication of functions, and diffusion of responsibility. For example, in Guyana, there is currently in existence a Timber Export Board, a Timbers Corporation, and a Forest Industries Corporation, all of which have responsibility for wood products.[20]

Associated with this emphasis on decentralization is a concern for participation. There are advantages inherent in decentralization of which one is releasing administrators from a constraint that limits their effectiveness in promoting development. In the society also, the trend toward rigid control, illustrated above with the example of trade unions, has prompted a contrary emphasis on the need for participation of local groups in a way that recognizes the positive contribution members of the society can, and should, be making. There is a need for reliance on local groups to help enforce the reforms as well as the determination of which operations, singly or in combination, are likely to constitute the minimum degree of intervention necessary to manage the economy.[21]

This type of participation is quite essential for the Caribbean microstates. Not only because it can develop the self-reliance necessary among the populace for accelerated development but also because it can result in the maintenance of bottom-up administration as opposed to top-down and institutional administration which tends to occur with economic expansion.[22]

In development administration, participation is the microperspective. It is the administration of systems at the grass-roots level. Ironically, participation has probably achieved more in development administration than any other aspect of the subject, yet it is only in recent times that it has received considerable attention in the literature on development administration, particularly as it applies to small nations. Goulet, for example, includes "optimum participation among development's strategic principles because unless efforts are made to widen participation, development will interfere with men's quest for esteem and freedom from manipulation."[23] Moreover, and as stated before, participation enhances the administrative process.

A fourth approach to administrative improvements carries the stress on participation further and is illustrated by the strategy that was intended in Grenada. In contrast to the previous approach, governmental administration is not seen as *the* instrument, or even *an* instrument, for promoting and achieving development but as a means of carrying out activities required of it by previous development in the whole society. In Grenada, under Bishop, the basic tenets of philosophy had revolved around the implementation of programs geared toward the provisions of basic needs, independence from Western capitalist ideologies, and the development of collective self-reliance with the socialist world. The revolutionary government had introduced policies and reformed administrative structures modeled on the Ujamaa concept and claimed to be building a system of "participatory democracy," involving the wider mobilization of the people within community councils and village assemblies while at the same time restoring order to the country's finances and economy by eliminating corruption and waste and by establishing effective control of recurrent expenditure.[24] Prime Minister Maurice Bishop had stated, categorically, that the approach of the government and the approach of the revolution was to make a conscious attempt to transform the economy and to seek to break the dependence on outside forces, laying the basis for a planned and progressive development.[25]

Still, at low levels of economic development, the demand for efficiency of government agencies is less urgent. The rhythm of life is slower and things move in set patterns. There is little difference between the ways of administration and the ways of life beyond the office.[26] On the other hand, however, higher levels of economic development create demands on the efficiency of government agencies while at the same time providing the input to allow the agencies to cope with the increasingly complex and technical tasks. Administrative systems tend to grow to cope with the developing needs of a modern society and the progress and expansion that result. Speed and flexibility become essential factors in the efficiency of public administration.

THE SIGNIFICANCE OF SIZE

Some additional attention to the issue of small size merits further discussion in this work. In the Caribbean microstates the unique problems of administration have generally been overlooked primarily because of those countries' lack of importance in global affairs and their remoteness. But small nations in the Caribbean tend to be plagued with a small administrative capacity, resulting from the lack of appropriate training and a pattern of living which carries over into the manner in which the administration of development is perceived. In St. Lucia and Dominica, for example, formal training programs are almost nonexistent. In Antigua and Montserrat there is some limited training but in both countries the civil service has degenerated into an inefficient bureaucracy where absenteeism, tardiness, and low productivity have become the order of the day. Moreover, there exists in a number of the government agencies no clearly defined job tasks for many of the civil servants and this in turn results in idleness and a fragmented pattern of development administration. This, of course, is one of the further problems of centralization despite the fact that microstates by their sheer size provide for greater familiarity, participation, and interaction among politicians, bureaucrats, and the populace.[27]

Murray, for example, has pointed out rather alarmingly that bureaucratization within an overpowerful and partly uncontrolled governmental administration is a problem which, although not peculiar to microstates, is understandable, given the circumstances of the microstates.[28] For the Caribbean the problem is even more pressing because of the deteriorating economic structure of the microstates there. Accepting, however, that the economic problems of Caribbean microstates are partly structural in nature, still the role of the administrative machinery looms large in the quest for economic progress and modernization. The administrative structure must be such, therefore, that it enhances "nation building." It must allow for systematic public decision making for the formulation of public policies and programs and allocating resources among them.

Small size may, as well, create barriers to institution building. In the eastern Caribbean, where personalistic political leadership is ascendant, a predictable limit is placed on the extent of openness that can be expected in the institutional *modus operandi* and this lack of openness may easily forestall the growth of interaction among the relevant social forces in society.[29]

Small size results not only in limitations but also challenges to and possibilities for the development administration machinery. It is therefore within this overall framework that integration and regional cooperation become important. Cooperation among Caribbean nations, but more so the developing microstates, can provide the access to resources, information, and the expertise needed to overcome the administrative constraints of small size. Such cooperation embraces truly cooperative relations among nations with similar administrative characteristics and should be pursued as a matter of regional policy to enhance the administration of development and the development of administration in Caribbean microstates. This can be accomplished through the existing regional institutions, such as CARICOM and CARICAD.

CONCLUSIONS

Developmental administration in the Caribbean is in a state of ineptness. The bureaucratic colonial administration has now been replaced by native politicians who exercise centralized authority and control with significant emphasis on politics. The emergence of ministerial administration and the development of the cabinet system have significantly altered the role and hence the status position of civil servants. From being the primary decision makers they have become the advisers; and evidently they have increasingly become advisers who are heard but seldom heeded. Thus, persons and groups seeking to influence policy increasingly direct their efforts toward the political actors. The politician is seen as the power figure and the civil servant is viewed as a clerk.[30] But these politicians have no notion of "development" or "modernization" or nation building and their major orientation is toward safeguarding their own positions, which is expressed as preserving "law and order,"[31] and maintaining and attracting political supporters.[32]

Development administration, however, is characterized by its purposes, its loyalties, its attitudes. The purposes of development administration are to stimulate and facilitate defined programs of social and economic progress. They are purposes of change, innovation, and movement, as contrasted to purposes of maintaining the status quo,[33] such as currently exists in the Caribbean.

These purposes are to apply policies as well as conduct programs of development for the enhancement of a nation. As such then, the bureaucracy for development administration must be accountable to the public, through its representatives. Bureaucratic loyalty in development administration must be to the people and not to its own vested institutional interests nor uncritically to sovereign political leaders as is the case in the majority of the Caribbean nations.

Administrative reform then, in the Caribbean, is overdue. Reform programs contain elements that stress improved political leadership, manpower planning and training, effective decentralization and communication, and popular participation. In such programs administration has an important part to play in the development effort. It is the instrument of accomplishment. In these programs, without proper and relevant development administration, a nation's economy is doomed to stagnation. In contrast to these programs, the strategy expressed currently for Grenada assigns a less central place to the administration, seeing the administration as an instrument to be developed and reformed as a result of previous economic development in the wider society.

For the majority of Caribbean nations the current concern is with the adjustment of their administration to meet the demands of development. The task of the political machinery must then be to develop structures that permit the public bureaucracy to function effectively in a changing environment, and which also must provide a flexibility within it to permit the bureaucracy to function as an agent of change.

NOTES

1. Kempe Ronald Hope, "Development Administration in Post-Independence Guyana," *International Review of Administrative Sciences* 43, no. 1 (1979), p. 69.

2. S.C. Dube, "Bureaucracy and Nation-Building in Transitional Societies," *International Social Science Journal* 16, no. 2 (1964), p. 233.

3. C.A.P. St. Hill, "Towards the Reform of the Public Services: Some Problems of Transitional Bureaucracies in Commonwealth Caribbean States," *Social and Economic Studies* 19 (March 1970), p. 143.

4. G.E. Mills, "Public Administration in the Commonwealth Caribbean: Evolution, Conflicts and Challenges," *Social and Economic Studies* 19 (March 1970), p. 15.

5. E. Jones and G.E. Mills, "Institutional Innovation and Change in the Commonwealth Caribbean," *Social and Economic Studies* 25 (December 1976), p. 330.

6. J.E. Greene, "Contemporary Politics in the English-Speaking Caribbean: Contradictions, Conflicts and Confusions," in *Contemporary Caribbean Issues*, ed. A.G. Cruz (Rio Piedras, Puerto Rico: Institute of Caribbean Studies, University of Puerto Rico, 1979), p. 89.

7. Edwin Jones, "Administrative Institution-Building in Jamaica: An Interpretation," *Social and Economic Studies* 23 (June 1974), pp. 268–86.

8. Jones and Mills, "Institutional Innovation," p. 330.

9. G.E. Mills, "Education and Training for the Public Services in the West Indies," *Journal of Administration Overseas* 5 (July 1966), pp. 156–57.

10. John C. Honey, *Toward Strategies for Public Administration Development in Latin America* (Syracuse: Syracuse University Press, 1968), p. 69.

11. T. Tsurutani, *The Politics of National Development* (New York: Chandler, 1973), p. 25.

12. Palmer, *Caribbean Dependence*, pp. 87–88.

13. Ibid., p. 96.

14. M.K. Bacchus, *Education for Development or Underdevelopment: Guyana's Educational System and Its Implications for the Third World* (Waterloo, Ontario: Wilfrid Laurier University Press, 1980), p. 52.

15. Kempe Ronald Hope, "The Emigration of High Level Manpower from Developing to Developed Countries with Reference to Trinidad and Tobago," *International Migration* 14, no. 3 (1976), p. 212.

16. Kempe Ronald Hope, "Improving Public Enterprise Management in Developing Countries," *Journal of General Management* 7 (Spring 1982), p. 81.

17. Caribbean Centre for Development Administration (CARICAD), *The Case of the Caribbean Centre for Development Administration* (Wildey, Barbados: CARICAD, 1981), p. 6.

18. Caribbean Centre for Development Administration (CARICAD), *Training of Trainers: Report on the Regional Workshop on Management Development and Training in the English-Speaking Caribbean* (Wildey, Barbados: CARICAD, 1980), pp. 5–6.

19. Kempe Ronald Hope and Aubrey Armstrong, "Toward the Development of Administrative and Management Capability in Developing Countries," *International Review of Administrative Sciences* 46, no. 4 (1980), p. 318.

20. Hope, *Development Policy*, p. 200.

21. Keith Griffin and Jeffrey James, *The Transition to Egalitarian Development* (New York: St. Martin's Press, 1981), pp. 68–69.

22. Coralie Bryant and Louise G. White, *Managing Development in the Third World* (Boulder, Colo.: Westview Press, 1982), pp. 218–24.

23. Denis Goulet, *The Cruel Choice: A New Concept in the Theory of Development* (New York: Atheneum, 1977), p. 148.

24. Anthony Payne, *Change in the Commonwealth Caribbean* (London: Chatham House Papers, Royal Institute of International Affairs, 1981), p. 16.

25. Maurice Bishop, *Address on the Occasion of the Second Anniversary of the Grenada Revolution*, People's Revolutionary Government, St. George's, Grenada, 1981, pp. 3–6.

26. L. Dabasi-Schweng, "The Influence of Economic Factors" in *Public Administration in Developing Countries*, ed. M. Kriesberg (Washington, D.C.: Brookings Institution, 1965), p. 21.

27. Jamal Khan, *Public Management: The Eastern Caribbean Experience* (Leiden: Department of Caribbean Studies, Royal Institute of Linguistics and Anthropology, 1982), p. 60.

28. David Murray, "Microstates: Public Administration for the Small and Beautiful," *Public Administration and Development* I (July–September 1981), p. 255.

29. Khan, *Public Management,* p. 61.

30. F.E. Nunes, "The Declining Status of the Jamaican Civil Service," *Social and Economic Studies* 23 (June 1974), p. 353.

31. Jean-Claude Garcia-Zamor, *The Ecology of Development Administration in Jamaica, Trinidad and Tobago, and Barbados* (Washington, D.C.: Organization of American States, 1977), p. 38.

32. George K. Danns, "Leadership and Corruption: An Analysis of Emergent Post-Colonial Rule in the Caribbean," *Transition* 3, no. 1 (1980), pp. 17–24.

33. George F. Gant, *Development Administration: Concepts, Goals, Methods* (Madison: University of Wisconsin Press, 1979), pp. 20–21.

PART VIII

CONCLUSION

19

Recent Economic Developments and Trends

BARBADOS

The relative openness of the Barbadian economy and its dependence on foreign exchange earnings from sugar, tourism, and manufacturing made it vulnerable to the slow recovery in most of Europe and Canada during 1981–83. Most significant was the decline in tourism, which had become the fastest growing sector of the economy and the principal foreign exchange earner. By the end of 1983, tourism, which accounts for well over one-half of gross foreign exchange earnings, declined by an estimated 8.5 percent in terms of real output despite an 8.1 percent increase in tourist arrivals. Also, sugar production, which now contributes less than one-fifth of total foreign exchange earnings, declined by 4 percent to a historic low of about three-fourths the average output level of the past decade.[1] Since tourism and sugar together generate almost one-sixth of GDP, their decline had a direct negative impact on the level of economic activity with the result that the only sectors showing substantial growth were nonsugar agricultural and petroleum.

On the fiscal side, central government current revenues increased from 24.6 percent of GDP in 1981 to an estimated 25.6 percent of GDP in 1983 while current expenditures declined from 23.6 percent of GDP in 1981 to 22.8 percent in 1983, with the result that central-government savings increased from 1 percent to 2.8 percent of GDP from 1981 to 1983. Capital expenditures also declined from 9.1 percent of GDP in 1981 to 6.6 percent in 1983, thereby reducing the overall central-government deficit from 8.1 percent of GDP in 1981 to 3.8 percent in 1983. The external public debt of Barbados decreased from US$334.4 million in 1981 to US$309 million in 1983. The debt is manageable, despite the heavy borrowings in 1981, and the debt service ratio remains below 6 percent.

More recent data indicate that the Barbados economy grew in real terms by about 2.4 percent during 1984, terminating the period of decline and stagnation which began in 1981. This growth was due to a bumper sugar harvest and a substantial increase in tourism.

It seems to be generally felt, and this author shares the same view, that despite Barbados's limited resource base, small domestic market, high degree of dependence on external markets, and high population density, there are a number of positive factors. These include the country's long history of constitutional democracy and social and political stability, its basically good infrastructure, its relatively equitable income distribution, its highly literate, well-trained, and disciplined labor force, its inherent attraction as a tourist destination, combined with the generally capable economic management of the authorities. Thus, Barbados is the only Commonwealth Caribbean nation that works efficiently and stands in good stead for continued future economic growth and development.[2] In the medium term the government's objectives are to diversify export products, reduce food dependency, and maintain a strong private sector. These strategies are embodied in the country's 1983–88 development plan.

GUYANA

The economy of Guyana continued to suffer further setbacks during 1981–84 with the external sector being struck the hardest. Bauxite production fell by approximately 40 percent in 1983, owing to market and labor problems and shutdown of production facilities. Real GDP declined by 20 percent between 1981 and 1983 and the public sector's overall deficit reached 50 percent of GDP. Unemployment was estimated in 1983 at 40 percent and the result has been a further worsening of social conditions.

Nevertheless, the economy recovered slightly in 1984 and GDP recorded a 4 percent growth. This recovery was the result of progress in agricultural production and the recovery of the mining sector, where bauxite production increased by more than 40 percent. However, despite this recovery and the implementation of measures designed to improve tax administration and collection, public sector finances continued to deteriorate and the total deficit reached almost 60 percent of GDP by the end of 1984 as a result of increasing government expenditure over revenues.

This deteriorating fiscal situation forced the government to take a number of stabilization measures. However, given the already high tax burden and the depressed state of the economy, there is currently little scope for further increases in revenues. Improvement in the government's financial situation was and is therefore dependent upon a reduction in expenditure and central government employment. To this end the government laid off some 25,000 employees during 1981–84 and discontinued the importation of such staples as split peas, wheat, and cooking oil, due to lack of foreign exchange. In addition, the government established an Export Development Fund to provide foreign exchange credits for imported inputs for export manufacturing and an Exports Promotion Council as well as an Industrial Promotion Council were established as forums for the private manufacturing sector and the government. Also, in 1984, the Guyana dollar was adjusted and effectively devalued by about 30 percent with respect to the basket-currency mechanism.[3]

Guyana's economic outlook for the late 1980s is one of further difficulty. Net international reserves are expected to decline further as export performance deteriorates. This in turn will give rise to considerable difficulty in financing the importation of necessary raw materials, spare parts, and other inputs. In light of this continued deterioration in the foreign exchange situation and a projected increase in external debt service payments, the government reached an agreement with its international commercial creditors whereby payments of principal were deferred during 1982–83 and these debts were converted into new, medium-term loans. However, this respite has been of little use and significant amounts of additional capital inflows now need to be acquired.[4] But, so far, Guyana has not announced an agreement with the International Monetary Fund and any rescheduling of outstanding obligations with the major creditor governments will depend on an agreement with the IMF. However, it is anticipated that the new administration of President Desmond Hoyte (who succeeded President Burnham on his death on August 6, 1985) will be seeking to come to terms with the IMF.

JAMAICA

Since 1980 Jamaica has embarked on a set of policies to move the economy closer to the free-market system. As a result, there has been a slight recovery in GDP growth from its negative trend in 1980 to an estimated 1 percent by the end of 1984. This growth is attributable to the recovery in agriculture and improvements in tourism as well as in the performance of the export manufacturing sector. The bauxite/alumina industry was adversely affected by the international recession and low demand for aluminum.

On the fiscal side, central-government current revenues increased from 25 percent of GDP in 1980 to approximately 30 percent of GDP by 1984. Current expenditures moved from 33 percent of GDP in 1980 to 34 percent in 1984, and the current savings was still negative at − 4 percent of GDP at the end of 1984. The deficit of the central government for the fiscal year ending in March 1984 was estimated at 15.5 percent of GDP. The primary reason for the increase in the deficit was the poor performance of revenues. The need for further borrowing abroad to finance public sector needs thus became necessary. The external public debt increased from US$1.9 billion in 1981 to approximately US$2.5 billion in 1983 and when the IMF debt is included the total external debt at the end of 1983 was US$3.2 billion with the debt service ratio reaching approximately 16.3 percent of exports.[5] In 1984, largely as a result of some rescheduling, public medium- and long-term debt is estimated to have increased by about US$500 million and service payments by an estimated 74 percent, to some 26 percent of export earnings.[6]

In response to the fiscal crisis, the government of Jamaica announced a number of policy measures. On the monetary side, an auction system was put into place to regulate and distribute available foreign exchange, based on bids for such exchange. The auction is held twice weekly by the Bank of Jamaica through a process of sealed bids and the exchange rate is then set at the clearing rate of the auction. Additionally, other monetary policies were put into effect to restrict inflationary growth of the money supply and domestic credit. The reserve ratio for commercial banks was increased, as was the bank rate.

Other policy measures included a reduction of the government workforce, restrictions on the travel of government officials, and the launching of AGRO 21. AGRO 21 was conceived in 1983 as a new thrust in agriculture commemorating the twenty-first anniversary of the independence of Jamaica. It is intended to put more land into agricultural production, to put more people to work, and to earn more foreign exchange.

The economic outlook for Jamaica looked somewhat favorable until the recently announced withdrawal of Reynolds Jamaica and Alcoa Minerals of Jamaica, which effectively shut down the bauxite industry. The government has attempted to recover from this setback by acquiring the alumina plant of Alcoa with Alcoa managing it on behalf of the government in an attempt to recover some of the foreign exchange that would have been lost had the plant been allowed to close permanently.

The country's promising growth sectors are primarily tourism and agriculture. Small-scale manufacturing is also expected to make a meaningful contribution to economic growth by taking advantage of the Caribbean Basin Initiative's trade and tax incentives. However, Jamaica's total economic recovery still hinges on the government's ability to reduce the budget deficit, increase international reserves, and further increase private-sector investment.

TRINIDAD AND TOBAGO

By the end of 1984 the economy of Trinidad and Tobago weakened in performance. Real GDP moved from a growth rate of 4.6 percent in 1981 to a decline of 6.4 percent in 1984. This was the result of a decline in output and prices of oil which began in 1980 and continued to have a negative impact on the level of economic activity, leading to a fall in total demand, a reduction of fixed investment, and an increase in the unemployment rate.[7]

Because of the gap between government revenue and expenditures, as a result of the reduction in oil revenues, current savings declined rapidly from 20.8 percent of GDP in 1981 to less than 1 percent by the end of 1984. The reduction in revenue also affected capital expenditures, which declined from 19.9 percent of GDP in 1981 to 17.1 percent of GDP in 1984, while the overall surplus/deficit of the central government moved from a positive 1.1 percent of GDP to − 17.0 percent.

Due to the downturn in oil revenues, the government put into effect a number of drastic measures that included budget cuts, higher rates for public utilities, more expensive fuels, and lower subsidies. Monetary policy resulted in the tightening of domestic credit and the allocation of available credit to priority productive sectors rather than to consumer credit. Additionally, the government implemented a system of foreign exchange controls to stem the outflow of foreign exchange for imports of consumer goods, travel, and private foreign remittance.[8] Also, in 1983, for the first time in several years, domestic tax rates were increased.

The economic outlook for Trinidad and Tobago is one of uphill recovery. Declining oil revenues will continue to increase the fiscal deficit unless there are further considerable cuts in government expenditures. Other sectors, such as agriculture, need to be revived and the problems of cost and productivity must be given some priority.

NOTES

1. Caribbean Development Bank, *Annual Report 1983*, p. 32.

2. See, for example, Inter-American Development Bank, *Economic and Social Progress,* 1983, p. 161.

3. Based on this mechanism, the exchange rate fluctuates weekly. At the end of 1985 the weekly exchange rate fluctuated between G$4.00 to G$4.50 = US$1.00.

4. See Kempe Ronald Hope, *Guyana: Politics and Development in an Emergent Socialist State* (Toronto: Mosaic Press, 1985), Chapter 1.

5. Inter-American Development Bank, *Economic and Social Progress,* 1984 p. 335.

6. Inter-American Development Bank, *Economic and Social Progress,* 1985 p. 301.

7. Caribbean Development Bank, *Annual Report 1983,* p. 42.

8. In December 1985 the government devalued its currency by 50 percent and established a dual rate. The old exchange rate of US$1.00 = TT$2.40 is being used for certain basic goods, drugs, and educational materials while the new rate is US$1.00 = TT$3.60 for all other transactions.

INDEX

ABOUT THE AUTHOR

KEMPE RONALD HOPE is Fulbright Professor of Economics and Public Policy in the Faculty of Social Sciences and Associate Research Fellow at the Institute of Social and Economic Research, University of the West Indies, Mona Campus, Jamaica. Dr. Hope, who holds graduate degrees from Rutgers and Syracuse universities, has published extensively on Third World development issues with general emphasis on the Caribbean and his books include: *Urbanization in the Commonwealth Caribbean* (1986); *Guyana: Politics and Development in an Emergent Socialist State* (1985); *The Dynamics of Development and Development Administration* (1984); *Recent Performance and Trends in the Caribbean Economy* (1980); *Development Policy in Guyana* (1979); and *The Post-War Planning Experience in Guyana* (1978).